LATIN AND GREEK TEXTS 8   ISSN 0951-7391

HORACE
ODES AND CARMEN SAECULARE

CW00551155

HORACE

Odes and Carmen Saeculare

with an English version in the original metres,

introduction and notes by

GUY LEE

FRANCIS CAIRNS

Published by Francis Cairns (Publications) Ltd
c/o The University, Leeds, LS2 9JT, Great Britain

Paperback edition 1999
Hardback edition first published 1998
Copyright © A.G. Lee, 1998

British Library Cataloguing in Publication
A catalogue record for this book is available from the British Library

ISBN 0 905205 96 0

Printed in Great Britain by
Redwood Books, Trowbridge, Wiltshire

TO THE COLLEGE OF
S[T] JOHN THE EVANGELIST,
CAMBRIDGE

CONTENTS

Preface   ix

Introduction
  The Life   xi
  The Odes   xii
  The Metres   xviii

Text and Translation
  Book One   2
  Book Two   58
  Book Three   96
  Book Four   158
  Carmen Saeculare   194

Differences from Garrod's revision
of Wickham's Oxford Classical Text   201

Explanatory Notes   203

Abbreviations and Select Bibliography   275

PREFACE

In 1956 J.B. Leishman published his *Translating Horace*, with the object of demonstrating to a sceptical readership that it was quite possible to reproduce Horatian lyric metres in English verse. Leishman's demonstration offered translations of thirty well-known Odes, a collection which displayed eight of the thirteen metrical systems used by Horace. It was a virtuoso performance about which Leishman himself was unduly but becomingly modest: 'My own attempt' he writes 'is far from perfect, but it does, I am convinced, indicate how the thing can and should be done, and I hope that it may encourage others to do better.'

Certainly, seven years later, when James Michie published his *The Odes of Horace*, the finest and most readable English version of the Odes, he was partially encouraged. 'Persuaded by Mr Leishman' he writes 'I have put ... thirteen odes (eleven of them Alcaic) into the original metres.' But thirteen out of 103 Odes (104 if we include the *Carmen Saeculare*) is not a large percentage, and this lucky number has encouraged me, not to try to do better than Michie (an improbability), but to try to do as well as Leishman for all four Books of the Odes plus *Carmen Saeculare*.

The Latin text is basically the vulgate, with differences from Garrod's revision of Wickham's Oxford Text recorded (pp.201–202).

I have provided skeleton notes, mostly designed to save the reader the trouble of consulting a classical dictionary, for this book is not aimed at scholars but primarily at lovers of poetry who wish to know what Horace says in his Odes and how he says it. The Bibliography lists the works I have consulted in its production.

My special thanks are due to: Professor Kenneth Quinn who read an earlier version of all four Books and the Introduction, Professor Wendell Clausen who read Books 1–3, Professor Neville Collinge and the late Dr Theodore Redpath who read Books 1 and 2, and Professor John Crook who read Book 4 and the *Carmen Saeculare*. Their criticisms and suggestions were invaluable. I am also very grateful to Professor Francis Cairns for helpful advice, Mrs Sandra Cairns for expert editorial assistance, Mrs Helen Lee for many shrewd comments and the late Miss Patricia Huskinson for skilled typing.

St John's College, Cambridge   *A.G.L.*

INTRODUCTION

THE LIFE

Horace's works come down to us virtually complete; they provide evidence for his life, his friends, his character and views, and even his physical appearance (*Epistles* 1.20.20–28); this evidence is supplemented by a *Vita Horati* deriving from Suetonius in the early second century A.D.

His full name was Quintus Horatius Flaccus. Born at Venusia in Apulia on 8th December 65 BC, he calls himself the son of an ex-slave who worked as a *coactor*, a kind of auctioneer's broker, buying and selling goods at auction on commission. His father must have done well at this job, for he could afford to have his son educated by the best teachers in Rome and to send him at the age of eighteen or nineteen to study in Athens.

Caesar's murder took place while Horace was at Athens (15th March 44 BC) and in August of that year Brutus the tyrannicide appeared and attended philosophical lectures, attracting many of the students, including Horace and Cicero's son, to the Republican cause against Antony and the young Octavian, Caesar's great-nephew and adopted son. Horace served under Brutus in Asia, impressed him enough to be made a military tribune (an office normally held by knights) and shared in his defeat at Philippi in the autumn of 42 BC.

He returned to Italy to find his father's property had been confiscated, probably during the proscription decreed by Antony, Lepidus, and Octavian, in which (according to Appian *Civil Wars* 4.5) 300 senators and 2000 knights were outlawed, their property confiscated, and rewards offered for their death. But Horace still had enough money to buy himself an administrative position as *scriba quaestorius* or secretary to the quaestors. This, though not a sinecure, would give him some time to read and write poetry.

His early work attracted the notice of the already established poets Virgil and Varius, who both spoke on his behalf to their patron Maecenas, Octavian's close friend and trusted adviser. Horace memorably describes his stammering introduction to the great man in 38 BC, and his acceptance as an *amicus* nine months later (*Satires* 1.6.54ff.). From then on his career was made.

He appeared first as a satirist in the tradition of Lucilius (the second-century inventor of Latin hexameter satire, an aggressive and autobiographical genre), publishing *Satires* 1 in 35 and 2 in 30 BC.

His next appearance was a literary impersonation; with his *Iambi* or *Epodes*, published in 30 BC, he became the Roman Archilochus, representing in Latin the iambic metres and belligerent spirit of that seventh-century Greek master of invective, himself reputedly the son of a slave mother.

Not long after 35 BC Maecenas gave Horace what he describes as a small estate in the Sabine Hills north-east of Tivoli, and this improvement in his financial and social status seems to have mellowed him. Certainly from his second literary impersonation in the *Odes* as the Roman Alcaeus (for which see the next section) the invective note has almost entirely disappeared.

Finally, returning to the dactylic hexameter in *Epistles* 1 (20 BC), he appears as himself, writing nineteen letters to friends and raising questions about how one ought to live. A second book of *Epistles* followed in 13 BC; it contains two letters, the first to Augustus (by the Princeps' own request), and both, like the earlier (or later?) *Ars Poetica*, concerned with literary criticism and how one ought to write.

About the same time he published a fourth book of *Odes*, having previously, as unofficial poet laureate, been commissioned by Augustus to celebrate the victories of his stepsons Drusus and Tiberius over the Alpine tribes Vindelici and Raeti in 15 BC (*Odes* 4.4 and 14 respectively). Not included in Book 4 is the *Carmen Saeculare*, a hymn in nineteen Sapphic stanzas to Apollo and Diana, written at Augustus' behest for performance by a choir of boys and girls at the Secular Games of 17 BC.

Horace in his fifties had reached the summit of his career: in the class-conscious society of his time, though son of an ex-slave, he had risen through friendship with Maecenas to friendship with Augustus himself; as Rome's greatest living poet he was even able, without giving offence, to refuse the emperor's invitation to become his private secretary. He never married, and on his deathbed (27th November 8 BC) he left his estate to Augustus, as Maecenas had done a few weeks earlier.

THE ODES

Horace's name for what we call his odes was *carmina*, 'songs', a literal Latin translation of the Greek word for songs, *odai*, itself a contracted form of the Homeric word, *aoidai*. He calls his singing 'Aeolian' (*Aeolium carmen* 3.30.13) because, as he explains at *Epistles* 1.19.32, he is Latinizing metres used by the Greek poet Alcaeus, a native of Mitylene on the island of Lesbos, writing around 600 BC in the Aeolic Greek dialect. Alcaeus belonged to one of the leading families of Lesbos who were engaged in a struggle for power on the island and in fighting to defend Lesbian territory on the Asian mainland. He wrote songs about politics and war, drinking-songs, love-songs, songs about Homeric heroes and hymns to the gods, for special occasions and for performance at drinking-parties (*symposia*) to the accompaniment of the lyre (hence 'lyric' verse).

Horace too, almost six hundred years later (the measure of our distance from Chaucer, say), wrote songs of the same kinds, often for performance at *conuiuia*, the Roman equivalent of the Greek *symposia*. Although Horace states explicitly that his words are designed to be set to music (4.9.4 *uerba loquor socianda chordis* 'I speak words for setting to lyre-strings') it is customary not to take him literally but to explain all his references to music and the lyre as conventional metaphors for the composition of lyric verse. Against this there is inscriptional evidence that his *Carmen Saeculare*, specially composed in Sapphics for the Secular Games of 17 BC, was sung by a choir of boys and girls. The sceptic must therefore admit that at least some of Horace's odes *could* be sung. As regards his description of himself as *Romanae fidicen lyrae* 'player of the Roman lyre' (4.3.23) and the reference to his own lyre-playing at a rehearsal of the *Carmen Saeculare* (4.6.35–36), Bonavia Hunt and Günther Wille take this literally too. Certainly lyre-playing was a common accomplishment among the Greeks, part indeed of a gentleman's education (see Cicero *Tusculans* 1.4). Horace as a philhellene interested in lyric poetry might well have learned to play its instrument, and in doing so he would simply have anticipated three Roman emperors: Nero (virtually a professional), Titus and Hadrian (gifted amateurs — see their respective *Vitae*).

To return to Alcaeus, the great library at Alexandria contained some ten papyrus rolls of his poetry, but today it survives in a small number of brief quotations cited by later authors and in a few papyrus fragments, so we can never compare a Horatian imitation with its complete Aeolic original. It is clear enough, however, from references to Roman life and Roman history in the odes, that Horace gives himself a very free hand. For example, he begins 1.37 with a literal translation of the first three words of Alcaeus' song in Alcaics celebrating the death of the tyrant Myrsilus: *Nunc est bibendum* 'It's time for drinking'; he continues with an allusion to a Roman religious custom and devotes the rest of the ode to an account of the defeat of Cleopatra at Actium in 31 BC and to her subsequent suicide in Egypt. Similarly, behind 1.9 stands an Alcaic poem about a great storm, frozen rivers, building up a fire, mixing wine and taking one's ease. The whole thing is Romanized by Horace, apart from the Greek name of young Thaliarchus, who, from line 9 onwards, is advised to trust in the gods, to live for the present, and to make the most of his youth.

Both these odes are dramatic monologues supposedly delivered at a symposium. In 1.37 the poet is addressing his boon-companions (*sodales*) but the scene is not described. In 1.9 he addresses another character, an adolescent, in a particular scene, which is described in part directly and in part by implication: it is winter; perhaps we are starting a party; the fire is made up and Sabine wine about to be poured; not far off snow-covered Mount Soracte can be seen.

In fact, most of Horace's odes are dramatic monologues, one-sided conversations sometimes or soliloquies on a particular occasion, some with background sketched in or implied, others with neither. The exceptions in Book 1 are: political verse (2, 12, 14), hymns (10, 21, 35), and an epic narrative (15).

The arrangement of the odes within each book must have received careful thought. The first nine odes of Book 1 are in nine different metres. Known as the Parade Odes they must be intended to display the poet's metrical virtuosity. Seven of them are tributes paid to specially important men: 1 Maecenas, 2 Augustus, 3 Virgil, 4 Sestius (consul in 23 BC, the year of publication), 6 Agrippa (Augustus' most trusted supporter and successful general), 7 Plancus (the consular who proposed in the Senate in 27 BC the title Augustus for Octavian). Presumably Pyrrha appears as number 5 in this distinguished company for variety and to remind the reader that love is a main theme of Aeolic lyric; she follows on naturally enough after the mention of Lycidas at the end of 4.

The nine Parade Odes have a counterpart in Book 2 which opens with eleven odes alternately in Alcaics and Sapphics. Similarly Book 3 opens with a special group of six odes in Alcaics, collectively known as the Roman Odes, whose first stanza forms a solemn introduction to all six poems as a new kind of poetry addressed to the younger generation.

First, last, and roughly middle positions in each book are specially important: 1.1 to Maecenas, 1.20 to Maecenas, 1.38 symbolic of Horace's poetry; 2.1 to Pollio, 2.12 to Maecenas, 2.20 again to Maecenas, about Horace's poetry; 3.16 to Maecenas, 3.30 about Horace's achievement (in the same metre as 1.1 and preceded by 3.29 to Maecenas).

Book 1 contains 38 odes, an unusual number for a collection of poems; more often collections consist of multiples of five poems. But it has been observed that if, in order to balance the 38 poems in Book 1, we count back 38 poems from 3.30, we arrive at 2.13, making 2.1–12 the middle section of the three books. Looking at these twelve poems we find that 2.1 and 12 are addressed to patrons, both authors; that 2.4 and 5, like 8 and 9, are erotic; that 6 and 7 in the middle of the group are addressed to special friends (a young and an old one), and that both have *mecum* in the first line and an oblique case of *amicus* in the last. Attempts to pair 2.2 and 3 with 10 and 11 as philosophical have met with resistance, but the other pairs are plausible enough. Possibly, then, Horace chose this middle position in Books 1 to 3 of his odes on purpose to emphasize the importance to him of friendship.

In his first published work (*Satires* 1.5.44) he had made that importance explicit:

> *Nil ego contulerim iucundo sanus amico*
>
> In my right mind, there's nothing I'd compare with a genial friend.

The Epicureans regarded friendship as one of the highest pleasures, and Horace was naturally epicurean in his tastes. The word *sanus* here implies a tacit contrast with the *insania* of the lover — with his *furor*. For Horace in middle age friendship was certainly a higher value than love.

His description of sexual jealousy at 1.13 is in competition with Sappho's well known Fragment 31 'He seems to me to be equal to a God ...' and with Catullus 51 translating Sappho, but its crude physiological and culinary details are designed to make the reader laugh, and its quiet ending suggests an ideal of close friendship rather than passion. Passion indeed is implicitly disapproved of in the phrase *puer furens* (1.13.11), though *furor* can be recommended in connexion with the return to Italy of an old army friend (2.7.26–28).

Horace has been much criticized for the supposed insincerity of his court poetry, the odes devoted to the praise of the grandest of all his friends, the emperor Augustus, or Caesar, as he more often calls him. Some readers regard these odes as mere propaganda produced at the suggestion of his patron Maecenas, but Fraenkel in his classic *Horace* (1957) more than restores the balance with his careful analysis of 'Odes concerned with Augustus'. 'Any critic of Horace' he writes (p.355) 'should at least admit that the poet himself believed in the ideas and the hopes which he made the themes of his patriotic odes, believed that it was Augustus who had saved the Roman world from utter ruin. The only alternative Horace could see to the rule of the Princeps was endless chaos.'

Here is a sample of the poetry in question taken from 4.5, Fraenkel's 'favourite ode':

> *Lucem redde tuae, dux bone, patriae.*
> *instar ueris enim uultus ubi tuus*
> *affulsit populo, gratior it dies*
>   *et soles melius nitent.*

> Bring, good leader, the light back to your fatherland.
> For whenever your face dawns like the spring upon
> Roman people the day passes more gratefully
>   And the sun has a better shine. (5–8)

The subtle craftsmanship of the Latin stanza, its rhyme, alliteration, assonance, and in the main clause (7–8) varied word-order do not obtrude and the total effect is disarmingly simple. For all their exaggeration the lines have a ring of sincerity — more so than, say, the lover's claim at Virgil *Eclogues* 7.59–60:

> *Phyllidis aduentu nostrae nemus omne uirebit,*
> *Iuppiter et laeto descendet plurimus imbri.*

> But when our Phyllis comes each coppice will be green
> And Jove descend abundantly in merry rain.

Ian Du Quesnay (1995) points out (p.157) that 'The stanza conflates three standard encomiastic topoi: the comparison of a return or arrival with the coming of spring after the cold of winter; the appearance or gaze of the ruler; and the comparison or identification of the ruler with the sun.' This is typical of Horace, who often operates with 'standard topoi' and commonplaces but makes them new by small unexpected changes, omissions and additions.

Odes 2.3 to Dellius will provide examples.

> *Aequam memento rebus in arduis*
> *seruare mentem ...*

> When things are steep remember to keep your mind
> Level ... (1–2)

The commonplace behind this opening is 'Keep your head'. Horace makes it his own by the double antithesis of 'steep' and 'level', 'things' and 'mind', by underlining the etymological connexion of *memini* and *mens*, and by using *aequa mens* for the more familiar *aequus animus* (cf. *aequanimitas*).

> *huc uina et unguenta et nimium breuis*
> *flores amoenae ferre iube rosae*
> > *dum res et aetas et Sororum*
> > *fila trium patiuntur atra*

> Command to bring here unguents and wine and blooms
> (Too transient, alas) of the lovely rose.
> > While things and time of life and those black
> > Threads of the Sisterly Three allow it. (13–16)

The commonplace here is (roughly) 'Let us eat and drink, for tomorrow we die'. Horace calls for an immediate symposium, asking for wine and its usual accompaniments of unguents and flowers. He specifies the flowers and matches the three ingredients of the symposium in the main clause with the three nouns in the *dum* clause (the third noun in each clause having dependent additions so as to form a so-called 'tricolon crescendo'). He includes a colour contrast of *atra* with *rosae*, personifies *fila* and refers to the Fates as the Three Sisters. Porphyrio, the 2nd/3rd century AD commentator, finds it necessary to explain: *dum ipsae Sorores patiuntur, hoc est, Parcae quarum fila sunt atra*, 'while the Sisters themselves allow it, that is the Parcae, whose threads are black.'

> *Omnes eodem cogimur, omnium*
> *uersatur urna serius ocius*
> > *sors exitura et nos in aeternum*
> > *exsilium impositura cumbae.*

> We all are herded toward the same place, and all
> Our lots are shaken up in the urn, to leap
> > Out soon or late and place us on the
> > Ferry to exile that lasts for ever. (25–28)

The commonplace here is 'We shall all die sooner or later'. The metaphor of cattle carries on from *uictima* 'sacrificial animal' in the previous line. The second metaphor shifts to a lottery, lines 25–27:

> > *omnium*
> *uer-sā-tur ur-nā ser-ius ocius*
> > *sors exitura*

vividly suggesting by sense and sound the constant shuffling of the lots in the urn and the jumping out of one in the elided final syllable of *exitura*. The third metaphor shifts to Charon's ferry in the Underworld, the two elisions of *-um* in 27 and 28 seeming to emphasize the never-ending exile. The word *exsilium* in the context of lots leaping out could hardly fail to remind the reader of *exsilire* 'to jump out' and would add a touch of humour to the gloom of the ending.

Such quatrains are easily memorable, especially as the Latin almost invariably contains fewer words than its English equivalent, even though both have the same number of syllables. So in this last example 17 Latin words are rendered by 36 English. English cannot hope to match the concision, dignity and sonority of Horace's Latin, let alone its convoluted word order (e.g. 2.3.25–28 above). In Latinizing these ancient Greek metres (see the next section) Horace has made of them something totally his own, unique and unrivalled.

THE METRES

One hopes that poetry-readers reading for pleasure will not be put off by the word 'metre' and its associations with complexity and limitation. There is no reason why such readers should bother at all about Horatian metres. If the translator has done his work properly they should be able intuitively to get the feel of the metre of each ode as it comes along, and they can therefore skip this section of the introduction with a clear conscience. How many readers of Auden's *In Memory of Sigmund Freud* know that it is supposed to be in Alcaics? And does such ignorance affect our appreciation of its poetry?

But for those inquiring spirits who are interested in the mechanics of poetry and who wish to know how each Horatian metre works the present section offers a general survey, omitting much additional detail of interest only to specialists.

The four books of Horace's odes comprise a total of 103 poems, each poem (except 4.8) consisting of a multiple of four lines and displaying one of thirteen metrical systems. These thirteen systems are listed below, roughly in the order of their frequency. (In what follows ˘ represents a short syllable, — long, and ≝ either short or long.)

1   **Alcaics:** a four line stanza used 37 times

$$\underset{\smile}{\simeq} - \smile - - / - \smile\smile - \smile \simeq$$
$$\underset{\smile}{\simeq} - \smile - - / - \smile\smile - \smile \simeq$$
$$\underset{\smile}{\simeq} - \smile - - - - \smile - \simeq$$
$$- \smile\smile - \smile\smile - \smile - \simeq$$

> *Odi profanum / uulgus et arceo.*
> *fauete linguis: / carmina non prius*
> *audita Musarum sacerdos*
> *uirginibus puerisque canto.* (3.1.1–4)

In lines 1 and 2 Horace regularly has a break between words after the fifth syllable.

Here is a rough English mnemonic:

> Lines one and two go / thus in Alcáic verse;
> Nine sýllables complete the third line;
> Four has a décasyllábic pattern.

In my English Alcaics the fifth syllable in lines one, two and three may be short, and the break between words in lines one and two may come after the sixth syllable. This is in fact a return to the freer practice of Alcaeus himself, which Horace, for whatever reason, chose to tighten up.

2   Asclepiad systems: used in a total of 34 odes. They come in five varieties built from the following metres:

(a) *Pherecratean*:

— — — — ᴗᴗ — ᵜ

cras donaberis haedo (3.13.3)

Here's your Phérecratéan.

(b) Glyconic:

— — — — ᴗᴗ — ᴗ ᵜ

magnas inter opes inops (3.16.28)

Here's how ev'ry Glycónic goes.

(c) *Lesser Asclepiad*:

— — / — ᴗᴗ — / — ᴗᴗ — / ᴗ ᵜ

multis / ille bonis / flebilis oc/cidit (1.24.9)

One more / chóriamb makes / Lesser Asclé/piad.

A choriamb is — ᴗᴗ —. Horace has a break between words after the sixth syllable. I follow the freer practice of Alcaeus.

(d) *Greater Asclepiad*:

— — / — ᴗᴗ — / — ᴗᴗ — / — ᴗᴗ — / ᴗ ᵜ

Nullam, / Vare, sacra / uite prius / seueris ar/borem (1.18.1)

With two / chóriambs more / you will have made / Greater Asclé/piad.

In Horace there is word-break after the sixth and tenth syllables. Here again I follow the freer practice of Alcaeus and Catullus.

2.1 First Asclepiad: Lesser Asclepiad repeated throughout, used for three odes.

Dicar, / qua uiolens / obstrepit Au/fidus (3.30.10)

2.2 Second Asclepiad: three Lesser Asclepiads plus a Glyconic, used for nine odes.

multis / ille bonis / flebilis oc/cidit,
nulli / flebilior / quam tibi, Ver/gili.
tu frus/tra pius heu / non ita cre/ditum
   poscis Quintilium deos, (1.24.9–12)

2.3 Third Asclepiad: two Lesser Asclepiads with a Pherecratean and Glyconic. Used for seven odes.

Quis mul/ta gracilis / te puer in / rosa
perfu/sus liquidis / urget odor/ibus
   grato, Pyrrha, sub antro?
     cui flavam religas comam? (1.5.1–4)

2.4 Fourth Asclepiad: Glyconic plus Lesser Asclepiad, used for twelve odes.

   audax omnia perpeti
gens hu/mana ruit / per uetitum / nefas. (1.3.25–26)

2.5 Fifth Asclepiad: Greater Asclepiad repeated throughout, used in three odes.

spem lon/gam reseces. / dum loquimur, / fugerit in/uida
aetas. / carpe diem, / quam minimum / credula pos/tero. (1.11.7–8)

My English Pherecrateans, Glyconics and Asclepiads may begin with — $\smile$ or $\smile$ — instead of — —. (N.B. The above numbering of the Asclepiad systems follows N–H; other authorities number them differently.)

3 Sapphics: a four line stanza used 25 times.

$$— \smile — — — / \smile\smile — \smile — \underline{\smile}$$
$$— \smile — — — / \smile\smile — \smile — \underline{\smile}$$
$$— \smile — — — / \smile\smile — \smile — \underline{\smile}$$
$$— \smile\smile — \underline{\smile}$$

tu pias laetis / animas reponis
sedibus uirgaque/ leuem coerces
aurea turbam, / superis deorum
gratus et imis. (1.10.17–20)

Sápphics show three lines / of eleven, then five
Sýllables thuswise.

In lines 1–3 Horace regularly has a word-break after the fifth syllable
or occasionally after the sixth. My English Sapphics may have a short
fourth syllable and may neglect the word-break after the fifth or sixth
syllable, in this following Catullus who followed the practice of
Sappho and Alcaeus. Here again, for whatever reason, Horace accepted
stricter limitations. Very occasionally my fourth line (the Adonic)
illustrates a conflict of metrical ictus and word accent, e.g. 1.25.12 'The
lunar dark time' and 3.27.76 'Commemorate you'.

After these seven systems there remain six other metres which are
used only once or twice.

4.1 First Archilochian: used twice.

— ‿‿ — ‿‿ — / ‿‿ — ‿‿ — ‿‿ — ‿

— ‿‿ — ‿‿ — ‿‿ — ‿

Quo nos cumque feret / melior fortuna parente,
  ibimus, o socii comitesque. (1.7.25–26)

First Archilóchian shows / a dactylic hexameter followed
  By a dactylic tetrameter thuswise.

4.2 Second Archilochian: used once.

— ‿‿ — ‿‿ — / ‿‿ — ‿‿ — ‿‿ — ‿

— ‿‿ — ‿ ‿

Diffugere niues, / redeunt iam gramina campis
  arboribusque comae (4.7.1–2)

In Archilóchian Two / a complete hexameter précedes
  Half a hexameter thus.

4.3 Third Archilochian: used once.

— ‿‿ — ‿‿ — / ‿‿ — ‿‿ / — ‿ — ‿ — —

‿ — ‿ — — / — ‿ — ‿ — —

Soluitur acris hiems / grata uice / ueris et Fauoni
  trahuntque siccas / machinae carinas (1.4.1–2)

Third Archilóchian, start/ing dactýlicly, / ends the line with trochees;
  Line two's iámbic, / but deficient thuswise.

For 'deficient' the technical term is 'catalectic', the last short syllable of the iambic line being lacking.

4.4 Greater Sapphic: used once.

> Lydia, dic per omnis
> te deos oro, / Sybarin // cur properes amando (1.8.1–2)

> Áristophánic first line
> Then a Sapphic start / with a clear //Áristophánic ending.

4.5 Hipponactian: used once.

$$\stackrel{\smile}{-} \, - \, \smile \, - \, \stackrel{\smile}{-} \, / \, - \, \smile \, - \, \smile \, - \, \stackrel{\smile}{-}$$

> Non ebur neque aureum
> mea renidet / in domo lacunar (2.18.1–2)

> Here's a Hípponáctian –
> Trocháic first line / plus iámbic second.

4.6 Ionics: used once.

$$\stackrel{\smile}{\smile} \, - \, - \, \stackrel{\smile}{\smile} \, - \, - \, \stackrel{\smile}{\smile} \, - \, - \, \stackrel{\smile}{\smile} \, - \, -$$

> Catus idem per apertum fugientis agitato
> grege ceruos iaculari ... (3.12.10–11)

Di-di dum-dum is repeated as the pattern in Iónics.

In scanning the lines of the English translation it may help to remember the following points.

1.   Although elisions such as *don't, I've, that's, you'll, belov'd, wing'd* are printed in the text, others are not. So, for example, depending on the metrical context words such as *driven, bidden, open* can be treated as one or two syllables; *difference, suffering, victory* as two or three; *favourable, intemperate, savagery* as three or four. Similarly a vowel ending a word may or may not elide with a vowel beginning the next word, e.g. *the inconstant* (1.1.7), *the unruffled* (1.5.8), *To aid* (1.2.26), *to a powerful* (1.5.16).

2.   *i, u* and *y* may be consonantal, reducing the word by one syllable, e.g.: *chariot* (1.1.4), *Icarian* (1.1.15), *Sestius* (1.4.14), *Lydia* (1.13.1), *tempestuous* (1.3.19), *gratefully I'll* (1.12.39), *carrying* (1.15.1), *Tityos and Geryon* (2.14.8).

3.　　Diphthongs may count as two syllables, e.g.: *our* (1.2.21), *hour* (2.16.31), *fire* (1.3.29), *clear* (1.22.1).

4.　　Some disyllables may count as monosyllables, e.g.: *prior* (1.8.14), *doing* (1.14.2), *cruel* (1.19.1), *power* (4.8.9)

5.　　The third syllable of dactylic words may be given secondary stress, turning the dactyl (— ⌣⌣) into a cretic (— ⌣ —); *eloquent* (1.10.1), *artfully* (1.10.3), *messenger* (1.10.6).

6.　　If a line seems to have too few syllables the reason may be found under 3; if too many, then under 1, 2 or 4. In this connexion one should remember that the final *e* in Greek girls' names is always pronounced (Barine, Chloe, Danae, Melpomene etc.) and that the ending *–eus* in Greek male names (Lynceus, Orpheus, Peleus etc.) is pronounced as one syllable except where a diaeresis indicates that it needs to be two (Proteüs 1.2.7). As regards Latin and Greek proper names the English metre will reveal where the stress falls, but very occasionally an accent is added, e.g. Albunéa (1.7.12), Pácorus (3.6.9), Cínara (4.1.4).

THE ODES

TEXT AND TRANSLATION

CARMINVM LIBER PRIMVS

I

Maecenas atauis edite regibus,
o et praesidium et dulce decus meum,
sunt quos curriculo puluerem Olympicum
collegisse iuuat metaque feruidis
euitata rotis palmaque nobilis   5
terrarum dominos euehit ad deos;
hunc, si mobilium turba Quiritium
certat tergeminis tollere honoribus;
illum, si proprio condidit horreo
quidquid de Libycis uerritur areis.   10
gaudentem patrios findere sarculo
agros Attalicis condicionibus
numquam demoueas, ut trabe Cypria
Myrtoum pauidus nauta secet mare.
luctantem Icariis fluctibus Africum   15
mercator metuens otium et oppidi
laudat rura sui; mox reficit ratis
quassas indocilis pauperiem pati.
est qui nec ueteris pocula Massici
nec partem solido demere de die   20
spernit, nunc uiridi membra sub arbuto
stratus, nunc ad aquae lene caput sacrae.
multos castra iuuant et lituo tubae
permixtus sonitus bellaque matribus
detestata. manet sub Ioue frigido   25
uenator tenerae coniugis immemor,
seu uisa est catulis cerua fidelibus,
seu rupit teretes Marsus aper plagas.
me doctarum hederae praemia frontium
dis miscent superis, me gelidum nemus   30
Nympharumque leues cum Satyris chori
secernunt populo, si neque tibias
Euterpe cohibet nec Polyhymnia
Lesboum refugit tendere barbiton.

ODES, BOOK ONE

1

Maecenas, the descendant of ancestral kings,
O protection and sweet title to fame for me,
Some there are who enjoy raising Olympic dust
In a chariot and close-shaving the turning-post
With hot wheels, and the palm-leaf of the champion   5
Uplifts them to the Gods, Lords of this world of ours.
Others like it if the inconstant electorate
Votes in crowds to promote them to the honours three;
Others too if they store up in their granaries
All the sweepings from off Libyan threshing-floors.   10
Those again who enjoy using a hoe to break
Up their family fields never will you dislodge
To cleave Myrtoan seas, even on Attalic terms,
As scared sailors aboard Cypriot timber-work.
While the African wind fights with Icarian waves   15
Frightened traders approve peace and their native town's
Countryside, but anon refit their shattered ships,
Unprepared to endure relative poverty.
Some there are who don't scorn cups of old Massic wine
Or subtracting a large part from the working day,   20
Sprawling now at full length under arbutus green,
Now perhaps by the calm source of a sacred stream.
Many live for the camp and for the sound of horns
Mixed with trumpets, for wars mothers abominate.
Under Jupiter's sky freezing, the hunter keeps   25
Watch, forgetting his soft-hearted young wife at home,
Should a hind have been caught sight of by faithful hounds
Or a Marsian boar broken the slender nets.
Me the ivy, reward of the poetic brow
Mingles with Gods above; me the cool woodland grove   30
And the Satyrs' and Nymphs' light-footed choruses
Separate from the crowd, if but Euterpe agree
Not to hush her reed pipe and Polyhymnia's
Not unwilling to string Lesbos's barbitos.

quodsi me lyricis uatibus inseres,   35
sublimi feriam sidera uertice.

II

Iam satis terris niuis atque dirae
grandinis misit pater et rubente
dextera sacras iaculatus arceis
terruit urbem,

terruit gentis, graue ne rediret   5
saeculum Pyrrhae noua monstra questae,
omne cum Proteus pecus egit altos
uisere montis,

piscium et summa genus haesit ulmo,
nota quae sedes fuerat columbis,   10
et superiecto pauidae natarunt
aequore dammae.

uidimus flauum Tiberim retortis
litore Etrusco uiolenter undis
ire deiectum monumenta regis   15
templaque Vestae,

Iliae dum se nimium querenti
iactat ultorem, uagus et sinistra
labitur ripa Ioue non probante u-
xorius amnis.   20

audiet ciuis acuisse ferrum
quo graues Persae melius perirent,
audiet pugnas uitio parentum
rara iuuentus.

quem uocet diuum populus ruentis   25
imperi rebus? prece qua fatigent
uirgines sanctae minus audientem
carmina Vestam?

But if you will include me among lyric bards   35
Then, my head through the clouds, I shall collide with stars.

2

Now enough of snow and of horrid hailstones
Has the Father showered on earth and letting
Fly with red right hand at our sacred summits
Frightened the City,

Frightened mankind lest there return the grievous   5
Age of Pyrrha weeping at unknown horrors
When the flocks of Proteüs all were driven to
Visit the high peaks

And when fish got stuck in the crowns of elmtrees
Which had been a favourite perch for pigeons,   10
And in the overflowing expanse were swimming
Terrified roe-deer.

We've seen yellow Tiber, his current twisted
Violently back from the Tuscan shore, race
On to hurl down royalty's monuments and   15
Temples of Vesta;

Boasting then to Ilia in her anguish
He was her avenger, against Jove's wishes
Over his left bank on the loose he slid, ux-
orious river.   20

Our young, thinned out by the guilt of parents,
Will be told how citizens, sharpening iron
Better used to slaughter aggressive Persians,
Fought one another.

Which of all the Gods can the people call on   25
To aid the falling empire? With what appeal can
Holy Virgins weary a Vesta who won't
Listen to their hymns?

cui dabit partis scelus expiandi
Iuppiter? tandem uenias precamur   30
nube candentis umeros amictus
augur Apollo;

siue tu mauis, Erycina ridens,
quam Iocus circum uolat et Cupido;
siue neglectum genus et nepotes   35
respicis auctor,

heu nimis longo satiate ludo,
quem iuuat clamor galeaeque leues
acer et Marsi peditis cruentum
uultus in hostem.   40

siue mutata iuuenem figura
ales in terris imitaris almae
filius Maiae patiens uocari
Caesaris ultor,

serus in caelum redeas diuque   45
laetus intersis populo Quirini,
neue te nostris uitiis iniquum
ocior aura

tollat; hic magnos potius triumphos,
hic ames dici pater atque princeps,   50
neu sinas Medos equitare inultos
te duce, Caesar.

III

Sic te diua potens Cypri,
sic fratres Helenae, lucida sidera,
uentorumque regat pater
obstrictis aliis praeter Iapyga,
nauis, quae tibi creditum   5
debes Vergilium finibus Atticis:
reddas incolumem precor
et serues animae dimidium meae.
illi robur et aes triplex
circa pectus erat, qui fragilem truci   10

6

Whom will Jove appoint to the role of expi-
ating our crime? Come, we beseech, at long last   30
With your gleaming shoulders in cloud enfolded,
Augur Apollo,

Or, if you prefer, Erycina laughing
While around fly Merriment and Desire,
Or, if you their sire are concerned for your race   35
And disowned grandsons,

Sated with your overlong game, alas, come
You whom war-cry pleases and polished helmets
And the Marsian infantry's watchful scowl at
Bloodthirsty foemen.   40

Or if you, wing'd son of the kindly Maia,
Changing shape on earth imitate a young man,
Suffering yourself to be nominated
Caesar's avenger,

Late may you return to the sky and gladly   45
Spend a long time here with Quirinus' people
Nor be carried off by a sudden whirlwind,
Vexed by our vices.

Rather may you here celebrate great Triumphs,
Here be known as Father and Foremost Roman,   50
Nor permit the Medes to ride out unpunished
While you rule, Caesar.

3

So may Cyprus's Goddess Queen,
So may Helena's twin brothers, unclouded stars,
And the Father of Winds (the rest
All tied up save the northwester Iapyx) guide
You, O ship, who've received on trust   5
Virgil's life and who owe him to the Attic shore:
There deliver him unimpaired,
I implore you, and save one who is half my soul.
There was hardwood and triple brass
Round his thorax who first launched a precarious   10

            commisit pelago ratem
primus, nec timuit praecipitem Africum
            decertantem Aquilonibus
nec tristis Hyadas nec rabiem Noti,
            quo non arbiter Hadriae   15
maior, tollere seu ponere uult freta.
            quem mortis timuit gradum
qui siccis oculis monstra natantia,
            qui uidit mare turbidum et
infamis scopulos Acroceraunia?   20
            nequiquam deus abscidit
prudens oceano dissociabili
            terras, si tamen impiae
non tangenda rates transiliunt uada.
            audax omnia perpeti   25
gens humana ruit per uetitum nefas,
            audax Iapeti genus
ignem fraude mala gentibus intulit.
            post ignem aetheria domo
subductum macies et noua febrium   30
            terris incubuit cohors
semotique prius tarda necessitas
            leti corripuit gradum.
expertus uacuum Daedalus aera
            pennis non homini datis;   35
perrupit Acheronta Herculeus labor.
            nil mortalibus ardui est:
caelum ipsum petimus stultitia neque
            per nostrum patimur scelus
iracunda Iouem ponere fulmina.   40

IV

Soluitur acris hiems grata uice ueris et Fauoni
        trahuntque siccas machinae carinas,
ac neque iam stabulis gaudet pecus aut arator igni
        nec prata canis albicant pruinis.
iam Cytherea choros ducit Venus imminente luna,   5
        iunctaeque Nymphis Gratiae decentes

Sailing ship on the cruel sea,
Neither fearing the swift onset of Africus
    In contention with Aquilo,
Nor the Hyades drear nor Notus' savagery,
    Than whom Adria has no more   15
Potent ruler to raise or to reduce his waves.
    What death's coming could he have feared
Who could watch with dry eyes sea-monsters swimming by,
    Who could face the tempestuous deep
And those infamous rocks the Acroceraunians?   20
    Providence has in vain divorced
Continents with the dissevering ocean-wave
    If, in spite of that, impious
Vessels leap over untouchable waterways.
    Daring every experience   25
Humankind rushes on, through what the Gods forbid.
    The rash son of Iapetus
Brought fire down for our race by unashamed deceit.
    After fire's removal from
Its etherial home, wasting disease and new   30
    Troops of fevers infested earth,
And the hitherto far-distant necessity
    Of death quickened its laggard pace.
Clever Daedalus made trial of empty air
    With those pinions denied to man.   35
Labouring Hercules burst open sad Acheron.
    Nothing's out of our mortal reach;
Heaven itself we attack, fools that we are, and by
    Our own wickedness won't allow
Jupiter to discard punitive thunderbolts.   40

4

Violent Winter relaxes in genial change to Spring and West Wind
    And down the shore machines are hauling dry hulls.
Now no longer do livestock enjoy being stalled or ploughman fireside
    And pastures are not glittering in white frost.
Under a full moon now there is dance led by Cytherean Venus   5
    And hand in hand the Nymphs and comely Graces

alterno terram quatiunt pede, dum grauis Cyclopum
    Vulcanus ardens uisit officinas.
nunc decet aut uiridi nitidum caput impedire myrto
    aut flore terrae quem ferunt solutae.   10
nunc et in umbrosis Fauno decet immolare lucis,
    seu poscat agna siue malit haedo.
pallida Mors aequo pulsat pede pauperum tabernas
    regumque turris. o beate Sesti,
uitae summa breuis spem nos uetat incohare longam;   15
    iam te premet nox fabulaeque Manes
et domus exilis Plutonia; quo simul mearis,
    nec regna uini sortiere talis
nec tenerum Lycidan mirabere, quo calet iuuentus
    nunc omnis et mox uirgines tepebunt.   20

V

Quis multa gracilis te puer in rosa
perfusus liquidis urget odoribus
    grato, Pyrrha, sub antro?
        cui flauam religas comam

simplex munditiis? heu quotiens fidem   5
mutatosque deos flebit et aspera
    nigris aequora uentis
        emirabitur insolens,

qui nunc te fruitur credulus aurea,
qui semper uacuam, semper amabilem   10
    sperat, nescius aurae
        fallacis. miseri, quibus

intemptata nites: me tabula sacer
uotiua paries indicat uuida
    suspendisse potenti   15
        uestimenta maris deo.

Make the ground shake with their rhythmical footwork & fiery Vulcan visits
    His heavy-duty Cyclopean workshops.
Now it is right to confine the glistening head with dark-green myrtle
    Or flowers which the loosened soil produces.   10
Now too in shadowy groves it is right to make sacrifice to Faunus —
    A kid, should he prefer, or else a ewe-lamb.
Pale Death kicks with indifferent foot at the door of pauper's cabin
    And royal palace. O born-lucky Sestius,
Life's brief total forbids our commitment to any longer-term hope.   15
    Soon Night will hold you fast and fabled Manes
And the intangible house of Pluto. When once you've made your way there
    You'll not throw dice to choose the king of drinking
Nor will you marvel at lovely young Lycidas, whom today the young men
    All rave about and soon the girls will fall for.   20

5

Who's the slip of a boy in a large wreath of rose
Drenched with liquid pomade pressing you, Pyrrha, so
    Under welcoming arbour?
        For whom braid you that auburn hair

Unobtrusively chic? Ah, he will often weep   5
At Gods and promise changed and in vain ignorance
    Be astonished at black winds
        Whipping up the unruffled sea

Who naïvely enjoys now your all-golden self,
Who expects you to be always available,   10
    Always lovable, not told
        How your air can deceive! Poor things

Those you dazzle untried! As for myself a shrine's
Votive tablet proclaims there on the wall that I've
    Dedicated my wet clothes   15
        To a powerful Ocean-God.

VI

Scriberis Vario fortis et hostium
uictor Maeonii carminis alite,
qua rem cumque ferox nauibus aut equis
    miles te duce gesserit.

nos, Agrippa, neque haec dicere nec grauem   5
Pelidae stomachum cedere nescii
nec cursus duplicis per mare Vlixei
    nec saeuam Pelopis domum

conamur, tenues grandia, dum pudor
imbellisque lyrae Musa potens uetat   10
laudes egregii Caesaris et tuas
    culpa deterere ingeni.

quis Martem tunica tectum adamantina
digne scripserit aut puluere Troico
nigrum Merionen aut ope Palladis   15
    Tydiden superis parem?

nos conuiuia, nos proelia uirginum
sectis in iuuenes unguibus acrium
cantamus uacui, siue quid urimur,
    non praeter solitum leues.   20

VII

Laudabunt alii claram Rhodon aut Mytilenen
        aut Epheson bimarisue Corinthi
moenia uel Baccho Thebas uel Apolline Delphos
        insignis aut Thessala Tempe;
sunt quibus unum opus est intactae Palladis urbem   5
        carmine perpetuo celebrare et
undique decerptae frondi praeponere oliuam;
        plurimus in Iunonis honorem
aptum dicet equis Argos ditisque Mycenas:
        me nec tam patiens Lacedaemon   10
nec tam Larisae percussit campus opimae
        quam domus Albuneae resonantis

6

You'll have Varius, that flyer of epic song,
To write you up as brave and the foe's conqueror
Wheresoever in ships or in the saddle fierce
    Soldiers fought under your command.

I won't take that as my subject, Agrippa, nor   5
The dire spleen of Achilles who refused to yield
Nor sea-travels of duplicitous Ulysses
    Nor Pelops' cruel family,

Themes too grand for my light verses, while modesty
And the Muse that controls the unwarlike lyre forbids   10
The imperfection of my wit to detract from great
    Caesar's glorification and yours.

Mars encased in his chain armour of adamant
Or else Meriones, black with the dust of Troy,
Or Tydides, a match by Pallas' help for Gods —   15
    Who will worthily write of these?

Give me parties, give me battles of passionate
Girls, whose nails have been cut, versus young men in love,
To sing, either heart-whole, or, if the heat is on,
    Still light-hearted as usual.   20

7

Others are welcome to praise far-famed Rhodos or Mytilene,
    Ephesus too or Isthmian Corinth's
Walls or Thebes that's specially known for Bacchus or Delphi
    Home of Apollo or Thessaly's Tempe.
Some there are whose only ambition is praising the Virgin   5
    Pallas' city in a long epic poem
And preferring her olive to foliage taken from elsewhere.
    Many a one to the glory of Juno
Celebrates Argos, ideal for horses, and wealthy Mycenae.
    But as for me neither tough Lacedaemon   10
Strikes such a chord in my heart nor the plain of fertile Larissa
    As Albunéa's reverberant grotto,

et praeceps Anio ac Tiburni lucus et uda
    mobilibus pomaria riuis.
albus ut obscuro deterget nubila caelo   15
    saepe Notus neque parturit imbris
perpetuos, sic tu sapiens finire memento
    tristitiam uitaeque labores
molli, Plance, mero, seu te fulgentia signis
    castra tenent seu densa tenebit   20
Tiburis umbra tui. Teucer Salamina patremque
    cum fugeret, tamen uda Lyaeo
tempora populea fertur uinxisse corona
    sic tristis adfatus amicos:
'quo nos cumque feret melior fortuna parente,   25
    ibimus, o socii comitesque,
nil desperandum Teucro duce et auspice Teucro.
    certus enim promisit Apollo
ambiguam tellure noua Salamina futuram.
    o fortes peioraque passi   30
mecum saepe uiri, nunc uino pellite curas:
    cras ingens iterabimus aequor.'

VIII

    Lydia, dic, per omnis
te deos oro, Sybarin cur properes amando
    perdere, cur apricum
oderit campum patiens pulueris atque solis,
    cur neque militaris   5
inter aequalis equitet, Gallica nec lupatis
    temperet ora frenis?
cur timet flauum Tiberim tangere? cur oliuum
    sanguine uiperino
cautius uitat neque iam liuida gestat armis   10
    bracchia, saepe disco,
saepe trans finem iaculo nobilis expedito?
    quid latet, ut marinae
filium dicunt Thetidis sub lacrimosa Troiae
    funera, ne uirilis   ·   15
cultus in caedem et Lycias proriperet cateruas?

Anio's sheer cascades, the sacred grove of Tiburnus,
      Orchards moistened by changeable channels.
Just as the white south wind will frequently wipe away clouds from   15
      Lowering skies nor labour to bring forth
Permanent rain, so you if you're wise will remember to limit
      Life's unhappiness and its afflictions,
Plancus, with mellow wine, whether camp with its well-polished eagles
      Holds you now or your favourite Tibur's   20
Dense shade later will hold. They say that Teucer, though leaving
      Father and Salamis island for exile,
Bound round his forehead moist with Lyaeus a garland of poplar,
      Thus consoling his friends in their sadness:
'Wheresoever a kinder Fate than my father may take us   25
      There we shall go, companions and comrades.
Never despair with Teucer as leader and Teucer as prophet,
      Seeing inerrant Apollo has promised
There'll be another ambiguous Salamis in a new country,
      O brave hearts who so often have suffered   30
Worse with me, use wine now to banish your worries. Tomorrow
      We'll be re-ploughing the limitless ocean.'

8

      Lydia, why in Heaven's name
All the rush to wreck Sybaris (tell me, I beg) with loving?
      Why does he so dislike the
Open Campus Martius though used to its dust and hot sun?
      Why does he not, a soldier   5
With his young contemporaries, ride on his horse, controlling
      Gallican mouth with wolf's-bit?
Why should he be frightened to touch yellowy Tiber? Why shun
      Worse than a viper's venom
Olive oil? No longer display bruises from wearing armour,   10
      Though he was once renowned for
Often hurling javelin or discus beyond the best mark?
      Why does he hide as legend
Says that sea-born Thetis' son did, prior to the tragic deaths at
      Ilion, lest a man's clothes   15
And behaviour forced him to face slaughter and Lycian squadrons?

IX

Vides ut alta stet niue candidum
Soracte nec iam sustineant onus
    siluae laborantes geluque
        flumina constiterint acuto.

dissolue frigus ligna super foco   5
large reponens atque benignius
    deprome quadrimum Sabina,
        o Thaliarche, merum diota.

permitte diuis cetera, qui simul
strauere uentos aequore feruido   10
    deproeliantis, nec cupressi
        nec ueteres agitantur orni.

quid sit futurum cras fuge quaerere et
quem Fors dierum cumque dabit, lucro
    appone, nec dulcis amores   15
        sperne puer neque tu choreas,

donec uirenti canities abest
morosa. nunc et Campus et areae
    lenesque sub noctem susurri
        composita repetantur hora,   20

nunc et latentis proditor intimo
gratus puellae risus ab angulo
    pignusque dereptum lacertis
        aut digito male pertinaci.

X

Mercuri, facunde nepos Atlantis,
qui feros cultus hominum recentum
uoce formasti catus et decorae
more palaestrae,

te canam, magni Iouis et deorum   5
nuntium curuaeque lyrae parentem,
callidum quidquid placuit iocoso
condere furto.

9

See how Soracte under thick-fallen snow
Stands up resplendent, nor can the labouring
    Woods any longer bear the load, and
        Rivers have flowed to a halt in sharp ice.

Thaw out the cold by piling the fire up   5
With plenty of logs and pouring more lavishly
    From its Sabine two-handled pitcher,
        O Thaliarchus. the four-year-old wine.

Leave all the rest to Gods, for as soon as they
Have laid the storm-winds battling it out upon   10
    The seething ocean, then are neither
        Cypresses shaken nor ancient rowans.

Beware of asking what may tomorrow bring,
And enter up as profit whatever day
    Good Luck may grant you, nor in boyhood   15
        Say No to sweet love-affairs and dances,

While youthful green is free from cantankerous
White hair. So now let Campus and public square
    And gentle whispers after nightfall
        Often be sought at an hour agreed on.   20

Sweet also now, betraying her hiding-place,
Is girlish laughter heard from a secret nook
    And keepsake snatched away from upper
        Arm or a seeming-reluctant finger.

10

Eloquent Mercurius, Atlas' grandson,
Who refined wild habits of early humans
Artfully by speech and the seemly customs
Of the palaestra,

You I'll sing, great Jupiter's and the Gods' own   5
Messenger, who fathered the curving lyre,
Clever too at hiding in playful theft what-
ever you fancy.

te, boues olim nisi reddidisses
per dolum amotas, puerum minaci   10
uoce dum terret, uiduus pharetra
risit Apollo.

quin et Atridas duce te superbos
Ilio diues Priamus relicto
Thessalosque ignis et iniqua Troiae   15
castra fefellit.

tu pias laetis animas reponis
sedibus uirgaque leuem coerces
aurea turbam, superis deorum
gratus et imis.   20

XI

Tu ne quaesieris, scire nefas, quem mihi, quem tibi
finem di dederint, Leuconoe, nec Babylonios
temptaris numeros. ut melius, quidquid erit, pati,
seu pluris hiemes seu tribuit Iuppiter ultimam,
quae nunc oppositis debilitat pumicibus mare   5
Tyrrhenum. sapias, uina liques, et spatio breui
spem longam reseces. dum loquimur, fugerit inuida
aetas: carpe diem quam minimum credula postero.

XII

Quem uirum aut heroa lyra uel acri
tibia sumis celebrare, Clio?
quem deum? cuius recinet iocosa
nomen imago

aut in umbrosis Heliconis oris   5
aut super Pindo gelidoue in Haemo,
unde uocalem temere insecutae
Orphea siluae,

Once, in your young days, when he tried to scare you
Using loud-mouthed threats should you not return his   10
Cows removed by cunning, Apollo laughed at
Losing his quiver.

Yes, and wealthy Priam with you as guide left
Ilium, eluding the proud Atridae
And Thessalian watch-fires and the encampment   15
Threatening his Troy.

You escort the souls of the good to Joyous
Mansions and with golden caduceus shepherd
The insubstantial many, belov'd by High Gods
And by the Lowest.   20

11

You are not to inquire (knowing's taboo) what limit Gods have set
To my life and to yours, Leuconoe. No Babylonian
Numerology! Far better endure whatever comes to pass,
Whether Jupiter vouchsafes any more winters or only this
Now exhausting the Tyrrhenian sea's breakers on pumice rocks.   5
Be a realist, keep straining the wine, and for our life's brief span
Cut back lengthier hope. While we converse Time the malevolent
Has flown. Harvest the day, trusting the next little as possible.

12

Say what man or hero you undertake to
Celebrate, Clio, on the lyre or shrill-tongued
Pipe? What God? Whose name will elusive Echo
Soon be repeating

Either on Mt Helicon's shady borders   5
Or on Pindus' summit or frosty Haemus
Whence the forest trees followed helter-skelter
Musical Orpheus

arte materna rapidos morantem
fluminum lapsus celerisque uentos,   10
blandum et auritas fidibus canoris
ducere quercus?

quid prius dicam solitis parentis
laudibus, qui res hominum ac deorum,
qui mare ac terras uariisque mundum   15
temperat horis?

unde nil maius generatur ipso
nec uiget quidquam simile aut secundum.
proximos illi tamen occupauit
Pallas honores   20

proeliis audax. neque te silebo,
Liber et saeuis inimica uirgo
beluis, nec te, metuende certa
Phoebe sagitta.

dicam et Alciden puerosque Ledae,   25
hunc equis, illum superare pugnis
nobilem; quorum simul alba nautis
stella refulsit,

defluit saxis agitatus umor,
concidunt uenti fugiuntque nubes   30
et minax, quod sic uoluere, ponto
unda recumbit.

Romulum post hos prius an quietum
Pompili regnum memorem an superbos
Tarquini fasces dubito an Catonis   35
nobile letum.

Regulum et Scauros animaeque magnae
prodigum Paulum superante Poeno
gratus insigni referam Camena
Fabriciumque.   40

hunc et incomptis Curium capillis
utilem bello tulit et Camillum
saeua paupertas et auitus apto
cum lare fundus.

With his mother's art to a standstill bringing
Swiftly-flowing rivers and rushing breezes, 10
Charmer who could lure with his singing lyre-strings
Long-eared oak-trees?

What shall I tell sooner than custom-sanctioned
Praises of that Parent who rules the affairs of
Men and Gods, the ocean and heaven and earth with 15
Varying seasons?

Whence no greater thing has been born than Himself
Nor can aught thrive similar or His second.
None the less next honours to Him has Pallas
Surely pre-empted, 20

Daring Warrior Maid, nor shall I omit you,
Liber, and the Virgin who's foe to savage
Beasts, nor you, Phoebus, to be dreaded for your
Accurate arrow.

Hercules I'll name too and Leda's twin boys, 25
One as champion rider, the other famed as
Pugilist, for soon as their silver star has
Shone out for sailors

Turbulent waters from the skerries drain down,
Stormy winds fall silent, the rain-clouds vanish, 30
And at sea (for such is their will) the breakers'
Menace becomes calm.

After these I doubt whether first to mention
Romulus, Pompilius' peaceful kingdom,
Collatine's proud rods, or the famous death of 35
Cato the Younger.

Regulus, the Scauri, and Paullus, lavish
Of his noble spirit as Punic victim,
Gratefully I'll record with Camena's glory,
Also Fabricius. 40

He and Dentatus and Camillus, useful
Fighting men, unshorn and unpolished, came from
Cruel lack of means and ancestral farms with
Homesteads in keeping.

21

crescit occulto uelut arbor aeuo   45
fama Marcelli: micat inter omnis
Iulium sidus uelut inter ignis
luna minores.

gentis humanae pater atque custos,
orte Saturno, tibi cura magni   50
Caesaris fatis data: tu secundo
Caesare regnes.

ille seu Parthos Latio imminentis
egerit iusto domitos triumpho
siue subiectos Orientis orae   55
Seras et Indos,

te minor latum reget aequus orbem:
tu graui curru quaties Olympum,
tu parum castis inimica mittes
fulmina lucis.   60

XIII

    Cum tu, Lydia, Telephi
ceruicem roseam, cerea Telephi
    laudas bracchia, uae meum
feruens difficili bile tumet iecur.
    tum nec mens mihi nec color   5
certa sede manet, umor et in genas
    furtim labitur, arguens
quam lentis penitus macerer ignibus.
    uror, seu tibi candidos
turparunt umeros immodicae mero   10
    rixae, siue puer furens
impressit memorem dente labris notam.
    non, si me satis audias,
speres perpetuum dulcia barbare
    laedentem oscula, quae Venus   15
quinta parte sui nectaris imbuit.
    felices ter et amplius
quos inrupta tenet copula nec malis

Like a tree it grows by unseen progression,   45
Fame of Marcellus, and among them all the
Julian star gleams, like the moon among the
Sky's lesser fires.

Father and Protector of human creatures,
Son of Saturn, Fate has entrusted you with   50
Care of our great Caesar; let Caesar rule as
Seconding Yourself,

Whether he has driven the Parthians threatening
Latium as captives in well-earned Triumph
Or the peoples next to the Orient border,   55
Chinese and Indians,

Under You he'll rule the wide world with justice.
You with heavy chariot will shake Olympus;
You at sacred grove's profanation hurl down
Enemy lightnings.   60

13

When you, Lydia, praise Telephus
And his neck (rosy pink!), Telephus *and* his arms
(Wax-smooth!) yuk, I can feel it, my
Liver boiling with sour bile and oedematous.
Then my mind and my colour change,   5
Shaken out of their fixed stance, and the moisture creeps
Down my cheeks, silent evidence
How I'm cooking inside over slow-burning fire.
I flare up when intemperate brawls
Fuelled by drinking have disfigured your shoulders' white, 10
Or that lunatic juvenile
Prints a mnemonic tooth-mark on your lower lip.
If you listen to my advice
You'll not hope for what lasts from a barbarian who
Spoils the sweetness of kisses in   15
The quintessence of her nectar by Venus dipped.
Three times fortunate they and more
Whom an unbroken bond holds and whose mutual love

23

    diuulsus querimoniis
suprema citius soluet amor die.   20

XIV

O nauis, referent in mare te noui
fluctus. o quid agis? fortiter occupa
    portum. nonne uides ut
        nudum remigio latus

et malus celeri saucius Africo   5
antemnaeque gemant ac sine funibus
    uix durare carinae
        possint imperiosius

aequor? non tibi sunt integra lintea,
non di, quos iterum pressa uoces malo.   10
    quamuis Pontica pinus,
        siluae filia nobilis,

iactes et genus et nomen inutile,
nil pictis timidus nauita puppibus
    fidit. tu nisi uentis   15
        debes ludibrium, caue.

nuper sollicitum quae mihi taedium,
nunc desiderium curaque non leuis,
    interfusa nitentis
        uites aequora Cycladas.   20

XV

Pastor cum traheret per freta nauibus
Idaeis Helenen perfidus hospitam,
ingrato celeris obruit otio
    uentos ut caneret fera

Nereus fata: 'mala ducis aui domum   5
quam multo repetet Graecia milite
coniurata tuas rumpere nuptias
    et regnum Priami uetus.

Undivided by grievances
Till the day of their death never will let them go.   20

14

O ship, you will be driven seaward again by fresh
Waves. O what are you doing? Bravely make haste to reach
    Harbour. Can you not see how
        Both your sides have been stripped of oars

And how, damaged by storm-winds out of Africa,   5
Mast and yard-arms are groaning, and the hull, without
    Ropes to gird it, can hardly
        Hold against the too masterful

Ocean? There's no intact sail-canvas left to you,
No Gods whom in your straits you can appeal to again.   10
    As pine timber from Pontus,
        Daughter of aristocratic woods,

You may boast of your birth and of a useless name,
But scared sailors have no trust in a painted poop.
    Watch out therefore, unless you're   15
        Set on being the butt of winds.

You, so lately my care-worn disillusionment
But now object of longing and no small concern,
    Must steer clear of the seas that
        Sunder glistening Cyclades.   20

15

When the treacherous sheepmaster was carrying off
Oversea his hostess Helen in Ida's fleet
Nereus smothered the swift breezes with undesired
    Calm in order to prophesy

A dire future: 'With ill omen you're leading home   5
Her whom Greece will reclaim with a great armament,
Having taken a joint oath to destroy your match
    And the old kingdom of Priamus.

heu heu, quantus equis, quantus adest uiris
sudor! quanta moues funera Dardanae 10
genti! iam galeam Pallas et aegida
    currusque et rabiem parat.

nequiquam Veneris praesidio ferox
pectes caesariem grataque feminis
imbelli cithara carmina diuides, 15
    nequiquam thalamo grauis

hastas et calami spicula Cnosii
uitabis strepitumque et celerem sequi
Aiacem: tamen heu serus adulteros
    crines puluere collines. 20

non Laertiaden, exitium tuae
genti, non Pylium Nestora respicis?
urgent impauidi te Salaminius
    Teucer, te Sthenelus sciens

pugnae, siue opus est imperitare equis, 25
non auriga piger. Merionen quoque
nosces. ecce furit te reperire atrox
    Tydides melior patre,

quem tu, ceruus uti uallis in altera
uisum parte lupum graminis immemor, 30
sublimi fugies mollis anhelitu,
    non hoc pollicitus tuae.

iracunda diem proferet Ilio
matronisque Phrygum classis Achillei:
post certas hiemes uret Achaicus 35
    ignis Iliacas domos.'

XVI

O matre pulchra filia pulchrior,
quem criminosis cumque uoles modum
    pones iambis, siue flamma
        siue mari libet Hadriano.

Ah how great is the sweat waiting for horse and man!
Alas, how many dead you bring the Dardan race!   10
Pallas this very day makes ready aegis and
    Helm and chariot and battle-lust.

Vainly truculent in Venus's patronage
You'll be combing your hair, and with the unwarlike lyre
You'll be sharing the songs women delight to hear.   15
    In the bedroom you'll vainly shun

Heavy lances and barbed arrows of Cnossian reed,
Noise of battle and Ajax in his swift pursuit.
None the less in the end, ah, you'll be powdering
    Those adulterous locks with dust.   20

There's Laërtiades, bringer of doom on your
Race, there's Pylian Nestor to be thinking of.
Unafraid in attack come Salaminian
    Teucer and Sthenelus, the skilled

Fighter, or, should the need come to manoeuvre steeds,   25
No bad charioteer. Meriones you'll meet
Too and look, there's berserk Diomed seeking you,
    His great father's superior,

From whom you, like a stag heedless of pasturage
Having seen in a far part of his glen a wolf,   30
Head thrown back and in fear panting will run away —
    Not the promise you made your love!

Achilles and his fleet's wrath will adjourn the day
Set for Ilium and mothers of Phrygia.
Certain winters must pass; then will Achaean fire   35
    Burn all Ilian buildings down.'

16

O lovely mother's even more lovely girl,
Please put what end you like to those libellous
    Iambics, whether by cremation
        Or in the depths of the Adriatic.

non Dindymene, non adytis quatit 5
mentem sacerdotum incola Pythius,
    non Liber aeque, non acuta
        si geminant Corybantes aera,

tristes ut irae, quas neque Noricus
deterret ensis nec mare naufragum 10
    nec saeuus ignis nec tremendo
        Iuppiter ipse ruens tumultu.

fertur Prometheus addere principi
limo coactus particulam undique
    desectam et insani leonis 15
        uim stomacho apposuisse nostro.

irae Thyesten exitio graui
strauere et altis urbibus ultimae
    stetere causae cur perirent
        funditus imprimeretque muris 20

hostile aratrum exercitus insolens.
compesce mentem: me quoque pectoris
    temptauit in dulci iuuenta
        feruor et in celeres iambos

misit furentem: nunc ego mitibus 25
mutare quaero tristia, dum mihi
    fias recantatis amica
        opprobriis animumque reddas.

XVII

Velox amoenum saepe Lucretilem
mutat Lycaeo Faunus et igneam
    defendit aestatem capellis
        usque meis pluuiosque uentos.

impune tutum per nemus arbutos 5
quaerunt latentis et thyma deuiae
    olentis uxores mariti
        nec uiridis metuunt colubras

Not Dindymene nor Pythian resident   5
So agitates priests' minds in the inner shrine,
    Nor Liber nor the Corybantes
        Clashing together the jangling cymbals,

As bitter anger, which neither Norican
Sword-blade can scare off nor the shipwrecking sea   10
    Nor savage fire nor Jupiter's self
        Hurtling down in terrific turmoil.

They say Prometheus, being compelled to add
Components cut from all other animals
    To primal clay, attached the maddened   15
        Lion's brute force to the human stomach.

'Twas anger brought Thyestes to merciless
Destruction and for towering cities proved
    The final reason why they perished
        Utterly and arrogant armies pressed down   20

The foeman's ploughshare over their flattened walls.
Control your temper. I too in youth's delight-
    ful season fell victim to hot blood's
        Fever and, furious, took to writing

High-speed iambics. Now, though, I seek to exchange   25
The sour for sweetness so long as you become
    My girl-friend, all insults recanted,
        And give me heart again — yours included.

17

Swift Faunus often exchanges Lycaeus for
Agreeable Lucretilis and protects
    My goats from fiery summer always
        And from the rain and the winds of winter.

Unharmed they wander through the protected grove   5
In search of arbutus and elusive thyme,
    Those wives of no sweet-smelling husband,
        Nor are their kidlings alarmed by any

nec Martialis haediliae lupos,
utcumque dulci, Tyndari, fistula   10
    ualles et Vsticae cubantis
        leuia personuere saxa.

di me tuentur, dis pietas mea
et musa cordi est. hic tibi copia
    manabit ad plenum benigno   15
        ruris honorum opulenta cornu.

hic in reducta ualle Caniculae
uitabis aestus et fide Teia
    dices laborantis in uno
        Penelopen uitreamque Circen.   20

hic innocentis pocula Lesbii
duces sub umbra, nec Semeleius
    cum Marte confundet Thyoneus
        proelia, nec metues proteruum

suspecta Cyrum, ne male dispari   25
incontinentis iniciat manus
    et scindat haerentem coronam
        crinibus immeritamque uestem.

XVIII

Nullam, Vare, sacra uite prius seueris arborem
circa mite solum Tiburis et moenia Catili.
siccis omnia nam dura deus proposuit neque
mordaces aliter diffugiunt sollicitudines.
quis post uina grauem militiam aut pauperiem crepat?   5
quis non te potius, Bacche pater, teque, decens Venus?
ac ne quis modici transiliat munera Liberi,
Centaurea monet cum Lapithis rixa super mero
debellata, monet Sithoniis non leuis Euhius,
cum fas atque nefas exiguo fine libidinum   10
discernunt auidi. non ego te, candide Bassareu,
inuitum quatiam nec uariis obsita frondibus
sub diuum rapiam. saeua tene cum Berecyntio
cornu tympana, quae subsequitur caecus Amor sui

Green serpents or wolves sacred to Roman Mars,
Whenever dulcet pipe-music, Tyndaris,   10
   Is heard to echo among the glens and
      Slippery boulders of sloped Ustica.

The Gods protect me — yes, and the Gods approve
My Muse and my devotion. From lavish horn
   Rich plenty of country honours here will   15
      Pour out abundantly into your lap.

In hidden valley here you'll evade the heat
Of Sirius and tell on your Teian strings
   Of two who suffered, loving one man,
      Penelopea and brittle Circe.   20

You here can drain innocuous Lesbian
Wine-cups in shade nor will Semeleïan
   Thyoneus with Mars' help engage in
      Wild battles nor, if suspected, need you

Be scared of headstrong Cyrus in case he might   25
Lay violent hands on you, not at all his match,
   And tear the garland clinging to your
      Hair and your innocent party-dress too.

18

Varus, you are to plant, first of all trees, none but the sacred vine
Around Cátilus' walls and the benign terrain of Tivoli.
For the God has proposed nothing but hard times for teetotallers
Nor can harrowing obsessions be dispelled any other way.
Who sounds off after drink on heavy campaigning or poverty   5
And not rather on you, Father of Wine, or, Venus fair, on you?
That no one should abuse moderate Liber's generosity
Centaurs warn, in their cups fighting a brawl out to the fatal end
With the Lapiths, and Sithonians warn, punished by Euhius   9
When in lechery's greed they make too small difference between what's right
And what's wrong. I will not unsettle you, radiant Bassareus,
Gainst your wishes or drag things better hid under that various
Leafage into the light. Therefore restrain barbarous tambourines,
Berecynthian horns too, with their camp-followers, blind Self-love

et tollens uacuum plus nimio Gloria uerticem   15
arcanique Fides prodiga, perlucidior uitro.

XIX

      Mater saeua Cupidinum
Thebanaeque iubet me Semelae puer
      et lasciua Licentia
finitis animum reddere amoribus.
      urit me Glycerae nitor   5
splendentis Pario marmore purius,
      urit grata proteruitas
et uultus nimium lubricus aspici.
      in me tota ruens Venus
Cyprum deseruit nec patitur Scythas   10
      et uersis animosum equis
Parthum dicere nec quae nihil attinent.
      hic uiuum mihi caespitem, hic
uerbenas, pueri, ponite turaque
      bimi cum patera meri: 15
mactata ueniet lenior hostia.

XX

Vile potabis modicis Sabinum
cantharis, Graeca quod ego ipse testa
conditum leui, datus in theatro
cum tibi plausus,

care Maecenas eques, ut paterni   5
fluminis ripae simul et iocosa
redderet laudes tibi Vaticani
montis imago.

Caecubum et prelo domitam Caleno
tu uides uuam: mea nec Falernae   10
temperant uites neque Formiani
pocula colles.

And Vainglory that lifts overly high her shallow-minded head   15
And the Trust that betrays mysteries, more diaphanous than glass.

19

         The cruel Mother of sweet Desires,
Theban Semele's boy, wanton Permissiveness,
         All as one are commanding me
To surrender to loves over (I thought) and done.
         Dazzling Glycera burns me (she   5
With more purity shines than the white Parian stone),
         Her provocative glamour burns
And the face that it's too risky to scrutinize.
         Venus falling upon me in force
Has migrated from Cyprus and forbidden me   10
         Talk of Scyths or of Parthian
Horsemen brave in retreat and such irrelevance.
         Here, boys, bring me fresh altar-turf.
Here's the place for the incense and the greenery
         And a bowl of wine two years old.   15
She will come the more gentle after a victim's slain.

20

You shall drink cheap Sabine from modest schooners,
Wine I sealed myself having stored it in a
Grecian jar that year when the Theatre audience
Gave you a big hand,

Dear Maecenas, knight, so the banks of Tiber   5
Your paternal river together with Mount
Vaticanus' rollicking echo sounded
Doubly your praises.

Caecuban and grapes that Calenian presses
Mellow you provide, but my tipple's never   10
Qualified by either Falernian vines or
Formian hillsides.

XXI

Dianam tenerae dicite uirgines,
intonsum pueri dicite Cynthium,
    Latonamque supremo
        dilectam penitus Ioui.

uos laetam fluuiis et nemorum coma,   5
quaecumque aut gelido prominet Algido
    nigris aut Erymanthi
        siluis aut uiridis Cragi;

uos Tempe totidem tollite laudibus
natalemque, mares, Delon Apollinis   10
    insignemque pharetra
        fraternaque umerum lyra.

hic bellum lacrimosum, hic miseram famem
pestemque a populo et principe Caesare in
    Persas atque Britannos   15
        uestra motus aget prece.

XXII

Integer uitae scelerisque purus
non eget Mauris iaculis neque arcu
nec uenenatis grauida sagittis,
    Fusce, pharetra,

siue per Syrtis iter aestuosas   5
siue facturus per inhospitalem
Caucasum uel quae loca fabulosus
    lambit Hydaspes.

namque me silua lupus in Sabina,
dum meam canto Lalagen et ultra   10
terminum curis uagor expeditis,
    fugit inermem,

quale portentum neque militaris
Daunias latis alit aesculetis
nec Iubae tellus generat, leonum   15
    arida nutrix.

21

Sing in honour of Diana, unmarried girls;
Boys, in honour of Cynthius with the flowing locks
    And of Leto so deeply
        Loved by mightiest Jupiter.

Sing her pleasure in streams, girls, and in forest leaves,   5
Whichsoever stand out on chilly Algidus
    Or from dark Erymanthine
        Woods or Lycian Cragus green,

While you males can exalt Tempe with equal praise,
Delos also, the island of Apollo's birth,   10
    And his glorious shoulder
        With full quiver and brother's lyre.

Tearful warfare, severe famine, and pestilence
From Rome's people and Prince Caesar he'll drive away
    On to Persia and Britain,   15
        Moved to action by your request.

22

One of upright life and a clear conscience
Needs no Moorish javelin nor a long bow
Nor a quiver laden with poisoned arrows,
Fuscus Aristius,

Even though preparing to travel through the   5
Sweltering Syrtes or the inhospitable
Caucasus or places that legendary
Hydaspes' stream laps;

For, as I was singing my Lalage and
Straying out of bounds, unafraid and carefree,   10
In Sabellian woodland a wolf fled from me
Though I was unarmed —

Monster such as neither the military
Land of Daunus feeds in its spacious oakwoods
Nor does Juba's country beget, that arid   15
Wet-nurse of lions.

pone me pigris ubi nulla campis
arbor aestiua recreatur aura,
quod latus mundi nebulae malusque
Iuppiter urget,   20

pone sub curru nimium propinqui
solis, in terra domibus negata:
dulce ridentem Lalagen amabo,
dulce loquentem.

XXIII

Vitas inuleo me similis, Chloe,
quaerenti pauidam montibus auiis
    matrem non sine uano
        aurarum et siluae metu.

nam seu mobilibus ueris inhorruit   5
aduentus foliis seu uirides rubum
    dimouere lacertae,
        et corde et genibus tremit.

atqui non ego te tigris ut aspera
Gaetulusue leo frangere persequor: 15
    tandem desine matrem
        tempestiua sequi uiro.

XXIV

Quis desiderio sit pudor aut modus
tam cari capitis? praecipe lugubris
cantus, Melpomene, cui liquidam pater
uocem cum cithara dedit.

ergo Quintilium perpetuus sopor   5
urget. cui Pudor et Iustitiae soror
incorrupta Fides nudaque Veritas
quando ullum inueniet parem?

Place me on bare tundra where not a single
Tree is freshened up by a breeze in summer,
That terrestrial region which mists and unkind
Jupiter harass,   20

Place me 'neath the chariot of the too close
Sun in lands prohibiting habitation:
I shall love my Lalage, her sweet laughter
And her sweet chatter.

23

You are running away, Chloe, just like a fawn
Seeking on the remote mountains her terrified
    Mother not without needless
        Fear of forest and fitful breeze.

For, if the advent of springtime has set shivering   5
Every lightly-hung leaf or if a green lizard
    Is disturbing a bramble,
        Trembling seizes her heart and knees.

And yet I'm not a fierce tiger or Gaetulan
Lion hard on your trail wanting to crunch you up.   10
    Time to part from your mother
        Now you're ready to take a man.

24

We should not be ashamed nor ever cease to mourn
Loss of one so belov'd. Teach me a song of grief,
O Melpomene. Your Father has given you
Liquid voice with the cithara.

So the sleep without end weighs on Quintilius.   5
But will Decency and, sister of Equity,
Incorruptible Good Faith, and the naked Truth
Ever happen upon his peer?

37

multis ille bonis flebilis occidit,
nulli flebilior quam tibi, Vergili.   10
tu frustra pius, heu, non ita creditum
poscis Quintilium deos.

quid si Threicio blandius Orpheo
auditam moderere arboribus fidem,
num uanae redeat sanguis imagini,   15
quam uirga semel horrida

non lenis precibus fata recludere
nigro compulerit Mercurius gregi?
durum: sed leuius fit patientia
quidquid corrigere est nefas.   20

XXV

Parcius iunctas quatiunt fenestras
iactibus crebris iuuenes proterui
nec tibi somnos adimunt amatque
ianua limen,

quae prius multum facilis mouebat   5
cardines. audis minus et minus iam
'me tuo longas pereunte noctes,
Lydia, dormis?'

in uicem moechos anus arrogantis
flebis in solo leuis angiportu   10
Thracio bacchante magis sub inter-
lunia uento,

cum tibi flagrans amor et libido
quae solet matres furiare equorum
saeuiet circa iecur ulcerosum,   15
non sine questu

laeta quod pubes hedera uirenti
gaudeat pulla magis atque myrto,
aridas frondes hiemis sodali
dedicet Euro.   20

He has passed on, bewailed by many decent men,
Though by none more bewailed, Virgil, than you. Alas,   10
Devout vainly you ask Gods for Quintilius,
In their keeping on other terms.

If with sweeter appeal than Thracian Orpheüs
You could finger the strings heard by the forest trees,
Could blood ever return to the insubstantial shade   15
When once Mercury's ruthless rod

Not disposed to unbar Fate to our human prayers
Will have penned it among his sombre flock of ghosts?
Hard indeed, but endurance will alleviate
What correction's forbidden to change.   20

25

Rarely now they come, the unruly young men
Rattling your closed shutters with volleyed gravel,
Robbing you of sleep, but the door and doorway
Hug one another,

Though, before, they opened on most obliging   5
Hinges. Less and less do you hear the cry now
'Lydia, all night long when I'm dying for you
How can you sleep on?'

You will weep, grown old in your turn, at lechers'
Arrogance, despised in some lonely alley   10
Where the north wind blusters more wildly during
The lunar dark time,

When in you the fire of love and lusting
Such as always maddens the dams of stallions
Rages round your ulcerous liver while you   15
Voice the complaint that

Young adults' exuberance takes more pleasure
In the greening ivy and dusky myrtle,
Dedicating desiccate leaves to winter's
Comrade the east wind.   20

XXVI

Musis amicus tristitiam et metus
tradam proteruis in mare Creticum
　　portare uentis, quis sub Arcto
　　　　rex gelidae metuatur orae,

quid Tiridaten terreat, unice　　　　　　　　　　　5
securus. o quae fontibus integris
　　gaudes, apricos necte flores,
　　　　necte meo Lamiae coronam,

Pimplei dulcis. nil sine te mei
prosunt honores: hunc fidibus nouis,　　　　　　　10
　　hunc Lesbio sacrare plectro
　　　　teque tuasque decet sorores.

XXVII

Natis in usum laetitiae scyphis
pugnare Thracum est: tollite barbarum
　　morem uerecundumque Bacchum
　　　　sanguineis prohibete rixis.

uino et lucernis Medus acinaces　　　　　　　　　5
immane quantum discrepat: impium
　　lenite clamorem, sodales,
　　　　et cubito remanete presso.

uultis seueri me quoque sumere
partem Falerni? dicat Opuntiae　　　　　　　　　10
　　frater Megyllae, quo beatus
　　　　uulnere, qua pereat sagitta.

cessat uoluntas? non alia bibam
mercede. quae te cumque domat Venus,
　　non erubescendis adurit　　　　　　　　　　15
　　　　ignibus, ingenuoque semper

amore peccas. quidquid habes, age
depone tutis auribus. a miser,
　　quanta laborabas Charybdi,
　　　　digne puer meliore flamma.　　　　　　20

26

The Muses' friend, I'll hand over pessimism
And every fear for turbulent winds to blow
    Away to Cretan seas, supremely
        Careless what king in the frozen zone's feared

Beneath the Bear, or what Tiridates dreads.   5
O you to whom untapped freshets bring delight,
    Entwine what flowers sun has opened,
        Entwine a coronal for my Lamia,

O sweet Pimpleïs, for without you the praise
I sing is empty. Him on new lyre-strings,   10
    Him to commemorate with Lesbian
        Plectrum befits you and your eight sisters.

27

To brawl with wine-cups meant for enjoyment's use
Is downright Thracian. Stop this uncivilized
    Behaviour and make sure that modest
        Bacchus is kept free of fights and bloodshed.

With wine and lamplight Parthian poniard   5
Is grossly incompatible. Comrades, please
    Just tone down this ungodly racket
        And recline, leaning upon your elbows.

I too, you're saying, ought to accept my share
Of dry Falernian? Then let Opuntian   10
    Megylla's lucky brother tell us
        What is the wound, what the dart he's dying of.

Determination fails you? But I'll not drink
On other terms. What Venus soever rules
    You, burns with flames you need not blush for.   15
        Always you fall for the free-born ladies!

And so whatever news you can give, come on,
Trust it to my safe hearing. — Alas, too bad!
    What a Charybdis you've been suffering!
        Boy, you deserve a far better mistress.   20

quae saga, quis te soluere Thessalis
magus uenenis, quis poterit deus?
    uix illigatum te triformi
        Pegasus expediet Chimaera.

XXVIII

Te maris et terrae numeroque carentis harenae
    mensorem cohibent, Archyta,
pulueris exigui prope litus parua Matinum
    munera, nec quicquam tibi prodest
aerias temptasse domos animoque rotundum   5
    percurrisse polum morituro.
occidit et Pelopis genitor, conuiua deorum,
    Tithonusque remotus in auras
et Iouis arcanis Minos admissus, habentque
    Tartara Panthoiden iterum Orco   10
demissum, quamuis clipeo Troiana refixo
    tempora testatus nihil ultra
neruos atque cutem morti concesserat atrae,
    iudice te non sordidus auctor
naturae uerique. sed omnis una manet nox   15
    et calcanda semel uia leti.
dant alios Furiae toruo spectacula Marti;
    exitio est auidum mare nautis;
mixta senum ac iuuenum densentur funera; nullum
    saeua caput Proserpina fugit.   20

me quoque deuexi rapidus comes Orionis
    Illyricis Notus obruit undis.
at tu, nauta, uagae ne parce malignus harenae
    ossibus et capiti inhumato
particulam dare; sic, quodcumque minabitur Eurus   25
    fluctibus Hesperiis, Venusinae
plectantur siluae te sospite, multaque merces,
    unde potest, tibi defluat aequo
ab Ioue Neptunoque sacri custode Tarenti.
    neglegis immeritis nocituram   30
postmodo te natis fraudem committere? fors et
    debita iura uicesque superbae

Is there a witch or wizard can set you free
With Thessaly's strong drugs? Is there even a God?
    Why, Pegasus will hardly loose you
        Tangled with that triple-faced Chimaera!

28

Though you could measure the sea and the land and the unnumbered
    You are confined, Archytas, near the   [sandgrains
Matine shore by a small contribution of exiguous dust,
    Nor is it any advantage to you now
That with your mind you explored aërial houses and ranged through
    The sky's vault, though destined to perish.   6
Pelops' father too passed away, though he shared the Gods' table,
    And Tithonus, though snatched up to heaven,
Minos also, though trusted with Jupiter's secrets; and Hades
    Holds Panthoides sent down to Orcus   10
Twice — though, when he unhooked that shield to prove he had lived in
    Trojan times, he then had surrendered
Nothing more than sinews and skin to the Goddess of black death —
    In your judgement no common expert
He on nature and truth. But one night waits for all creatures   15
    And death's road must be trodden once only.
Some the Furies present as a public show to morose Mars;
    Greedy sea is disaster for sailors;
Funerals of old and of young are crowded wholesale together;
    There's no head grim Proserpina misses.   20

I too was drowned in Illyrian waves by Notus, destructive
    Adjutant of setting Orion.
But please, sailor, don't you be unkind and refuse to provide my
    Unburied bones and head with a little
Share of the shifting sand — in return, however much Eurus   25
    Threatens Hesperian waves, may Venusia's
Forests be thrashed without danger to you, and plentiful payment
    Flow down whence it can to your lap from
Fair-minded Jove and Neptune, the guardian of holy Tarentum.
    Are you not worried about your committing   30
Crime that will one day hurt your innocent children? For maybe
    Rights unpaid and haughty requital

te maneant ipsum: precibus non linquar inultis,
  teque piacula nulla resoluent.
quamquam festinas, non est mora longa: licebit   35
  iniecto ter puluere curras.

XXIX

Icci, beatis nunc Arabum inuides
gazis et acrem militiam paras
    non ante deuictis Sabaeae
        regibus horribilique Medo

nectis catenas? quae tibi uirginum   5
sponso necato barbara seruiet?
    puer quis ex aula capillis
        ad cyathum statuetur unctis

doctus sagittas tendere Sericas
arcu paterno? quis neget arduis   10
    pronos relabi posse riuos
        montibus et Tiberim reuerti,

cum tu coemptos undique nobilis
libros Panaeti Socraticam et domum
    mutare loricis Hiberis,   15
        pollicitus meliora, tendis?

XXX

O Venus regina Cnidi Paphique,
sperne dilectam Cypron et uocantis
ture te multo Glycerae decoram
transfer in aedem.

feruidus tecum puer et solutis   5
Gratiae zonis properentque Nymphae
et parum comis sine te Iuuentas
Mercuriusque.

Wait for yourself. I shall not be left with prayers unanswered
    And no atonement will ever absolve you.   34
Though you are pressed for time the delay is short. Having thrown three
    Handfuls of dust over me you can run off.

29

Iccius, do you now covet Arabia's
Rich treasure and prepare for a fierce campaign
    Against the so far undefeated
        Rulers of Sheba, and rivet fetters

For dreaded Parthian? Will some barbarian bride   5
Whose groom you've killed in battle become your slave?
    Some boy from royal court with perfumed
        Tresses be set up as your wine-waiter,

Though trained in shooting Serican arrow-heads
From father's bowstring? Who would deny that streams   10
    Which find their level can flow backwards
        Up the steep hillside and Tiber turn round

When you propose to barter Panaetius'
Distinguished writings purchased from far and wide
    And Socrates' household for Spanish   15
        Breastplates in spite of your better promise?

30

Cnidian and Paphian Queen, O Venus,
Spurn belovèd Cyprus and emigrate to
Glycera's fair shrine, who is calling you with
Plentiful incense.

Hasten, bringing with you the passionate Boy   5
And the Nymphs and Graces with loosened girdles,
Youth that's hardly socialized without you,
Mercury also.

XXXI

Quid dedicatum poscit Apollinem
uates? quid orat de patera nouum
    fundens liquorem? non opimae
        Sardiniae segetes feracis,

non aestuosae grata Calabriae   5
armenta, non aurum aut ebur Indicum,
    non rura quae Liris quieta
        mordet aqua taciturnus amnis.

premant Calena falce quibus dedit
fortuna uitem, diues et aureis   10
    mercator exsiccet culillis
        uina Syra reparata merce,

dis carus ipsis, quippe ter et quater
anno reuisens aequor Atlanticum
    impune. me pascunt oliuae,   15
        me cichorea leuesque maluae.

frui paratis et ualido mihi,
Latoe, dones et precor integra
    cum mente nec turpem senectam
        degere nec cithara carentem.   20

XXXII

Poscimus, si quid uacui sub umbra
lusimus tecum, quod et hunc in annum
uiuat et pluris, age dic Latinum,
barbite, carmen,

Lesbio primum modulate ciui,   5
qui ferox bello tamen inter arma,
siue iactatam religarat udo
litore nauim,

Liberum et Musas Veneremque et illi
semper haerentem puerum canebat   10
et Lycum nigris oculis nigroque
crine decorum.

31

From consecrated Phoebus what boon is bard
Beseeching? What his prayer as he pours the year's
    New grapejuice from the chalice? Not for
        Fertile Sardinia's bumper harvests

Nor sweltering Calabria's much admired
Livestock nor gold and Indian ivory
    Nor country estate which Liris nibbles
        With quiet water, a taciturn stream.

Let those whose luck allows it cut back their vines
With Calene knife, and prosperous merchant drain   10
    From golden goblets vintages which
        He has acquired with goods from Syria,

Gods' favourite too, as three and four times a year
He navigates unscathed the Atlantic main.
    But as for me, my fare is olives —   15
        Olives and chicory and light mallows.

Latoan, grant me enjoyment of what's to hand
Together with good health and a mind, I pray,
    Undamaged, and to pass an old age
        Neither repulsive nor lacking lyric.   20

32

I beseech you, barbitos, if at leisure
In the shade we've sported with verse together,
Come and voice a lyric in Latin lasting
This year and longer.

By a Lesbian citizen you were first played,   5
Who though fierce in war, yet between attacks or
After tying up on the rain-wet shore his
Storm-beaten vessel

Used to sing of Liber, the Muses, Venus,
And the Boy in constant attendance on her,   10
And of Lycus too with his beautiful black
Ringlets and black eyes.

o decus Phoebi et dapibus supremi
grata testudo Iouis, o laborum
dulce lenimen mihi cumque salue   15
rite uocanti.

XXXIII

Albi, ne doleas plus nimio memor
immitis Glycerae, neu miserabilis
decantes elegos, cur tibi iunior
    laesa praeniteat fide.

insignem tenui fronte Lycorida   5
Cyri torret amor, Cyrus in asperam
declinat Pholoen; sed prius Apulis
    iungentur capreae lupis

quam turpi Pholoe peccet adultero.
sic uisum Veneri, cui placet imparis   10
formas atque animos sub iuga aenea
    saeuo mittere cum ioco.

ipsum me melior cum peteret Venus,
grata detinuit compede Myrtale
libertina, fretis acrior Hadriae   15
    curuantis Calabros sinus.

XXXIV

Parcus deorum cultor et infrequens,
insanientis dum sapientiae
    consultus erro, nunc retrorsum
        uela dare atque iterare cursus

cogor relictos. namque Diespiter,   5
igni corusco nubila diuidens
    plerumque, per purum tonantis
        egit equos uolucremque currum,

Turtleshell, applauded at feasts of highest
Jupiter, O glory of Phoebus, O sweet
Consolation in trouble, be gracious when I   15
Duly invoke you.

33

Don't grieve, Albius, excessively brooding on
Cruel Glycera. Stop droning out pitiful
Elegiacs on faith broken, demanding why
    You're outshone by a younger man.

There's Lycóris (a low forehead her famous point)   5
Smouldering with a grand passion for Cyrus. But
Cyrus turns to sharp-tongued Phóloe. Sooner though
    Will deer mate with Apulian wolves

Than will Pholoe do wrong with that ugly rake.
Such is Venus's will, who is content to send   10
Ill-matched bodies and minds under her brazen yoke
    In a merciless comedy.

I myself when pursued by a more classy love
Was held fast by an ex-slave on a welcome chain —
By name Myrtale, even wilder than Adria's   15
    Breakers curving Calabrian bays.

34

A thrifty and occasional worshipper
While I professed a crazy philosophy
    And went astray, I find myself forced
        Now to sail back and again go over

The course I'd left behind. For Diespiter,   5
Who normally divides with his lightning flash
    Cloud cover, drove his thundering horses
        And flying chariot through a clear sky,

quo bruta tellus et uaga flumina,
quo Styx et inuisi horrida Taenari   10
    sedes Atlanteusque finis
        concutitur. ualet ima summis

mutare et insignem attenuat deus
obscura promens: hinc apicem rapax
    Fortuna cum stridore acuto   15
        sustulit, hic posuisse gaudet.

XXXV

O diua gratum quae regis Antium,
praesens uel imo tollere de gradu
    mortale corpus uel superbos
        uertere funeribus triumphos,

te pauper ambit sollicita prece   5
ruris colonus, te dominam aequoris
    quicumque Bithyna lacessit
        Carpathium pelagus carina.

te Dacus asper, te profugi Scythae
urbesque gentesque et Latium ferox   10
    regumque matres barbarorum et
        purpurei metuunt tyranni,

iniurioso ne pede proruas
stantem columnam neu populus frequens
    ad arma, cessantis ad arma   15
        concitet imperiumque frangat.

te semper anteit saeua Necessitas,
clauos trabalis et cuneos manu
    gestans aenos nec seuerus
        uncus abest liquidumque plumbum.   20

te Spes et albo rara Fides colit
uelata panno sed comitem abnegat,
    utcumque mutata potentis
        ueste domos inimica linquis.

At which insensate Earth and meandering streams,
The Styx and hateful Taenarus' grim abode   10
    And the Atlantean bounds were shaken.
        God has the power to change the lowest

To highest and can humble celebrities,
Promoting the unknown. Fortune the predator
    With shrill scream lifts her crown from one head   15
        Happily placing it on another.

35

O Goddess ruling your belov'd Antium,
Prepared to raise up even from the lowest rank
    Our mortal bodies and to transform
        Arrogant Triumphs to funeral mourning,

Poor tenant farmers court you with anxious prayer   5
As countryside's queen, so too as ocean's queen
    Whoever challenges Carpathian
        Seas in a Thynian merchant vessel.

Of you nomadic Scyths and rough Dacians,
Cities and tribes and bellicose Latium   10
    And mothers of barbarian kings and
        Purple-clad potentates live in terror,

In case with unjust foot you should overturn
The standing pillar, or the packed populace
    Should call 'To arms, to arms' the laggards,   15
        Breaking authority's hold on power.

Always before you walks grim Necessity
Equipped with outsize beam-nails and dowel-pins
    And brazen wedges; present too are
        Exigent clamps and, for melting down, lead.   20

Attending you are Hope and rare Loyalty
White-clad, but they refuse their companionship
    Whenever in changed garb you leave the
        Homes of the great as an adversary.

at uulgus infidum et meretrix retro   25
periura cedit, diffugiunt cadis
    cum faece siccatis amici
        ferre iugum pariter dolosi.

serues iturum Caesarem in ultimos
orbis Britannos et iuuenum recens   30
    examen Eois timendum
        partibus Oceanoque rubro.

eheu cicatricum et sceleris pudet
fratrumque. quid nos dura refugimus
    aetas? quid intactum nefasti   35
        liquimus? unde manum iuuentus

metu deorum continuit? quibus
pepercit aris? o utinam noua
    incude diffingas retusum in
        Massagetas Arabasque ferrum.   40

XXXVI

        Et ture et fidibus iuuat
placare et uituli sanguine debito
        custodes Numidae deos,
qui nunc Hesperia sospes ab ultima
        caris multa sodalibus,   5
nulli plura tamen diuidit oscula
        quam dulci Lamiae, memor
actae non alio rege puertiae
        mutataeque simul togae.
Cressa ne careat pulchra dies nota,   10
        neu promptae modus amphorae
neu morem in Salium sit requies pedum,
        neu multi Damalis meri
Bassum Threicia uincat amystide,
        neu desint epulis rosae   15
neu uiuax apium neu breue lilium.
        omnes in Damalin putris
deponent oculos, nec Damalis nouo

Yet fickle mob and fraudulent prostitute   25
Then turn their backs, and once every winecask's drained
    (The dregs included) friends play truant,
        Being too crafty to share the burden.

Look after Caesar who is about to attack
The world's-end Britons, guard his most recent swarm   30
    Of young men threatening Eoan
        Boundaries and the Red Ocean's coastline.

Our scars, alas, our crime, and our brothers' blood
Bring shame upon us. What has our cruel age
    Recoiled from? What unnatural deed   35
        Left unattempted? Has fear of Heaven

Restrained our young men's hands? Is there any shrine
They've not despoiled? If only you'd forge afresh
    The blunted iron on some new anvil
        Gainst the Massagetae and the Arabs!   40

36

      With incense and the lyre and calf's
Blood as promised it's our pleasure to gratify
      Gods that watch over Numida,
Who now safely returned from far Hesperia
      Shares with dearest companions   5
Many kisses, with none, however, more than with
      His sweet Lamia, remembering
How his boyhood was spent under no other king,
      And the toga assumed with him.
Let this beautiful day not lack a Cretan mark.   10
      Let's not ration the opened jar.
Give no rest to the feet, dance like the Salii.
      Don't let hard-drinking Damalis
Win the contest with Bassus at the Thracian sconce.
      Let the feast have its roses and   15
Long-lived celery and lilies that last a day.
      All will fix upon Damalis
Tender come-hither looks, but Damalis will not

diuelletur adultero
lasciuis hederis ambitiosior.   20

XXXVII

Nunc est bibendum, nunc pede libero
pulsanda tellus, nunc Saliaribus
  ornare puluinar deorum
    tempus erat dapibus, sodales.

antehac nefas depromere Caecubum   5
cellis auitis, dum Capitolio
  regina dementis ruinas
    funus et imperio parabat

contaminato cum grege turpium
morbo uirorum, quidlibet impotens   10
  sperare fortunaque dulci
    ebria. sed minuit furorem

uix una sospes nauis ab ignibus,
mentemque lymphatam Mareotico
  redegit in ueros timores   15
    Caesar ab Italia uolantem

remis adurgens, accipiter uelut
mollis columbas aut leporem citus
  uenator in campis niualis
    Haemoniae, daret ut catenis   20

fatale monstrum: quae generosius
perire quaerens nec muliebriter
  expauit ensem nec latentis
    classe cita reparauit oras,

ausa et iacentem uisere regiam   25
uultu sereno, fortis et asperas
  tractare serpentes, ut atrum
    corpore combiberet uenenum,

Be divorced from her new lover,
Clinging closer than exuberant ivy clings.   20

37

It's time for drinking, time with unfettered feet
To beat the ground in dances, high time today
    To furnish the Gods' cushioned couches
        With Saliarian banquets, comrades.

From patriarchal bins it was sacrilege   5
Till now to bring out Caecuban, while the queen
    Was plotting mindless ruin for the
        Capitoline and an end to Empire,

Among her pervert company of disease-
polluted 'males', intemperately hoping for   10
    The moon, and with her sweet good fortune
        Drunk, but the madness was checked when hardly

A single ship escaped the consuming flames,
And Caesar brought back fearful reality
    To a mind deranged by Mareotic,   15
        While she fled Italy, by pursuing

Her close with his oared galleys, as sparrowhawk
Pursues the gentle dove or a hunter brisk
    The leveret on plains of snowy
        Thessaly, so he could load with fetters   20

The deadly deviant. She, though, determining
To die more nobly, neither was terrified
    As women are by sword nor changed course
        With her swift fleet for some hidden refuge,

But dared go see her palace in its collapse   25
With brow serene, and handle courageously
    Her angry serpents so that she could
        Drink with her body their blackest venom,

deliberata morte ferocior,
saeuis Liburnis scilicet inuidens   30
    priuata deduci superbo
        non humilis mulier triumpho.

XXXVIII

Persicos odi, puer, apparatus,
displicent nexae philyra coronae,
mitte sectari rosa quo locorum
sera moretur.

simplici myrto nihil allabores   5
sedulus cura: neque te ministrum
dedecet myrtus neque me sub arta
uite bibentem.

The more defiant having resolved to die,
And loth, no doubt, that barbarous Liburnians   30
    Should bring her here dethroned for pompous
       Triumph, a woman but not submissive.

38

I detest all Persian extravagance, boy.
Garlands bound with bast of the linden displease.
Quit the search for where in the neighbourhood late
Roses may linger.

Mind you take pains not to elaborate on   5
Simple myrtle. Myrtle's not unbecoming
Wear for you the waiter nor me while drinking
Under a dense vine.

CARMINVM LIBER ALTER

I

Motum ex Metello consule ciuicum
bellique causas et uitia et modos
    ludumque Fortunae grauisque
        principum amicitias et arma

nondum expiatis uncta cruoribus,   5
periculosae plenum opus aleae,
    tractas et incedis per ignis
        suppositos cineri doloso.

paulum seuerae Musa tragoediae
desit theatris: mox ubi publicas   10
    res ordinaris, grande munus
        Cecropio repetes cothurno,

insigne maestis praesidium reis
et consulenti, Pollio, curiae,
    cui laurus aeternos honores   15
        Delmatico peperit triumpho.

iam nunc minaci murmure cornuum
perstringis auris, iam litui strepunt,
    iam fulgor armorum fugacis
        terret equos equitumque uultus.   20

audire magnos iam uideor duces
non indecoro puluere sordidos
    et cuncta terrarum subacta
        praeter atrocem animum Catonis.

Iuno et deorum quisquis amicior   25
Afris inulta cesserat impotens
    tellure, uictorum nepotes
        rettulit inferias Iugurthae.

ODES, BOOK TWO

1

The civic turmoil from Celer's consulship,
War's origins, mistakes and development,
    The play of Fortune and the fateful
        Friendships of principals, and their weapons

Defiled with bloodshed still unatoned today,   5
A dicey, indeed a dangerous, enterprise
    Your subject; you are marching over
        Fires concealed by deceptive ashes.

The Muse of austere Tragedy for a while
Must leave the theatre; when you have chronicled   10
    Our state affairs, then you'll resume your
        Great contribution to the Attic buskin,

Well-known defence of sorrowful litigants
And senators in conference, Pollio,
    For whom the bay procured eternal   15
        Dignity in your Dalmatian Triumph.

Already now with menacing blare of horns
You rasp our ears, already the bugles scream
    And flashing weapons terrify the
        Runaway horses and horsemen's faces.   20

Already I seem to hear the great generals
Begrimed, but not dishonourably, with dust,
    And of the whole world subjugated
        Save for the terrible will of Cato.

Juno and Gods who, friendlier to Africans,   25
Had fled the land their weakness could not avenge,
    Have sacrificed his conquerors' grandsons
        In expiation to dead Jugurtha.

quis non Latino sanguine pinguior
campus sepulcris impia proelia   30
   testatur auditumque Medis
      Hesperiae sonitum ruinae?

qui gurges aut quae flumina lugubris
ignara belli? quod mare Dauniae
   non decolorauere caedes?   35
      quae caret ora cruore nostro?

sed ne relictis, Musa, procax iocis
Ceae retractes munera neniae;
   mecum Dionaeo sub antro
      quaere modos leuiore plectro.   40

II

Nullus argento color est auaris
abdito terris, inimice lamnae
Crispe Sallusti, nisi temperato
splendeat usu.

uiuet extento Proculeius aeuo   5
notus in fratres animi paterni;
illum aget penna metuente solui
Fama superstes.

latius regnes auidum domando
spiritum quam si Libyam remotis   10
Gadibus iungas et uterque Poenus
seruiat uni.

crescit indulgens sibi dirus hydrops
nec sitim pellit, nisi causa morbi
fugerit uenis et aquosus albo   15
corpore languor.

redditum Cyri solio Phraäten
dissidens plebi numero beatorum
eximit Virtus populumque falsis
dedocet uti   20

What plain has not been fattened with Latin blood
And does not testify with its many graves   30
    To godless battles and the tumult,
        Heard by the Medes, of Hesperia's downfall?

What channel or what river is ignorant
Of mournful war? What sea have not Daunian
    Mass casualties foully stained? What   35
        Quarter or border's without our spilt gore?

But don't abandon badinage, cheeky Muse,
To resurrect the genre of the Cean dirge:
    With me in Dionean grotto
        Look for the tunes of a lighter plectrum.   40

2

Silver has no brightness when buried in the
Miser's subsoil, Crispus Sallustius, you
Enemy of plate when it doesn't shine with
Reasonable use.

Proculeius after his death will live long,   5
Known as fatherlike in his care for brothers.
He'll be borne on wings that are loth to droop by
Fame the survivor.

You can rule more widely by mastering mind's
Greed than if you added to distant Gades   10
Libya, and united both Punic peoples
Under one governor.

Dreaded dropsy grows by its self-indulgence
And can never drive away thirst unless the
Trouble's cause retreats from the veins, and watery   15
Tiredness from blanched flesh.

Reason disagrees with the Plebs in striking
Off the list of happy men King Phraätes,
Now restored to Cyrus's throne, and wants the
Masses to unlearn   20

uocibus, regnum et diadema tutum
deferens uni propriamque laurum,
quisquis ingentis oculo irretorto
spectat aceruos.

III

Aequam memento rebus in arduis
seruare mentem, non secus in bonis
    ab insolenti temperatam
        laetitia, moriture Delli,

seu maestus omni tempore uixeris,   5
seu te in remoto gramine per dies
    festos reclinatum bearis
        interiore nota Falerni.

quo pinus ingens albaque populus
umbram hospitalem consociare amant   10
    ramis? quid obliquo laborat
        lympha fugax trepidare riuo?

huc uina et unguenta et nimium breuis
flores amoenae ferre iube rosae,
    dum res et aetas et sororum   15
        fila trium patiuntur atra.

cedes coemptis saltibus et domo
uillaque flauus quam Tiberis lauit,
    cedes et exstructis in altum
        diuitiis potietur heres.   20

diuesne prisco natus ab Inacho
nil interest an pauper et infima
    de gente sub diuo moreris,
        uictima nil miserantis Orci.

omnes eodem cogimur, omnium   25
uersatur urna serius ocius
    sors exitura et nos in aeternum
        exsilium impositura cumbae.

False descriptions, offering a crown, secure rule,
And unfading bays to the one who seeing
    Massive heaps of treaure can pass without a
        Single look backwards.

3

When things are steep, remember you have to keep
A level mind; likewise when the going's good
    To tone down all extravagant re-
        joicing: for Death is on stand-by, Dellius,

Whether you've spent your lifetime in total gloom   5
Or lying back at ease on secluded grass
    Have treated yourself every feast day
        To a Falernian of choicest vintage.

For what do lofty pine and the poplar white
Love co-extending shady hospitality   10
    Of branches? Why does truant water
        Labour to rush in a twisting channel?

Command to bring here unguents and wine and blooms
(Too transient, alas) of the lovely rose,
    While things and time of life and those black   15
        Threads of the Sisterly Three allow it.

You'll leave the estates you purchased, the house in town,
The country seat yellow Tiberinus laves;
    You'll leave the riches you have piled up
        High, and an heir will obtain possession.   20

Rich scion of primordial Inachus
Or poor, of lowest origin, sojourning
    In the open, makes no difference — you'll fall
        Victim to Orcus who pities no one.

We all are herded toward the same place, and all   25
Our lots are shaken up in the urn, to leap
    Out, soon or late, and place us on the
        Ferry to exile that lasts forever.

IV

Ne sit ancillae tibi amor pudori,
Xanthia Phoceu: prius insolentem
serua Briseis niueo colore
mouit Achillem;

mouit Aiacem Telamone natum   5
forma captiuae dominum Tecmessae;
arsit Atrides medio in triumpho
uirgine rapta,

barbarae postquam cecidere turmae
Thessalo uictore et ademptus Hector   10
tradidit fessis leuiora tolli
Pergama Grais.

nescias an te generum beati
Phyllidis flauae decorent parentes;
regium certe genus et penatis   15
maeret iniquos.

crede non illam tibi de scelesta
plebe delectam neque sic fidelem,
sic lucro auersam potuisse nasci
matre pudenda.   20

bracchia et uultum teretesque suras
integer laudo; fuge suspicari
cuius octauum trepidauit aetas
claudere lustrum.

V

Nondum subacta ferre iugum ualet
ceruice, nondum munia comparis
    aequare nec tauri ruentis
        in uenerem tolerare pondus.

circa uirentis est animus tuae   5
campos iuuencae, nunc fluuiis grauem
    solantis aestum, nunc in udo
        ludere cum uitulis salicto

64

4

Don't be ashamed of loving a girl in service,
Xanthias Phoceüs. The slave Briseïs
Long ago entranced with her pale complexion
Haughty Achilles,

And Tecmessa entranced as a captive with her   5
Loveliness her lord Telamonian Ajax,
While Atrides burned in mid-triumph for the
Virgin he'd kidnapped

After Troy's barbarian squadrons fell to
Thessaly's great victor, and loss of Hector   10
Handed Pergama over to weary Greeks, an
Easier conquest.

How d'you know the parents of fair-haired Phyllis
Won't make rich in-laws and won't bring you credit?
She's of royal birth, I'm convinced, lamenting   15
Unfair Penates.

Tell yourself your sweetheart has not been picked from
Wicked Plebs, that trust such as hers and lack of
Interest in profit could not have sprung from
Scandalous mother.   20

I approve, heart-whole, of her arms, her face, her
Shapely legs, so please will you stop suspecting
One whose life has brought to a speedy end his
Fortieth winter.

5

Not yet with docile neck has she stamina
To bear the yoke, not yet is she adequate
    For yoke-mate's duties nor can stand the
        Weight of a bull into Venus pitching.

The fancies of your heifer revolve around   5
Green meadows, sometimes solacing heavy heat
    In running streams, now passionately
        Longing to frolic with calves among the

praegestientis. tolle cupidinem
immitis uuae: iam tibi liuidos   10
    distinguet autumnus racemos
        purpureo uarius colore.

iam te sequetur: currit enim ferox
aetas et illi quos tibi dempserit
    apponet annos; iam proterua   15
        fronte petet Lalage maritum,

dilecta quantum non Pholoe fugax,
non Chloris albo sic umero nitens
    ut pura nocturno renidet
        luna mari Cnidiusue Gyges,   20

quem si puellarum insereres choro,
mire sagacis falleret hospites
    discrimen obscurum solutis
        crinibus ambiguoque uultu.

VI

Septimi, Gadis aditure mecum et
Cantabrum indoctum iuga ferre nostra et
barbaras Syrtis, ubi Maura semper
aestuat unda,

Tibur Argeo positum colono   5
sit meae sedes utinam senectae,
sit modus lasso maris et uiarum
militiaeque.

unde si Parcae prohibent iniquae,
dulce pellitis ouibus Galaesi   10
flumen et regnata petam Laconi
rura Phalantho.

ille terrarum mihi praeter omnis
angulus ridet, ubi non Hymetto
mella decedunt uiridique certat   15
baca Venafro,

Damp osier-beds. Get rid, then, of your desire
For unripe grapes; soon autumn the many-hued   10
    Will differentiate the blue-grey
        Clusters with colourful purple for you.

Soon she'll be chasing you, for relentless Time
Careering on will credit to her the years
    He's stolen from you. Soon with brazen   15
        Front will your Lalage seek a husband,

Belov'd as flighty Pholoe never was
Nor Chloris whose white shoulder would gleam as when
    At night a cloudless moon is mirrored
        On the sea's surface, or Cnidian Gyges   20

Who, if you planted him in a group of girls,
Could bluff discerning strangers amazingly,
    The difference made problematic
        By his long hair and hermaphrodite looks.

6

Though you'd go with me to Cadiz, Septimius,
And the Cantabri who reject our yoke, and
Barbarous Syrtes where Moroccan tides are
Forever seething,

Tibur colonized by an Argive farmer   5
I'd prefer as haven for my retirement,
The end for one who's weary of sea and travel
And army service.

But, if Fate's unfairness debar me from there,
I would seek Galaesus, the river sweet to   10
Leather-coated sheep, and the rural realm of
Spartan Phalanthus.

There, beyond the rest, is the corner of our
World that smiles on me, where the honey's quite as
Good as Hymettus, and the berry rivals   15
Verdant Venafrum,

uer ubi longum tepidasque praebet
Iuppiter brumas et amicus Aulon
fertili Baccho minimum Falernis
inuidet uuis.   20

ille te mecum locus et beatae
postulant arces; ibi tu calentem
debita sparges lacrima fauillam
uatis amici.

VII

O saepe mecum tempus in ultimum
deducte Bruto militiae duce,
    quis te redonauit Quiritem
        dis patriis Italoque caelo,

Pompei, meorum prime sodalium?   5
cum quo morantem saepe diem mero
    fregi coronatus nitentis
        malobathro Syrio capillos.

tecum Philippos et celerem fugam
sensi relicta non bene parmula,   10
    cum fracta uirtus et minaces
        turpe solum tetigere mento.

sed me per hostis Mercurius celer
denso pauentem sustulit aere;
    te rursus in bellum resorbens   15
        unda fretis tulit aestuosis.

ergo obligatam redde Ioui dapem
longaque fessum militia latus
    depone sub lauru mea nec
        parce cadis tibi destinatis.   20

obliuioso leuia Massico
ciboria exple, funde capacibus
    unguenta de conchis. quis udo
        deproperare apio coronas

Where the spring's long-lasting and Jove dispenses
Warmth in wintertime, and the vale of Aulon,
Fertile Bacchus' friend, has least cause to envy
Grapes of Falernum.   20

That's the posting and the luxurious stronghold
Summons you and me; it is there you'll sprinkle
Tributary tears on the still warm ash of
Your friend the lyrist.

7

Oh, often led with me to what seemed our life's
Last moments, under Brutus's leadership —
    Who's given you back as civilian
        To ancestral Gods and Italian skies,

Pompeius, first of all my companions?   5
With you I've broken up many a boring day
    With unmixed wine, my garlanded hair
        Gleaming with Syrian malobathrum.

Together we experienced Philippi
And headlong rout, my buckler ignobly dumped,   10
    When 'Virtue' broke and those who threatened
        Touched with their chins the inglorious ground.

But me swift-wingèd Mercury carried off
In epic mist through the enemy, terrified,
    While you were sucked back into war by   15
        Currents that swept you on through its wild surge.

So duly pay the feast you owe Jupiter
And laying body down underneath my bay,
    Tired as you are by long campaigning,
        Kill off the wine-jars intended for you.   20

Brim-full fill up with Massic amnesia
Smooth tulip-glasses. Pour from capacious shells
    The perfumes. Who will quickly twine moist
        Garlands of celery or of myrtle?

curatue myrto? quem Venus arbitrum   25
dicet bibendi? non ego sanius
    bacchabor Edonis: recepto
        dulce mihi furere est amico.

VIII

Vlla si iuris tibi peierati
poena, Barine, nocuisset umquam,
dente si nigro fieres uel uno
turpior ungui,

crederem: sed tu simul obligasti   5
perfidum uotis caput, enitescis
pulchrior multo iuuenumque prodis
publica cura.

expedit matris cineres opertos
fallere et toto taciturna noctis   10
signa cum caelo gelidaque diuos
morte carentis.

ridet hoc, inquam, Venus ipsa, rident
simplices Nymphae ferus et Cupido
semper ardentis acuens sagittas   15
cote cruenta.

adde quod pubes tibi crescit omnis,
seruitus crescit noua nec priores
impiae tectum dominae relinquunt
saepe minati.   20

te suis matres metuunt iuuencis,
te senes parci miseraeque nuper
uirgines nuptae, tua ne retardet
aura maritos.

And whom will Venus choose to be toastmaster? 25
Myself, I'll rave it up as insanely as
   The Edonians. It's sheer delight for
      Me to go mad when a friend has come home.

8

If, for all your promises broken, any
Punishment, Barine, had ever harmed you,
If by one black tooth or discoloured nail you
   Grew at all ugly,

I'd believe you. But, when you put at risk your 5
Faithless head on oath, you begin to shine out
Lovelier by far and emerge the young men's
   Centre of attention.

Yes, it pays you well to swear falsely by your
Mother's buried ashes, by silent night-time's 10
Stars with heaven's vault and the Gods whom ice-cold
   Death never touches.

Even Venus laughs at it, I assure you.
The artless Nymphs laugh too and that cruel youngster
Cupid, ever sharpening fiery darts on 15
   Blood-spattered whetstone.

You're the one, what's more, all the young grow up for,
Grow up your new slaves, but the earlier lot still
Won't desert the house of their perjured mistress,
   Though they keep threatening. 20

Mothers all fear you for their ignorant cubs,
Mean old men fear you and unhappy new brides
Lately virgin fear you in case your fragrance
   Holds back their husbands.

IX

Non semper imbres nubibus hispidos
manant in agros aut mare Caspium
    uexant inaequales procellae
        usque nec Armeniis in oris,

amice Valgi, stat glacies iners   5
mensis per omnis aut Aquilonibus
    querceta Gargani laborant
        et foliis uiduantur orni:

tu semper urges flebilibus modis
Mysten ademptum nec tibi uespero   10
    surgente decedunt amores
        nec rapidum fugiente solem.

at non ter aeuo functus amabilem
plorauit omnis Antilochum senex
    annos, nec impubem parentes   15
        Troilon aut Phrygiae sorores

fleuere semper. desine mollium
tandem querelarum et potius noua
    cantemus Augusti tropaea
        Caesaris et rigidum Niphaten,   20

Medumque flumen gentibus additum
uictis minores uoluere uertices
    intraque praescriptum Gelonos
        exiguis equitare campis.

X

Rectius uiues, Licini, neque altum
semper urgendo neque, dum procellas
cautus horrescis, nimium premendo
litus iniquum.

auream quisquis mediocritatem   5
diligit, tutus caret obsoleti
sordibus tecti, caret inuidenda
sobrius aula.

9

Not always does rain pour from the clouds upon
Bedraggled farmland, nor is the Caspian Sea
    Forever buffeted by gusting
        Storm-winds, nor up on Armenia's borders,

Friend Valgius, does ice remain motionless   5
For all the twelve months, or by the northern blasts
    Are the oakwoods of Garganus troubled
        And manna-ashes bereft of leafage,

But you in mournful measure continually
Bemoan the loss of Mystes; your passion won't   10
    Give way when Hesperus is rising
        Nor when he flees from the ravening Sun.

Yet the ancient who saw three generations out
Did not lament belovèd Antilochus
    Lifelong, nor parents and his Phrygian   15
        Sisters forever shed tears for Troilus

The adolescent. Cease your effeminate
Complaints at long last, and let us rather sing
    Of Caesar Augustus' most recent
        Victory-trophies and stark Niphates   20

And how the Parthian river, now added to
The conquered races, rolls more submissive crests,
    And how within fixed bounds Geloni
        Gallop their horses on undersized plains.

10

You will live more rightly, Licinius, if you
Neither make always for deep water nor through
Cautious dread of tempests too closely hug the
Dangerous coastline.

Anyone in love with the Golden Mean plays   5
Safe, avoids the squalor of run-down lodgings,
Sensibly avoids a palatial house too
As cause of envy.

saepius uentis agitatur ingens
pinus et celsae grauiore casu 10
decidunt turres feriuntque summos
fulgura montis.

sperat infestis, metuit secundis
alteram sortem bene praeparatum
pectus. informis hiemes reducit 15
Iuppiter, idem

summouet. non, si male nunc, et olim
sic erit: quondam citharae tacentem
suscitat Musam neque semper arcum
tendit Apollo. 20

rebus angustis animosus atque
fortis appare; sapienter idem
contrahes uento nimium secundo
turgida uela.

XI

Quid bellicosus Cantaber et Scythes,
Hirpine Quincti, cogitet Hadria
    diuisus obiecto, remittas
        quaerere nec trepides in usum

poscentis aeui pauca. fugit retro 5
leuis iuuentas et decor, arida
    pellente lasciuos amores
        canitie facilemque somnum.

non semper idem floribus est honor
uernis neque uno luna rubens nitet 10
    uultu: quid aeternis minorem
        consiliis animum fatigas?

cur non sub alta uel platano uel hac
pinu iacentes sic temere et rosa 15
    canos odorati capillos,
        dum licet, Assyriaque nardo

It's the giant pine that is oftener shaken
By the gales, high towers that tumble down with
Heavier collapse; it's the mountain-tops make   10
Targets for lightning.

Well-conditioned minds in distress are hopeful,
Fearful in good times, of the opposite fate.
Though He brings around unattractive winters,   15
Jupiter also

Moves them on. Today may be bad; tomorrow
Won't be so too. Sometimes Apollo wakes his
Silent lyric Muse and is not forever
Stretching his bowstring.   20

When in difficulties reveal your strength and
Spirit. Likewise it will be prudent of you,
When the wind's too favourable, to reef your
Bellying canvas.

11

What warlike Cantabri, or the Scythians
Far back of Adria's barrier, may intend,
        Hirpinus Quinctius, cease inquiring
                Nor be afraid to take full advan

Of life that asks but little. Unwrinkled y   h,   5
Good looks, recede behind us as middl   e,
        Grey-haired and desiccant, dismiss
                Light-hearted loves and untro   ed slumber.

Flowers can't forever flourish in vern   loom
Nor blushing moon shine on with the   fsame face.   10
        What use is there in wearying your
                Mind that can't cope with eternal scheming?

Why, under lofty platanus or this pine,
Stretched out in comfort carelessly, while we may,
        Our grizzled hair perfumed with roses   15
                And with Assyrian nard anointed,

potamus uncti? dissipat Euhius
curas edacis. quis puer ocius
   restinguet ardentis Falerni
      pocula praetereunte lympha?   20

quis deuium scortum eliciet domo
Lyden? eburna dic age cum lyra
   maturet, incomptam Lacaenae
      more comam religata nodo.

XII

Nolis longa ferae bella Numantiae
nec durum Hannibalem nec Siculum mare
Poeno purpureum sanguine mollibus
   aptari citharae modis

nec saeuos Lapithas et nimium mero   5
Hylaeum domitosque Herculea manu
Telluris iuuenes, unde periculum
   fulgens contremuit domus

Saturni ueteris; tuque pedestribus
dices historiis proelia Caesaris,   10
Maecenas, melius ductaque per uias
   regum colla minacium.

me dulces dominae Musa Licymniae
cantus, me uoluit dicere lucidum
fulgentis oculos et bene mutuis   15
   fidum pectus amoribus;

quam nec ferre pedem dedecuit choris
nec certare ioco nec dare bracchia
ludentem nitidis uirginibus sacro
   Dianae celebris die.   20

num tu quae tenuit diues Achaemenes
aut pinguis Phrygiae Mygdonias opes
permutare uelis crine Licymniae
   plenas aut Arabum domos,

Why don't we drink? For Euhius will dispel
The cares that eat us. — Which of the boys will first
    Cool down with water flowing-by our
        Goblets of fiery-strong Falernian?   20

And who will lure out Lyde, the hard-to-get
Call-girl, from home? Go tell her to hurry here
    With ivory lyre, her unkempt tresses
        Tied in a knot, the Laconian fashion.

12

Fierce Numantia's long wars, stubborn Hannibal,
The Sicilian sea purple with Punic blood —
You'd not wish for such harsh themes to be made to fit
    The soft tones of the cithara.

Nor wild Lapiths and Hylaeus too full of wine   5
And the children of Earth conquered by Hercules
When their dangerous fling caused the bright shining home
    Of old Saturn to shake with fear.

Besides, you will narrate better yourself in prose
As historian, Maecenas, the many fights   10
Caesar won and describe menacing kings, their necks
    In chains, led through the streets of Rome.

I however have been willed by the Muse to praise
The sweet singing of my lady Licymnia
And her glistening bright eyes and her tender heart   15
    Firmly faithful in mutual love,

Whom it hasn't disgraced either to tread the dance
Or join battles of wit or to move supple arms
Among trimly attired virgins disporting on
Crowded Diana's sacred day.   20

All the worldly estate of rich Achaemenes,
The Mygdonian wealth of fertile Phrygia,
Lavish Arabic homes — would you agree to exchange
    For these one of Licymnia's locks

cum flagrantia detorquet ad oscula   25
ceruicem aut facili saeuitia negat
quae poscente magis gaudeat eripi,
    interdum rapere occupet?

XIII

Ille et nefasto te posuit die,
quicumque primum, et sacrilega manu
    produxit, arbos, in nepotum
        perniciem opprobriumque pagi;

illum et parentis crediderim sui   5
fregisse ceruicem et penetralia
    sparsisse nocturno cruore
        hospitis; ille uenena Colcha

et quidquid usquam concipitur nefas
tractauit, agro qui statuit meo   10
    te, triste lignum, te caducum
        in domini caput immerentis.

quid quisque uitet numquam homini satis
cautum est in horas. nauita Bosphorum
    Thynus perhorrescit neque ultra   15
        caeca timet aliunde fata,

miles sagittas et celerem fugam
Parthi, catenas Parthus et Italum
    robur: sed improuisa leti
        uis rapuit rapietque gentis.   20

quam paene furuae regna Proserpinae
et iudicantem uidimus Aeacum
    sedesque discretas piorum et
        Aeoliis fidibus querentem

Sappho puellis de popularibus,   25
et te sonantem plenius aureo,
    Alcaee, plectro dura nauis,
        dura fugae mala, dura belli.

When she's bending her neck down to your burning kiss   25
Or refusing a kiss with playful cruelty
Which, more badly than her suitor, she wishes stolen
    And sometimes is the first to steal?

13

He planted you out, Tree, on an evil day
(Whoever first it was) and with impious hand
    Then brought you up to cause the district
        Scandal and posterity disaster.

I could believe he actually broke his own   5
Poor father's neck and spattered the Household Gods
    With blood of guest in midnight murder.
        He must have dealt in the drugs of Colchis

And every abomination conceivable,
The brute who stationed you on my property,   10
    Malignant timber, you to topple
        On your proprietor's innocent head.

From hour to hour no human is wary enough
Of what to avoid. The Thynian mariner   15
    Will dread the Bosphorus, beyond that
        Fearing no unforeseen fate from elsewhere.

Our soldiers fear the arrows and speedy flight
Of Parthians, Parthians chains and Italian hearts-
    of-oak, but still it's the unexpected
        Death-blow has taken and will take most off,   20

How close I came to seeing the realm of wan
Proserpina, and Aeacus on the bench,
    The abodes allotted to the pious,
        Sappho complaining upon Aeolian

Lyre-strings about the girls, her compatriots,   25
And you, Alcaeus, sounding in fuller tones
    With golden quill hard times on shipboard,
        Hard times in exile and warfare's hard times.

utrumque sacro digna silentio
mirantur umbrae dicere, sed magis   30
    pugnas et exactos tyrannos
        densum umeris bibit aure uulgus.

quid mirum, ubi illis carminibus stupens
demittit atras belua centiceps
    auris et intorti capillis   35
        Eumenidum recreantur angues?

quin et Prometheus et Pelopis parens
dulci laborem decipitur sono
    nec curat Orion leones
        aut timidos agitare lyncas.   40

XIV

Eheu fugaces, Postume, Postume,
labuntur anni nec pietas moram
    rugis et instanti senectae
        afferet indomitaeque morti,

non si trecenis quotquot eunt dies,   5
amice, places illacrimabilem
    Plutona tauris, qui ter amplum
        Geryonen Tityonque tristi

compescit unda, scilicet omnibus,
quicumque terrae munere uescimur,   10
    enauiganda, siue reges
        siue inopes erimus coloni.

frustra cruento Marte carebimus
fractisque rauci fluctibus Hadriae,
    frustra per autumnos nocentem   15
        corporibus metuemus Austrum:

uisendus ater flumine languido
Cocytos errans et Danai genus
    infame damnatusque longi
        Sisyphus Aeolides laboris.   20

The shades admire them both as they utter things
That earn a sacred hush, but the common crowd   30
    Packed shoulder-tight have thirstier ears for
        Battles and tyrants deposed and banished.

What wonder, when that beast of a hundred heads
Lets fall his black ears, stunned by their monodies,
    And serpents intertwined among the   35
        Locks of the Eumenides are rested?

Yes, even Prometheus and Pelops' father too
Are tricked by sweet sound out of their suffering
    Nor does Orion then desire to
        Chase after lions and timid lynxes.   40

14

Those fugitives (ah, Postumus, Postumus!)
The years, they slip by, nor can religion bring
    Delay to wrinkles and old age's
        Onset and death the unconquerable,

Not even though you killed every fleeting day   5
Three hundred bulls, my friend, to conciliate
    Illachrymable Pluto, who curbs
        Tityos and Geryon the triple giant

With gloomy water, which it is very sure
That all of us who feed on the gifts of earth   10
    Must voyage over, whether we be
        Kings or impoverished tenant farmers.

In vain we keep away from bloodthirsty Mars
And Adriatic breakers that roar and hiss,
    In vain through autumn days are worried   15
        Lest the Sirocco should harm our bodies.

Cocytus must be faced, with his feeble stream
Meandering dark, and Danaüs' shameful brood,
    And, serving sentence of hard labour,
        Sisyphus Aeolides, forever.   20

linquenda tellus et domus et placens
uxor, neque harum quas colis arborum
    te praeter inuisas cupressos
        ulla breuem dominum sequetur.

absumet heres Caecuba dignior   25
seruata centum clauibus et mero
    tinget pauimentum superbo,
        pontificum potiore cenis.

XV

Iam pauca aratro iugera regiae
moles relinquent, undique latius
    extenta uisentur Lucrino
        stagna lacu platanusque caelebs

euincet ulmos. tum uiolaria et   5
myrtus et omnis copia narium
    spargent oliuetis odorem
        fertilibus domino priori,

tum spissa ramis laurea feruidos
excludet ictus. non ita Romuli   10
    praescriptum et intonsi Catonis
        auspiciis ueterumque norma:

priuatus illis census erat breuis,
commune magnum; nulla decempedis
    metata priuatis opacam   15
        porticus excipiebat Arcton

nec fortuitum spernere caespitem
leges sinebant, oppida publico
    sumptu iubentes et deorum
        templa nouo decorare saxo.   20

Earth must be left and home and belovèd wife
And out of all the trees you are growing here
    There's not a single one will follow
        You their brief lord save the hateful cypress.

A worthier heir will use up the Caecuban   25
One hundred keys kept locked and will splash the floor
    Of marble with the pride of neat wine
        Choicer and stronger than pontiffs' banquets.

15

Quite soon palatial mansions will leave the plough
But little acreage, and on every side
    Ponds more extensive than the Lucrine
        Lake will be seen, and the bachelor plane

Evict the elm. Then violet- and myrtle-beds   5
And wealth of every bloom to delight the nose
    Will scatter scent where olive groves once
        Gave a rich crop to the previous owner.

Then thickly branching laurels will form a shield
Against assaults of heat. Very different this   10
    From Romulus' and bearded Cato's
        Augural edict and ancient practice.

For them their private property list was short,
The common wealth great. There was no colonnade
    Laid out by private ten-foot rods to   15
        Capture the cool of the shady Great Bear,

Nor did the laws allow one to disregard
Fortuitous turf, but they decreed that towns
    And temples of the Gods be adorned at
        Public expense and with newly-cut stone.   20

XVI

Otium diuos rogat in patenti
prensus Aegaeo, simul atra nubes
condidit lunam neque certa fulgent
sidera nautis,

otium bello furiosa Thrace, 5
otium Medi pharetra decori,
Grosphe, non gemmis neque purpura ue-
nale nec auro.

non enim gazae neque consularis
summouet lictor miseros tumultus 10
mentis et curas laqueata circum
tecta uolantis.

uiuitur paruo bene, cui paternum
splendet in mensa tenui salinum
nec leuis somnos timor aut cupido 15
sordidus aufert.

quid breui fortes iaculamur aeuo
multa? quid terras alio calentis
sole mutamus patriae? quis exsul
se quoque fugit? 20

scandit aeratas uitiosa nauis
Cura nec turmas equitum relinquit,
ocior ceruis et agente nimbos
ocior Euro.

laetus in praesens animus quod ultra est 25
oderit curare et amara lento
temperet risu: nihil est ab omni
parte beatum.

abstulit clarum cita mors Achillem,
longa Tithonum minuit senectus: 30
et mihi forsan, tibi quod negarit,
porriget hora.

16

Calm is what those caught in the open Aegean
Ask the Gods for, soon as the gloomy cloud rack
Hides the moon and stars are no longer shining
Clearly for sailors.

Driven mad by war it's for calm that Thrace asks   5
And for calm the Medes with their painted quivers,
Grosphus, though it cannot be bought with jewels
Or purple or gold.

No exotic treasure or consul's lictor
Can disperse the miserable disorders   10
Of the mind or worries that flutter round the
Rich coffered ceiling.

Life is good on little for one whose father's
Saltcellar shines bright on a frugal table,
Nor does fear or miserly greed purloin his   15
Unburdened slumber.

Why in our short life do we boldly target
So much? Why for lands that an alien sun
Warms exchange our own? Has an exile ever
Fled from himself too?   20

Noxious Care will board the bronze-plated galley
And keep pace with squadrons of mounted horsemen,
Than a stag more swift and more swift than Eurus
Driving the rain-clouds.

Let a mind that's pleased with the present shun all   25
Care for what's beyond and with tolerant smile
Lighten disappointments, for no one's ever
Totally lucky.

Speedy death made off with renowned Achilles,
Long old age is wasting away Tithonus,   30
And to me perhaps will the hour bring what
It has denied you.

te greges centum Siculaeque circum-
mugiunt uaccae, tibi tollit hinnitum
apta quadrigis equa, te bis Afro   35
murice tinctae

uestiunt lanae: mihi parua rura et
spiritum Graiae tenuem Camenae
Parca non mendax dedit et malignum
spernere uulgus.   40

XVII

Cur me querelis exanimas tuis?
nec dis amicum est nec mihi te prius
    obire, Maecenas, mearum
        grande decus columenque rerum.

a, te meae si partem animae rapit   5
maturior uis, quid moror altera,
    nec carus aeque nec superstes
        integer? ille dies utramque

ducet ruinam. non ego perfidum
dixi sacramentum: ibimus, ibimus   10
    utcumque praecedes, supremum
        carpere iter comites parati.

me nec Chimaerae spiritus igneae
nec si resurgat centimanus Gyas
    diuellet umquam: sic potenti   15
        Iustitiae placitumque Parcis.

seu Libra seu me Scorpios aspicit
formidolosus, pars uiolentior
    natalis horae, seu tyrannus
        Hesperiae Capricornus undae,   20

utrumque nostrum incredibili modo
consentit astrum: te Iouis impio
    tutela Saturno refulgens
        eripuit uolucrisque Fati

You've a hundred flocks and Sicilian milch cows
Mooing all around and for you there whinny
Chariot-racing mares and you wear wool twice dyed   35
In Afric's murex,

While to me there's given by a truly sparing
Fate a small estate and a Greek Camena's
Frugal inspiration, and disregard for
The envious vulgar.   40

17

You're killing me, Maecenas, with your complaints.
But why? It's not God's pleasure nor is it mine
    That you, great glory and culmination
        Of my existence, should die before me.

Ah, if as half my soul you are carried off   5
By premature force, why should I linger on,
    Your other half, surviving neither
        Equally dear nor a whole man. That day

Will ruin us both. This is no treacherous pledge
I've given you. Together we'll go, we'll go   10
    Whenever you lead on, companions
        Ready to share in the final journey.

Me neither shall the fiery Chimaera's breath
Nor hundred-handed Gyas if he revive,
    From you part ever: such the will of   15
        Justice all-powerful and the Parcae.

For whether Libra or perilous Scorpio
Looks after me as being my horoscope's
    More forceful part or Capricornus
        Absolute Lord of the Western Ocean,   20

Your star and mine are, in an incredible
Way, both concordant. Jupiter's guardianship,
    Refulgent against impious Saturn,
        Saved you from him and slowed down the rapid

tardauit alas, cum populus frequens   25
laetum theatris ter crepuit sonum:
    me truncus illapsus cerebro
        sustulerat, nisi Faunus ictum

dextra leuasset, Mercurialium
custos uirorum. reddere uictimas   30
    aedemque uotiuam memento:
        nos humilem feriemus agnam.

XVIII

    Non ebur neque aureum
mea renidet in domo lacunar,
    non trabes Hymettiae
premunt columnas ultima recisas
    Africa neque Attali   5
ignotus heres regiam occupaui
    nec Laconicas mihi
trahunt honestae purpuras clientae.
    at fides et ingeni
benigna uena est pauperemque diues   10
    me petit: nihil supra
deos lacesso nec potentem amicum
    largiora flagito,
satis beatus unicis Sabinis.

    truditur dies die   15
nouaeque pergunt interire lunae:
    tu secanda marmora
locas sub ipsum funus et sepulcri
    immemor struis domos
marisque Bais obstrepentis urges   20
    summouere litora,
parum locuples continente ripa.
    quid quod usque proximos
reuellis agri terminos et ultra
    limites clientium   25
salis auarus? pellitur paternos
    in sinu ferens deos
et uxor et uir sordidosque natos.

Wing-beat of Fate, that day when the populace   25
Crowding the theatre granted you triple applause.
    A tree-trunk falling on my skull had
        Carried me off, had not Faunus lightened

The blow with his right hand, the protector he
Of Mercury's collegians. Don't forget   30
    To pay a votive shrine and victims:
        I shall be offering a modest ewe-lamb.

18

    Neither gold nor ivory
Of panelled ceiling scintillates in my home.
    No Hymettan architraves
Press down on columns quarried in remotest
        Africa, nor do I own   5
As unknown heir of Attalus a palace,
    Nor can well-born protégées
Of mine be seen trailing Laconian purples.
    Still, I've honesty and wit
(A generous outcrop) and rich people court me   10
    Though I'm poor. I pester Heaven
For nothing further, nor solicit from my
    Powerful friend more lavish gifts,
Blest richly enough with only my dear Sabines.

    Day shoves yesterday aside   15
And new moons press on to their disappearance.
    You, with death at hand, contract
For marble to be cut, and build your houses
    Not remembering the tomb,
But where the sea is thundering at Baiae   20
    Hurry to push back the shore,
Not rich enough so long as coast confines you.
    Even worse, persistently
You rip up neighbours' landmarks and in more greed
    Overleap the boundaries   25
Of your own clients. Out they're driven together,
    Wife and husband clutching to
Their bosoms Household Gods and ragged children.

nulla certior tamen
rapacis Orci sede destinata   30
    aula diuitem manet
erum. quid ultra tendis? aequa tellus
        pauperi recluditur
regumque pueris, nec satelles Orci
    callidum Promethea   35
reuexit auro captus. hic superbum
        Tantalum atque Tantali
genus coercet, hic leuare functum
        pauperem laboribus
uocatus atque non uocatus audit.   40

XIX

Bacchum in remotis carmina rupibus
uidi docentem, credite posteri,
    Nymphasque discentis et auris
        capripedum Satyrorum acutas.

euhoe, recenti mens trepidat metu   5
plenoque Bacchi pectore turbidum
    laetatur; euhoe, parce Liber,
        parce graui metuende thyrso.

fas peruicacis est mihi Thyiadas
uinique fontem lactis et uberes   10
    cantare riuos atque truncis
        lapsa cauis iterare mella;

fas et beatae coniugis additum
stellis honorem tectaque Penthei
    disiecta non leni ruina   15
        Thracis et exitium Lycurgi.

tu flectis amnis, tu mare barbarum,
tu separatis uuidus in iugis
    nodo coerces uiperino
        Bistonidum sine fraude crinis.   20

Yet no hall more certainly
Awaits its wealthy lord than his appointed   30
    Seat in grasping Orcus' realm.
Why strive for more? Earth, equal and impartial,
    Opens both for paupers and
For royal children, nor did Orcus' henchman
    For a gold bribe ferry back   35
Duplicitous Prometheus. He imprisons
    Tantalus the proud and all
Of Tantalus' descendants. He, when summoned —
    Yes, and when unsummoned too —
Gives ear to free the poor whose toil is over.   40

19

I've seen, among unvisited mountain crags,
Lord Bacchus teaching dithyrambs (it's the truth,
    Posterity!), Nymphs memorizing
    And the sharp ears of goat-foot Satyrs.

Eu-oi, my mind is trembling with new-born dread   5
And feels confused delight in a heart inspired
    By Bacchus. *Eu-oi*, spare me, Liber,
    Spare me, dread Lord of the fearful thyrsus!

Now I may sing of strenuous Thyades,
Of springs that flow with wine and of rivers rich   10
    In milk, describing once again how
    Honey exuded from hollow tree-trunks;

May sing of how the crown of your honoured wife
Was placed among the stars, and of Pentheus' hall
    Thrown down by no mild earthquake, and of   15
    Thracian Lycurgus' extermination.

You turn the rivers, tame the barbaric sea,
You, soaked with wine among inaccessible
    High peaks, bind up quite harmlessly the
    Bistonids' tresses with knotted vipers.   20

tu, cum parentis regna per arduum
cohors Gigantum scanderet impia,
    Rhoetum retorsisti leonis
        unguibus horribilique mala;

quamquam choreis aptior et iocis   25
ludoque dictus non sat idoneus
    pugnae ferebaris; sed idem
        pacis eras mediusque belli.

te uidit insons Cerberus aureo
cornu decorum leniter atterens   30
    caudam et recedentis trilingui
        ore pedes tetigitque crura.

XX

Non usitata nec tenui ferar
penna biformis per liquidum aethera
    uates neque in terris morabor
        longius inuidiaque maior

urbis relinquam. non ego, pauperum   5
sanguis parentum, non ego quem uocas,
    dilecte Maecenas, obibo
        nec Stygia cohibebor unda.

iam iam residunt cruribus asperae
pelles et album mutor in alitem   10
    superne nascunturque leues
        per digitos umerosque plumae.

iam Daedaleo notior Icaro
uisam gementis litora Bosphori
    Syrtisque Gaetulas canorus   15
        ales Hyperboreosque campos;

me Colchus et qui dissimulat metum
Marsae cohortis Dacus et ultimi
    noscent Geloni, me peritus
        discet Hiber Rhodanique potor.   20

And when the Giants' impious company
Was climbing up to heaven, your father's realm,
  You hurled back Rhoetus with your lion's
    Talons and terror-inspiring muzzle.

Supposedly more fit for the dancing-floor   25
And games and jesting, you were considered not
  Well qualified for fighting; still you
    Proved to be central in peace and war both.

When Cerberus saw you in your majesty
With golden horn, unhurtful he gently wagged   30
  His tail, and touched your feet and legs with
    Triple-tongued mouth as you made your way back.

20

On pinions neither chic nor conventional
I'll soar through the empyrean, a twi-form bard,
  Nor shall I linger earth-bound for much
    Longer — victorious over envy

I'll leave the cities. No, as for me, 'the blood   5
Of humble parents,' me whom you choose to invite,
  Belovèd Maecenas, I'll not die —
    Never be hemmed in by Stygian waters.

Already rough skin's forming upon my legs;
My upper half is metamorphosing to   10
  A snow-white bird, and downy feathers
    Sprout from my fingers and either shoulder.

Than Daedalean Icarus better known
I'll visit soon the Bosphorus' sounding shore
  As tuneful swan, and the Gaetúlan   15
    Syrtes and Hyperborean tundra.

By Colchians and Dacians who hide their fear
Of Marsian cohorts I shall be known, and by
  Furthest Geloni; me the well-read
    Drinkers of Ebro and Rhone will study.   20

absint inani funere neniae
luctusque turpes et querimoniae;
    compesce clamorem ac sepulcri
      mitte superuacuos honores.

No dirges, please, at my hollow funeral,
No unseemly grief or murmur of discontent.
    Suppress the wailing and don't even
        Order my tomb — it's a needless tribute.

CARMINVM LIBER TERTIVS

I

Odi profanum uulgus et arceo.
fauete linguis: carmina non prius
   audita Musarum sacerdos
      uirginibus puerisque canto.

regum timendorum in proprios greges,   5
reges in ipsos imperium est Iouis,
   clari Giganteo triumpho,
      cuncta supercilio mouentis.

est ut uiro uir latius ordinet
arbusta sulcis, hic generosior   10
   descendat in Campum petitor,
      moribus hic meliorque fama

contendat, illi turba clientium
sit maior: aequa lege Necessitas
   sortitur insignis et imos;   15
      omne capax mouet urna nomen.

destrictus ensis cui super impia
ceruice pendet, non Siculae dapes
   dulcem elaborabunt saporem,
      non auium citharaeque cantus   20

somnum reducent: somnus agrestium
lenis uirorum non humilis domos
   fastidit umbrosamque ripam,
      non Zephyris agitata tempe.

desiderantem quod satis est neque   25
tumultuosum sollicitat mare
   nec saeuus Arcturi cadentis
      impetus aut orientis Haedi,

ODES, BOOK THREE

1

The uninitiate vulgar I hate and ban.
Keep guard on language. Poetry hitherto
    Unheard of, as the Muses' priest, I
        Sing for our unmarried girls and young men.

Dread kings have power over the flocks they own   5
But Jove has power over the kings themselves,
    Renowned for Gigantean Triumph,
        Shifting the world with a lifted eyebrow.

It's true that A more widely than B lays out
His trees in rows; another as candidate   10
    Goes down more nobly born to Mars' Field;
        This one in conduct and reputation

Is leading; that one comes with a bigger crowd
Of clients: still, impartial Necessity
    Draws lots for V I Ps and lowest —   15
        In her big urn every name is shuffled.

For one with drawn sword over his impious neck
Suspended no Sicilian banqueting
    Can ever elaborate sweet savours
        Nor can the music of bird or lyre   20

Bring back his sleep. But merciful sleep does not
Disdain the humble dwellings of country folk,
    Their shady river-banks and scenic
        Forested valleys by Zephyrs ruffled.

The man contented with a sufficiency   25
Is never worried by the tumultuous sea
    Or by the fierce aggressiveness of
        Setting Arcturus or Haedus rising

non uerberatae grandine uineae
fundusque mendax, arbore nunc aquas 30
    culpante, nunc torrentia agros
        sidera, nunc hiemes iniquas.

contracta pisces aequora sentiunt
iactis in altum molibus: huc frequens
    caementa demittit redemptor 35
        cum famulis dominusque terrae

fastidiosus; sed Timor et Minae
scandunt eodem quo dominus, neque
    decedit aerata triremi et
        post equitem sedet atra Cura. 40

quodsi dolentem nec Phrygius lapis
nec purpurarum sidere clarior
    delenit usus nec Falerna
        uitis Achaemeniumque costum,

cur inuidendis postibus et nouo 45
sublime ritu moliar atrium?
    cur ualle permutem Sabina
        diuitias operosiores?

II

Angustam amice pauperiem pati
robustus acri militia puer
    condiscat et Parthos ferocis
        uexet eques metuendus hasta

uitamque sub diuo et trepidis agat 5
in rebus. illum ex moenibus hosticis
    matrona bellantis tyranni
        prospiciens et adulta uirgo

suspiret, eheu, ne rudis agminum
sponsus lacessat regius asperum 10
    tactu leonem, quem cruenta
        per medias rapit ira caedes.

Or by his vineyards when they are lashed with hail
Or by a cheating farm when his orchards blame   30
    Now cloudbursts, now the sun's heat scorching
        Cornfields and now unexpected cold-spells.

The fishes feel their watery world reduced
By deeply laid blocks where the assiduous
    Contractor with his staff and the owner   35
        Tired of the land lowers tons of rubble

As filling-in, but Terror and Menaces
Can clamber up as high as the owner and
    Black Worry go aboard the brass-bound
        Trireme and ride on the horseman's pillion.   40

But if the use of purples more radiant
Than any star, if marble from Phrygia,
    Falernian vines and Persian perfumes
        Cannot console one in pain or sorrow,

Then why should I uprear an imposing hall   45
In modern style with envy-provoking porch?
    Or why exchange my Sabine vale for
        Wealth that is even more labour-intensive?

2

The boy whom active service is toughening up
Must learn to suffer poverty's pinch as friend
    And harass the ferocious Parthians,
        Lancer formidable for his spear-thrust,

And spend his life in the open on dangerous   5
Commissions. Him from the enemy battlements
    The consort of the warrior tyrant,
        Watching afar with her grown-up daughter,

Will sigh 'Alas', afraid lest the royal betrothed,
A tiro on campaign, should provoke the lion   10
    Unsafe to handle, whom bloodthirsty
        Anger drives on through the midst of slaughter.

dulce et decorum est pro patria mori:
mors et fugacem persequitur uirum
    nec parcit imbellis iuuentae   15
        poplitibus timidoque tergo.

Virtus repulsae nescia sordidae
intaminatis fulget honoribus
    nec sumit aut ponit securis
        arbitrio popularis aurae: 20

Virtus recludens immeritis mori
caelum negata temptat iter uia
    coetusque uulgaris et udam
        spernit humum fugiente pinna.

est et fideli tuta silentio   25
merces: uetabo, qui Cereris sacrum
    uulgarit arcanae, sub isdem
        sit trabibus fragilemque mecum

soluat phaselon: saepe Diespiter
neglectus incesto addidit integrum;   30
    raro antecedentem scelestum
        deseruit pede Poena claudo.

III

Iustum et tenacem propositi uirum
non ciuium ardor praua iubentium,
    non uultus instantis tyranni
        mente quatit solida neque Auster,

dux inquieti turbidus Hadriae,   5
nec fulminantis magna manus Iouis:
    si fractus illabatur orbis,
        impauidum ferient ruinae.

hac arte Pollux et uagus Hercules
enisus arcis attigit igneas,   10
    quos inter Augustus recumbens
        purpureo bibet ore nectar.

It's sweet and right to die for one's native land.
Death also catches up with the man who flees,
    And has no mercy on the hamstrings   15
        And timid backs of unwarlike youngsters.

Not knowing drab defeat at the polls Manhood
Shines ever bright with unsullied victories
    Nor takes up nor lays down the axes
        Bidden by the breath of the people's favour.   20

Manhood that opens heaven above to those
Unworthy of death dares go the forbidden way
    And spurns all contact with the vulgar
        And with dank earth on evasive pinions.

Trustworthy silence also will have a sure   25
Requital. I'll forbid any publicist
    Of secret Ceres' ritual to
        Share the same roof or unmoor a fragile

Sailboat with me, for often Diespiter
When slighted mixes guilty with innocent,   30
    But limping Punishment has seldom
        Failed to catch sinners despite their head start.

3

A righteous man and steadfast in his resolve
No voters' passion calling for evil deeds
    No frown of peremptory tyrant
        Ever will shake from his settled purpose —

Not Auster, restless Adria's boisterous lord,
Nor mighty hand of thunderbolt-hurling Jove.
    Were heaven's dome to crack and topple,
        Struck by the debris he'll never panic.

Thus Pollux and migratory Hercules
Strove on and reached the fiery citadel,   10
    Between whom Augustus reclining
        Later will drink ruddy-lipped the nectar.

hac te merentem, Bacche pater, tuae
uexere tigres indocili iugum
   collo trahentes, hac Quirinus   15
      Martis equis Acheronta fugit,

gratum elocuta consiliantibus
Iunone diuis: 'Ilion, Ilion
   fatalis incestusque iudex
      et mulier peregrina uertit   20

in puluerem, ex quo destituit deos
mercede pacta Laomedon, mihi
   castaeque damnatum Mineruae
      cum populo et duce fraudulento.

iam nec Lacaenae splendet adulterae   25
famosus hospes nec Priami domus
   periura pugnaces Achiuos
      Hectoreis opibus refringit,

nostrisque ductum seditionibus
bellum resedit. protinus et grauis   30
   iras et inuisum nepotem,
      Troica quem peperit sacerdos,

Marti redonabo. illum ego lucidas
inire sedes, discere nectaris
   sucos et adscribi quietis   35
      ordinibus patiar deorum.

dum longus inter saeuiat Ilion
Romamque pontus, qualibet exsules
   in parte regnanto beati;
      dum Priami Paridisque busto   40

insultet armentum et catulos ferae
celent inultae, stet Capitolium
   fulgens triumphatisque possit
      Roma ferox dare iura Medis.

horrenda late nomen in ultimas   45
extendat oras, qua medius liquor
   secernit Europen ab Afro,
      qua tumidus rigat arua Nilus.

For such deserving, tigers transported you,
O Father Bacchus, bearing the yoke upon
    Their obstinate necks, and Quirinus   15
        Acheron-bound fled in Mars's chariot,

While Juno gave a welcome address among
The Gods in council: 'Ilion, Ilion,
    A deadly and adulterous judge,
        Paired with an alien woman, turned you   20

To ashes — since the day when Laomedon
Left Gods without their promised reward, accursed
    By me and by the chaste Minerva,
        You and your people and cheating leader.

No longer shines for Spartan adulteress   25
Her infamous guest, nor does the perjured house
    Of Priam with Hector's assistance
        Beat back the aggressive Achaeans' onset;

The war that our refractory feuds prolonged
Has now subsided. Forthwith my grievous wrath   30
    And hatred of my grandson whom the
        Ilian priestess produced I'll give up

For Mars's sake, allowing him entry to
The heavenly realms of light, to experience
    The taste of nectar and enrolment   35
        In the now peaceable ranks of Godhead.

As long as wide sea chafes between Ilion
And Rome, so long can the exiles be fortunate
    And rule whatever land they favour.
        Only if on Paris' tomb and Priam's   40

The cattle trample, and the wild animals
Hide cubs in safety, then let the Capitol
    In splendour stand and warlike Rome ad-
        minister justice to conquered Parthians.

Feared greatly far and wide, let her spread her name   45
To the uttermost extremities where the straits
    Dissever Africa from Europe,
        Where swollen Nile inundates the flat fields.

aurum irrepertum et sic melius situm,
cum terra celat, spernere fortior   50
   quam cogere humanos in usus
      omne sacrum rapiente dextra,

quicumque mundo terminus obstitit,
hunc tanget armis, uisere gestiens
   qua parte debacchentur ignes,   55
      qua nebulae pluuiique rores.

sed bellicosis fata Quiritibus
hac lege dico, ne nimium pii
   rebusque fidentes auitae
      tecta uelint reparare Troiae.   60

Troiae renascens alite lugubri
fortuna tristi clade iterabitur
   ducente uictrices cateruas
      coniuge me Iouis et sorore.

ter si resurgat murus aeneus   65
auctore Phoebo, ter pereat meis
   excisus Argiuis, ter uxor
      capta uirum puerosque ploret.'

non hoc iocosae conueniet lyrae.
quo, Musa, tendis? desine peruicax   70
   referre sermones deorum et
      magna modis tenuare paruis.

IV

Descende caelo et dic age tibia
regina longum Calliope melos,
   seu uoce nunc mauis acuta,
      seu fidibus citharaque Phoebi.

auditis? an me ludit amabilis   5
insania? audire et uideor pios
   errare per lucos, amoenae
      quos et aquae subeunt et aurae.

More resolute to scorn undiscovered gold
(Gold better placed, accordingly, underground)   50
    Than gather it for human use by
        Laying profane hands on all that's sacred,

Whatever confines limit this world of ours,
She'll reach them with her weaponry, keen to see
    The zones where dance in Bacchic frenzy   55
        Fiery heatwaves or fogs and drizzle.

I tell the fierce Quirites their future, though
With this proviso: let them not (dutiful
    To excess and trusting in their power)
        Think of rebuilding ancestral Troy's roofs.

Troy's Fortune, resurrected with sinister
Omen, will re-enact her disastrous fall,
    While I lead on victorious squadrons,
        Jupiter's sister and wedded consort.

Suppose its wall three times should arise in bronze   65
With Phoebus' help, three times would it be destroyed,
    Hacked down by my Argives, three times for
        Husband and children would captive wives weep ...'

But this will never do for the playful lyre.
Why try so hard, Muse? Don't be persistent. Stop   70
    Reporting speeches of the Gods and
        Slighting a grand theme with paltry quatrains.

4

Come down from heaven and render upon the pipe,
Calliope my queen, a long melody,
    Or with a clear voice, if you now wish,
        Or on the kithara-strings of Phoebus. —

Do you hear it? Or does ravishing ecstasy   5
Delude me? I seem to hear and to wander through
    Muse-haunted woodland where refreshing
        Zephyrs and rivulets softly enter.

me fabulosae Volture in Apulo
nutricis extra limina Pulliae   10
    ludo fatigatumque somno
        fronde noua puerum palumbes

texere, mirum quod foret omnibus,
quicumque celsae nidum Acherontiae
    saltusque Bantinos et aruum   15
        pingue tenent humilis Forenti,

ut tuto ab atris corpore uiperis
dormirem et ursis, ut premerer sacra
    lauroque collataque myrto,
        non sine dis animosus infans.   20

uester, Camenae, uester in arduos
tollor Sabinos, seu mihi frigidum
    Praeneste seu Tibur supinum
        seu liquidae placuere Baiae.

uestris amicum fontibus et choris   25
non me Philippis uersa acies retro,
    deuota non exstinxit arbos
        nec Sicula Palinurus unda.

utcumque mecum uos eritis, libens
insanientem nauita Bosphorum   30
    temptabo et urentis harenas
        litoris Assyrii uiator,

uisam Britannos hospitibus feros
et laetum equino sanguine Concanum,
    uisam pharetratos Gelonos   35
        et Scythicum inuiolatus amnem.

uos Caesarem altum, militia simul
fessas cohortes abdidit oppidis,
    finire quaerentem labores
        Pierio recreatis antro;   40

uos lene consilium et datis et dato
gaudetis, almae. scimus ut impios
    Titanas immanemque turbam
        fulmine sustulerit caduco,

A child on Voltur Mount in Apulia
Beyond my wet-nurse Pullia's cottage-door   10
    When I was tired with play and sleeping
        Fairytale woodpigeons covered me with

Fresh-fallen leaves, a marvel to all the folk
Of Acherontia's eyrie among the hills,
    The woodland pasturage of Bantia   15
        And the rich loam of low-lying Forentum,

How I could sleep with body uninjured by
Black vipers and bears, how I was overlaid
    With sacred bay and gathered myrtle,
        Toddler courageous, divinely favoured.   20

I'm yours, Camenae, yours when I make the ascent
To arduous Sabines or when I'm entertained
    By cool Praeneste or laid-back Tibur
        Or by the liquid appeal of Baiae.

Because I love your fountains and dancing choir,   25
The routed line of battle at Philippi,
    The accursèd tree, and Palinurus'
        Sicilian breakers could not destroy me.

Whenever you are with me I'll gladly face
As sailor the unpredictable Bosphorus   30
    Or else as wayfarer the burning
        Sands of Assyria's distant coastline;

I'll visit stranger-hating Britannia
And Cóncani who relish the blood of mares,
    I'll visit quiver-hung Geloni and   35
        Scythian river and come to no hurt.

As soon as high-born Caesar has hidden away
His battle-wearied cohorts in country towns
    And sought to terminate his labours,
        You in Pierian cave refresh him.   40

You, Kindly Ones, give gentle advice and when
It's given rejoice. We know how the impious
    Titanes and the Giant gang were
        Sent to their doom by his thunderbolt who

qui terram inertem, qui mare temperat 45
uentosum et urbis regnaque tristia,
    diuosque mortalisque turmas
        imperio regit unus aequo.

magnum illa terrorem intulerat Ioui
fidens iuuentus horrida bracchiis 50
    fratresque tendentes opaco
        Pelion imposuisse Olympo.

sed quid Typhoeus et ualidus Mimas
aut quid minaci Porphyrion statu,
    quid Rhoetus euulsisque truncis 55
        Enceladus iaculator audax

contra sonantem Palladis aegida
possent ruentes? hinc auidus stetit
    Vulcanus, hinc matrona Iuno et
        numquam umeris positurus arcum, 60

qui rore puro Castaliae lauit
crinis solutos, qui Lyciae tenet
    dumeta natalemque siluam,
        Delius et Patareus Apollo.

uis consili expers mole ruit sua; 65
uim temperatam di quoque prouehunt
    in maius; idem odere uiris
        omne nefas animo mouentis.

testis mearum centimanus Gyas
sententiarum, notus et integrae 70
    temptator Orion Dianae
        uirginea domitus sagitta.

iniecta monstris Terra dolet suis
maeretque partus fulmine luridum
    missos ad Orcum; nec peredit 75
        impositam celer ignis Aetnen,

incontinentis nec Tityi iecur
reliquit ales, nequitiae additus
    custos; amatorem trecentae
        Pirithoum cohibent catenae. 80

Controls the passive earth and the wind-blown sea 45
And cities and the realms of the mournful dead,
    Divinities and troops of mortals,
        One and alone with impartial power.

Great terror they inflicted on Jupiter,
That arrogant young crew with their swarm of hands, 50
    Those brothers striving hard to pile Mount
        Pelion onto tree-grown Olympus.

But could Typhoeus and the robust Mimas
Or could Porphyrion's menacing stature or
    Could Rhoetus and Enceladus, that 55
        Insolent hurler of uptorn tree-trunks,

Stand any chance, attacking the thunderous shield
Of Pallas — the aegis? Here stood the ravening
    Vulcanus, here Matrona Juno and
        One who will never drop bow from shoulder, 60

Who washes in pure dew of Castalia
His loosened tresses, ruler of Lycia's
    Thorn-thickets and his native woodland,
        Delian and Patarean Apollo.

Force lacking counsel fails through its own excess; 65
Force wisely managed even the Gods approve
    And strengthen, while abominating
        Force that premeditates every horror.

Gyas the hundred-handed is evidence
For my opinion and the notorious 70
    Orion, pure Diana's would-be
        Rapist, subdued by her virgin arrow.

Piled over her monstrosities Earth feels pain
And mourns her offspring sent by the thunderbolt
    To ghastly Orcus, nor can swift fire 75
        Eat away superimposed Mount Etna

Nor has the bird, assigned to his lechery
As warder, left the liver of Tityos
    The dissolute. Three hundred shackles
        Limit Pirithous' womanizing. 80

V

Caelo tonantem credidimus Iouem
regnare: praesens diuus habebitur
    Augustus adiectis Britannis
        imperio grauibusque Persis.

milesne Crassi coniuge barbara   5
turpis maritus uixit et hostium —
    pro curia inuersique mores! —
        consenuit socerorum in armis,

sub rege Medo Marsus et Apulus,
anciliorum et nominis et togae   10
    oblitus aeternaeque Vestae,
        incolumi Ioue et urbe Roma?

hoc cauerat mens prouida Reguli
dissentientis condicionibus
    foedis et exemplo trahenti   15
        perniciem ueniens in aeuum,

si non periret immiserabilis
captiua pubes: 'signa ego Punicis
    affixa delubris et arma
        militibus sine caede' dixit   20

'derepta uidi, uidi ego ciuium
retorta tergo bracchia libero
    portasque non clausas et arua
        Marte coli populata nostro.

auro repensus scilicet acrior   25
miles redibit: flagitio additis
    damnum. neque amissos colores
        lana refert medicata fuco

nec uera uirtus, cum semel excidit,
curat reponi deterioribus.   30
    si pugnat extricata densis.
        cerua plagis, erit ille fortis,

5

Because he thunders we have believed that Jove
Is King in Heaven: Augustus will prove a God
    On earth by adding to the Empire
        Troublesome Parthians and Britanni.

Have Crassus' troops lived on with barbarian wives   5
In shameful wedlock, reaching old age — alas
    For Senate and perverted values! —
        Fighting their enemy kinsmen's battles?

Marsi or Apulians under a Parthian king,
Forgetting toga, name and *ancilia*   10
    And everlasting Vesta, while both
        Jove and the city of Rome are standing?

Of this the prescient thinking of Regulus
Gave warning when rejecting those infamous
    Conditions and the precedent which   15
        Promised disaster in future years

Unless our captured soldiers were ruthlessly
Eliminated: 'Eagles' said he 'I've seen
    Displayed in Carthaginian shrines and
        Stripping of armour from legionaries   20

Without a fight. Free citizens too I've seen
Pinioned, their arms in shackles behind their backs,
    And city gates not closed and fields laid
        Waste by our army re-cultivated.

Bought back with gold what soldier do you suppose   25
Comes home the braver? That's simply adding loss
    To disgrace. Wool with dye once doctored
        Never regains its initial colour;

True valour likewise once it is thrown away,
You'll never replace in the degenerate.   30
    If roedeer freed from closely woven
        Nets ever fight, then a man will prove brave

qui perfidis se credidit hostibus,
et Marte Poenos proteret altero,
    qui lora restrictis lacertis   35
        sensit iners timuitque mortem.

hic unde uitam sumeret inscius,
pacem duello miscuit: o pudor!
    o magna Carthago probrosis
        altior Italiae ruinis!'   40

fertur pudicae coniugis osculum
paruosque natos ut capitis minor
    ab se remouisse et uirilem
        toruus humi posuisse uultum,

donec labantis consilio patres   45
firmaret auctor numquam alias dato
    interque maerentis amicos
        egregius properaret exul.

atqui sciebat quae sibi barbarus
tortor pararet: non aliter tamen   50
    dimouit obstantis propinquos
        et populum reditus morantem

quam si clientum longa negotia
diiudicata lite relinqueret
    tendens Venafranos in agros   55
        aut Lacedaemonium Tarentum.

VI

Delicta maiorum immeritus lues,
Romane, donec templa refeceris
    aedesque labentis deorum et
        foeda nigro simulacra fumo.

dis te minorem quod geris, imperas.   5
hinc omne principium, huc refer exitum:
    di multa neglecti dederunt
        Hesperiae mala luctuosae.

Who's handed his life over to treacherous foes,
And trample Poeni down in a second war
  When he has meekly felt the rawhide   35
    Tight on his arms and has feared to face death.

This man, not knowing how to secure his life,
Confuses peace with war. O the shame of it!
  O mighty Carthage, glorified by
    Italy's most ignominious ruin!   40

They say that drawing back from his chaste wife's kiss
And little children (since he had forfeited
  A citizen's full rights) he fixed his
    Masculine gaze on the ground, grim-visaged,

Till he had strengthened wavering Senators   45
With counsel never given before or since
  And hurried from among his grieving
    Friends into unprecedented exile.

Just what the cruel torturer had in store
For him he well knew, nevertheless he pushed   50
  Aside opposing kinsfolk and the
    Public who tried to delay his way back

As though he left behind the demanding case
Of some dependant, settlement gained at last,
  And made for his Venafran acres   55
    Or Lacedaemonian Tarentum.

6

Though innocent you'll pay for your forebears' sins,
O Roman, till the day you restore the Gods'
  Great temples and dilapidated
    Shrines and their images fouled by black smoke.

You rule because you're humble towards the Gods.   5
Thence all begins, to them refer every end.
  The Gods neglected have brought many
    Evils on long-suffering Hesperia.

iam bis Monaeses et Pacori manus
inauspicatos contudit impetus 10
    nostros et adiecisse praedam
        torquibus exiguis renidet.

paene occupatam seditionibus
deleuit urbem Dacus et Aethiops,
    hic classe formidatus, ille 15
        missilibus melior sagittis.

fecunda culpae saecula nuptias
primum inquinauere et genus et domos:
    hoc fonte deriuata clades
        in patriam populumque fluxit. 20

motus doceri gaudet Ionicos
matura uirgo et fingitur artibus
    iam nunc et incestos amores
        de tenero meditatur ungui.

mox iuniores quaerit adulteros 25
inter mariti uina neque eligit
    cui donet impermissa raptim
        gaudia luminibus remotis,

sed iussa coram non sine conscio
surgit marito, seu uocat institor 30
    seu nauis Hispanae magister,
        dedecorum pretiosus emptor.

non his iuuentus orta parentibus
infecit aequor sanguine Punico
    Pyrrhumque et ingentem cecidit 35
        Antiochum Hannibalemque dirum,

sed rusticorum mascula militum
proles, Sabellis docta ligonibus
    uersare glebas et seuerae
        matris ad arbitrium recisos 40

portare fustis, Sol ubi montium
mutaret umbras et iuga demeret
    bubus fatigatis, amicum
        tempus agens abeunte curru.

Twice now Monaeses' and Pácorus's troops
Have pulverized ill-omened attacks of ours   10
    And grin with glee at having added
        Rich Roman loot to their paltry chokers.

Dacian and Ethiopian foes almost
Destroyed the City busied with civil strife,
    The second formidable at sea, the   15
        First better skilled with projectile arrows.

Our century, prolific in vices, first
Polluted marriage, family, and the home.
    Disaster channelling from this source
        Poured in a flood over country and people.   20

Pubescent girls are keen to be taught depraved
Ionic dances; trained up in wanton wiles
    Precociously they are obsessed by
        Illicit loves from their tenderest years.

And next they look for younger adulterers   25
At husband's drinking-parties nor do they choose
    To whom to give forbidden pleasures
        Hurriedly and with the lights extinguished,

But, bidden, stand up publicly with the full
Consent of husband, whether a salesman call   30
    Or master of some Spanish vessel,
        High-paying buyer of degradation.

Not sprung from such parents were the Roman young
Who dyed Sicilian waters with Punic blood
    And smote Antiochus the Mighty,   35
        Devilish Hannibal, and King Pyrrhus.

But they were manly offspring of peasant troops
Brought up to turn the clods with Sabellian-
    type mattocks and to carry home cut
        Firewood at a punctilious mother's   40

Dictation, when the Sun-God was lengthening
The mountain shadows, taking away the yokes
    From weary oxen and bringing friendly
        Hours of rest as his chariot vanished.

damnosa quid non imminuit dies?   45
aetas parentum peior auis tulit
    nos nequiores, mox daturos
        progeniem uitiosiorem.

VII

Quid fles, Asterie, quem tibi candidi
primo restituent uere Fauonii
    Thyna merce beatum,
        constantis iuuenem fide

Gygen? ille Notis actus ad Oricum   5
post insana Caprae sidera frigidas
    noctes non sine multis
        insomnis lacrimis agit.

atqui sollicitae nuntius hospitae,
suspirare Chloen et miseram tuis   10
    dicens ignibus uri,
        temptat mille uafer modis.

ut Proetum mulier perfida credulum
falsis impulerit criminibus nimis
    casto Bellerophontae   15
        maturare necem refert,

narrat paene datum Pelea Tartaro,
Magnessam Hippolyten dum fugit abstinens,
    et peccare docentis
        fallax historias monet.   20

frustra: nam scopulis surdior Icari
uoces audit adhuc integer. at tibi
    ne uicinus Enipeus
        plus iusto placeat caue,

quamuis non alius flectere equum sciens   25
aeque conspicitur gramine Martio
    nec quisquam citus aeque
        Tusco denatat alueo.

Iniquitous Time, what does it not debase?   45
Our fathers' generation, inferior
    To our grandsires', bred us more immoral,
        Soon to produce even worse descendants.

7

Why weep, Asterie, when, at the start of spring,
Cloudless winds from the west will restore him to you
    Blest with Thynian freightage,
        That young man ever true of heart —

Gyges? Driven by south winds into Oricum,   5
After Capra the wild goat's constellation rose,
    Sleepless, not without many
        Tears, he passes the chilly nights.

Nonetheless his forlorn hostess's go-between
Telling how Chloe sighs, how the poor darling burns   10
    With a passion that's like yours,
        Slily tempts him a thousand ways:

Relates how a disloyal wife with her fraudulent
Accusations impelled Proetus the credulous
    To arrange sudden death for   15
        Over-faithful Bellerophon;

How, while running from Magnessan Hippolyte,
Peleus' abstinence nearly ended in Tartarus,
    And more stories are cited
        Craftily — to encourage vice.   20

In vain. Deafer than Icarian rocks he hears
What is said and remains constant.
    But as for you, don't let neighbour Enipeus
        Please you more than he ought to do,

On the Martian grass though the spectator sees   25
No one equally well trained to control his mount
    Nor does anyone swim so
        Fast as he down the Tuscan stream.

prima nocte domum claude neque in uias
sub cantu querulae despice tibiae   30
    et te saepe uocanti
        duram difficilis mane.

VIII

Martiis caelebs quid agam Kalendis,
quid uelint flores et acerra turis
plena miraris positusque carbo in
caespite uiuo,

docte sermones utriusque linguae?   5
uoueram dulcis epulas et album
Libero caprum prope funeratus
arboris ictu.

hic dies anno redeunte festus
corticem adstrictum pice dimouebit   10
amphorae fumum bibere institutae
consule Tullo.

sume, Maecenas, cyathos amici
sospitis centum et uigiles lucernas
perfer in lucem: procul omnis esto   15
clamor et ira.

mitte ciuilis super urbe curas:
occidit Daci Cotisonis agmen,
Medus infestus sibi luctuosis
dissidet armis,   20

seruit Hispanae uetus hostis orae
Cantaber sera domitus catena,
iam Scythae laxo meditantur arcu
cedere campis.

neglegens ne qua populus laboret,   25
parce priuatus nimium cauere et
dona praesentis cape laetus horae:
linque seuera.

Lock your door when the night falls and do not look down
To the street at the pipe's pitiful serenade,   30
    And though often called cruel
        Still go on being obstinate.

8

What am I, a bachelor, doing on the
First of March? Why flowers and casket full of
Incense? Why the charcoal arranged on fresh-cut
Turf, you are wondering,

Master of researches in either language?   5
I had vowed to Liber a tasty banquet
And a white he-goat when I nearly snuffed it,
Felled by a tree's fall.

As the year comes round this convivial day
Shall extract the cork, firmly fixed with pitch seal,   10
From a wine-jar ordered to tipple smoke when
Tullus was consul.

Drink a hundred measures of this, Maecenas,
To your friend's escape and prolong the wakeful
Candlelight till dawn, and be far from us all   15
Shouting and anger.

Drop the politician's concern about Rome.
Fallen is Dacian Cotiso's army column,
Noxious Medes in arms for their own destruction
Fight one another.   20

Cantabri, our old enemies along the
Spanish coast, face slavery, tamed by late chains.
Even Scyths are planning with bows unstrung to
Give up their grasslands.

Take it easy and don't as a private person   25
Agonize about the great public's troubles.
Gladly seize the gifts of the present moment.
Leave serious business.

IX

Donec gratus eram tibi
nec quisquam potior bracchia candidae
    ceruici iuuenis dabat,
Persarum uigui rege beatior.

    'donec non alia magis   5
arsisti neque erat Lydia post Chloen,
    multi Lydia nominis
Romana uigui clarior Ilia.'

    me nunc Thressa Chloe regit,
dulcis docta modos et citharae sciens,   10
    pro qua non metuam mori,
si parcent animae fata superstiti.

    'me torret face mutua
Thurini Calais filius Ornyti,
    pro quo bis patiar mori,   15
si parcent puero fata superstiti.'

    quid si prisca redit Venus
diductosque iugo cogit aeneo,
    si flaua excutitur Chloe
reiectaeque patet ianua Lydiae?   20

    'quamquam sidere pulchrior
ille est, tu leuior cortice et improbo
    iracundior Hadria,
tecum uiuere amem, tecum obeam libens.'

X

Extremum Tanain si biberes, Lyce,
saeuo nupta uiro, me tamen asperas
porrectum ante foris obicere incolis
plorares Aquilonibus.

audis quo strepitu ianua, quo nemus   5
inter pulchra satum tecta remugiat
uentis et positas ut glaciet niues
puro numine Iuppiter?

9

While you found me agreeable
And no other young man dearer than I could throw
    Round your beautiful neck his arms,
I was truly alive, richer than Persian kings.

'While you burned for no other more   5
Nor did Lydia come second to Chloe, then
    I was truly alive, a great
Name, a Lydia more famed than Rome's Ilia.'

Thracian Chloe's my mistress now,
Skilled sweet singer and expert on the cithara,   10
    For whom I'm not afraid to die
If the Fates will but let my very soul survive.

'Thurian Calaïs, Ornytus'
Son, is searing me now with a love-torch we share,
    For whom I'll suffer double death   15
If the Fates will but let my darling boy survive.'

Say the old Venus returns and brings
Those now parted beneath her brazen yoke, what then?
    Say blonde Chloe is shaken off
And for Lydia thrown out the door opens wide?   20

'Though he's fairer than any star,
Though you're lighter than cork, apt to get angrier
    Than the stormy Adriatic sea,
I'd love living with you, gladly with you I'd die.'

10

If you drank of the Don, Lyce, among the Scyths
As the wife of a brute, still you would shed a tear,
Were I laid at your rough door, to expose me to
All the resident northerlies.

Can't you hear how the door rattles and how the trees   5
In your elegant court planted are moaning loud
In this gale, and with unclouded divinity
How Jove freezes the lying snow?

ingratam Veneri pone superbiam,
ne currente retro funis eat rota.   10
non te Penelopen difficilem procis
Tyrrhenus genuit parens.

o quamuis neque te munera nec preces
nec tinctus uiola pallor amantium
nec uir Pieria paelice saucius   15
curuat, supplicibus tuis

parcas, nec rigida mollior aesculo
nec Mauris animum mitior anguibus:
non hoc semper erit liminis aut aquae
caelestis patiens latus.   20

XI

Mercuri — nam te docilis magistro
mouit Amphion lapides canendo —
tuque, testudo, resonare septem
callida neruis,

nec loquax olim neque grata, nunc et   5
diuitum mensis et amica templis,
dic modos, Lyde quibus obstinatas
applicet auris,

quae uelut latis equa trima campis
ludit exsultim metuitque tangi   10
nuptiarum expers et adhuc proteruo
cruda marito.

tu potes tigris comitesque siluas
ducere et riuos celeris morari;
cessit immanis tibi blandienti   15
ianitor aulae,

Cerberus, quamuis furiale centum
muniant angues caput eius atque
spiritus taeter saniesque manet
ore trilingui.   20

Rid yourself of the pride Venus abominates,
Lest the windlass should spin back and the rope fly loose.   10
Your Tyrrhenian dad sired no Penelope
To turn down every follower.

O though neither will gifts nor any prayer avail
Nor the pallor of poor lovers tinged blue with cold
Nor your husband obsessed by his Pierian moll   15
To deflect you, yet spare the lives

Of your suppliants, no softer than rigid oak
Nor more gentle of heart than Mauretanian snakes
Though you are. Not for aye will this physique of mine
Stand your doorstep and heaven's floods.   20

11

Mercury (for tutored by you Amphion
Learned to shift stone blocks by the power of song) and
Turtleshell, you too, adept at responding
To seven lyre-strings,

Voiceless once nor pleasing, but nowadays the
Friend of rich men's tables and holy places,
Speak a tune which Lyde can't help but lend an
Obstinate ear to.

Like a three-year-old filly wildly frisking
On the open plain she's afraid of being touched,   10
Ignorant of wedlock and too unripe yet
For a rough husband.

You can lure to follow you forest trees and
Tigers, and slow down rapid-flowing rivers;
Once to your enchantment the vasty Hall's gate-   15
keeper surrendered,

Cerberus, despite the one hundred serpents
Fortifying his head like the Furies, and his
Evil-smelling breath and the slobber drooling
From his three-tongued mouth.   20

quin et Ixion Tityosque uultu
risit inuito; stetit urna paulum
sicca, dum grato Danai puellas
carmine mulces.

audiat Lyde scelus atque notas   25
uirginum poenas et inane lymphae
dolium fundo pereuntis imo
seraque fata,

quae manent culpas etiam sub Orco.
impiae — nam quid potuere maius? —   30
impiae sponsos potuere duro
perdere ferro.

una de multis face nuptiali
digna periurum fuit in parentem
splendide mendax et in omne uirgo   35
nobilis aeuum,

'surge' quae dixit iuueni marito,
'surge, ne longus tibi somnus unde
non times detur; socerum et scelestas
falle sorores,   40

quae uelut nactae uitulos leaenae
singulos eheu lacerant: ego illis
mollior nec te feriam neque intra
claustra tenebo.

me pater saeuis oneret catenis,   45
quod uiro clemens misero peperci;
me uel extremos Numidarum in agros
classe releget.

i pedes quo te rapiunt et aurae,
dum fauet nox et Venus, i secundo   50
omine et nostri memorem sepulcro
scalpe querelam.'

Yes, and even Tityos and Ixion
Couldn't help but smile. For a time the urn stood
Dehydrated while your delightful song charmed
Danaus' daughters.

Lyde must be told of those virgins' crime and   25
Famous punishment of the barrel emptied
By the water draining away through its base
And the delayed fate

Which awaits wrongdoing in Orcus also.
Wicked girls, what worse could they ever have done?   30
Wicked, they were able with ruthless steel to
Murder their bridegrooms.

One alone there was who deserved the wedding-
Torch, a brilliant liar towards her perjured
Father and a virgin for every future   35
Era ennobled.

'Quick, get up!' she said to her youthful husband,
'Quick, get up now, lest a long sleep be given you
Whence you least expect. Trick your father-in-law and
Criminal cousins   40

Who like lionesses on bull-calves pouncing
Savage each her own, alas! I, than they more
Merciful, will neither attack you nor keep
Prisoner behind bars.

Me let father load with inhuman fetters   45
Since I spared in pity my helpless husband.
Let him even exile me by ship to furthest
Fields of Numidia.

Go, wherever feet and the breezes take you,
While the night and Venus permit. With good luck   50
Go, and on a tombstone engrave a sad verse
As my memorial.'

XII

Miserarum est neque amori
dare ludum neque dulci
mala uino lauere, aut exanimari metuentis
patruae uerbera linguae.

tibi qualum Cythereae   5
puer ales, tibi telas
operosaeque Mineruae studium aufert, Neobule,
Liparaei nitor Hebri

simul unctos Tiberinis
umeros lauit in undis,   10
eques ipso melior Bellerophonte, neque pugno
neque segni pede uictus,

catus idem per apertum
fugientis agitato
grege ceruos iaculari et celer arto latitantem   15
fruticeto excipere aprum.

XIII

O fons Bandusiae, splendidior uitro,
dulci digne mero non sine floribus,
cras donaberis haedo,
cui frons turgida cornibus

primis et uenerem et proelia destinat;   5
frustra, nam gelidos inficiet tibi
rubro sanguine riuos
lasciui suboles gregis.

te flagrantis atrox hora Caniculae
nescit tangere, tu frigus amabile   10
fessis uomere tauris
praebes et pecori uago.

fies nobilium tu quoque fontium
me dicente cauis impositam ilicem
saxis, unde loquaces   15
lymphae desiliunt tuae.

12

It's a girl's fate not to let love
Have its due fling nor with sweet wine
Wash away all her afflictions or to lose heart being frightened
    Of the tongue-lash of an uncle.

Cytherea's winged youngster   5
Steals your basket, Neobule,
Steals your hand-loom and your interest in the labour of Minerva,
    Soon as radiant Liparean

Hebrus washes well-oiled shoulders
In the ripples of the Tiber,   10
As a horseman better even than Bellerophon, unbeaten
    Both at boxing and at sprinting.

Clever also at the spearing
Of a stag flying in the open
When the herd's roused, and the quickest at extracting any wild boar   15
    Lying low in tangled thicket.

13

O Bandusian spring, glistening more than glass,
Most deserving of sweet wine and of flowers too,
    Yours a kidling tomorrow
        Whose brow swollen with nascent horns

Forecasts Venus for him, head-to-head fights as well;   5
Vainly though, for this offspring of the mischievous
    Caprine herd shall discolour
        Your cold stream with his dark red blood.

You the sweltering Dog Star's unrelenting hour
Does not know how to touch, you for the roaming flock   10
    And ox tired by the ploughshare
        Can provide a delightful cool.

You shall also become one of the famous springs
As I tell of the oak growing above the cave
    From whose rocks your loquacious   15
        Waters leap in their downward rush.

XIV

Herculis ritu modo dictus, o plebs,
morte uenalem petiisse laurum
Caesar Hispana repetit penatis
uictor ab ora.

unico gaudens mulier marito   5
prodeat iustis operata diuis
et soror clari ducis et decorae
supplice uitta

uirginum matres iuuenumque nuper
sospitum; uos, o pueri et puellae   10
iam uirum expectate, male ominatis
parcite uerbis.

hic dies uere mihi festus atras
exiget curas: ego nec tumultum
nec mori per uim metuam tenente   15
Caesare terras.

i pete unguentum, puer, et coronas
et cadum Marsi memorem duelli,
Spartacum si qua potuit uagantem
fallere testa.   20

dic et argutae properet Neaerae
murreum nodo cohibere crinem:
si per inuisum mora ianitorem
fiet abito.

lenit albescens animos capillus   25
litium et rixae cupidos proteruae:
non ego hoc ferrem calidus iuuenta
consule Planco.

XV

          Vxor pauperis Ibyci,
tandem nequitiae fige modum tuae
          famosisque laboribus;
maturo propior desine funeri

128

14

Hercules-like lately reported, O Plebs,
To have sought the laurel that's bought by dying,
Caesar seeks again his Penates, as the
Victor from Spain's coast.

Let his wife, well pleased with her peerless husband,   5
In religious thanks to the just Gods come forth,
And our famous general's sister, and, with
Suppliant headband

Beautified, the mothers of virgins and young
Soldiers safe home lately. But you, O boys and   10
Girls, await a real man, avoiding any
Word of ill omen.

For myself this day will be truly festive,
Banishing black cares. I shall fear no civil
Strife or death by violence while the earth's in   15
Caesar's safe keeping.

Go and look for ointment, my boy, and garlands
And a jar recalling the Marsian conflict,
If there's one somewhere could escape marauding
Spartacus' notice.   20

Also bid melodious Neaera make haste
And confine her hair in a knot, myrrh-scented.
If her hateful janitor raise objection,
Give up and come back.

Whitening hair gentles the power of passion   25
Predisposed to quarrels and reckless brawling.
I would not have stood that in youthful heat when
Plancus was consul.

15

Wife of indigent Ibycus,
At long last you should leave off misbehaviour
     And your labours of ill repute.
Ever nearer a non-premature grave give up

inter ludere uirgines   5
et stellis nebulam spargere candidis.
            non, siquid Pholoen satis,
et te, Chlori, decet: filia rectius
            expugnat iuuenum domos,
pulso Thyias uti concita tympano.   10
            illam cogit amor Nothi
lasciuae similem ludere capreae:
            te lanae prope nobilem
tonsae Luceriam, non citharae decent
            nec flos purpureus rosae   15
nec poti uetulam faece tenus cadi.

XVI

Inclusam Danaen turris aenea
robustaeque fores et uigilum canum
tristes excubiae munierant satis
            nocturnis ab adulteris,

si non Acrisium uirginis abditae   5
custodem pauidum Iuppiter et Venus
risissent: fore enim tutum iter et patens
            conuerso in pretium deo.

aurum per medios ire satellites
et perrumpere amat saxa potentius   10
ictu fulmineo; concidit auguris
            Argiui domus ob lucrum

demersa exitio; diffidit urbium
portas uir Macedo et subruit aemulos
reges muneribus; munera nauium   15
            saeuos illaqueant duces.

crescentem sequitur cura pecuniam
maiorumque fames: iure perhorrui
late conspicuum tollere uerticem,
            Maecenas, equitum decus.   20

Playing among the unmarried girls,   5
Give up casting a cloud over resplendent stars.
        What suits Pholoe well enough
Doesn't also suit you, Chloris. Your daughter's right
        To try storming the young men's homes,
A Bacchante on a high, driven by a beating drum.   10
        Love for Nothus is forcing her
Like a mischievous roe-deer to cavort and play.
        What suits you is to spin the wool
Shorn near famous Luceria, and not citharas
        Nor the rose's vermilion bloom   15
Nor casks drained to the dregs, now that you're middle aged.

16

Brazen tower and oak door and the frightening
Vigilance of her watchdogs would have proved enough
Of a barrier to guard imprisoned Danae
        From nocturnal adulterers,

Had not Venus and Jove laughed at Acrisius,   5
Panic-stricken custodian of the hidden girl;
For the way would be quite safe and accessible,
        When the God was transformed to cash.

Gold loves finding its way through any bodyguard
And demolishing stone, being more powerful   10
Than the thunderbolt's shock. Lucre it was that caused
        The Argive soothsayer's house to fall,

Ruined utterly. Through gifts Macedonia's king
Split apart city-gates and undermined the power
Of his royal opponents, and a gift can net   15
        Fearsome Admirals of the Fleet.

Worry and hunger for still more are the consequence
Of increase in one's wealth. Rightly have I recoiled
From upraising my head high in the public gaze,
        Maecenas, paragon of knights.   20

quanto quisque sibi plura negauerit,
ab dis plura feret: nil cupientium
nudus castra peto et transfuga diuitum
    partis linquere gestio,

contemptae dominus splendidior rei,   25
quam si quidquid arat impiger Apulus
occultare meis dicerer horreis,
    magnas inter opes inops.

purae riuus aquae siluaque iugerum
paucorum et segetis certa fides meae   30
fulgentem imperio fertilis Africae
    fallit sorte beatior.

quamquam nec Calabrae mella ferunt apes
nec Laestrygonia Bacchus in amphora
languescit mihi nec pinguia Gallicis   35
    crescunt uellera pascuis,

importuna tamen pauperies abest
nec, si plura uelim, tu dare deneges.
contracto melius parua cupidine
    uectigalia porrigam   40

quam si Mygdoniis regnum Alyattei
campis continuem. multa petentibus
desunt multa: bene est cui deus obtulit
    parca quod satis est manu.

XVII

Aeli uetusto nobilis ab Lamo —
quando et priores hinc Lamias ferunt
    denominatos et nepotum
        per memores genus omne fastus

auctore ab illo ducit originem,   5
qui Formiarum moenia dicitur
    princeps et innantem Maricae
        litoribus tenuisse Lirim

The more things anyone can do without, the more
He will get from the Gods. Stripped I enlist with those
Who have mastered desire, and I am overjoyed
    To change sides and desert the rich,

More distinguished as lord of a despised estate   25
Than if everyone knew I was concealing in
My barns all that the hard-working Apulian ploughs,
    In great riches a pauper still.

My small channel of clear water, my one or two
Woodland acres, the crops I can rely upon,   30
Are luck greater than Proconsul of opulent
    Africa can appreciate.

No Calabrian bees bring me their honeycombs
Nor is Bacchus's wine mellowing now for me
In a Formian jar nor do my fleeces grow   35
    Thick on Gallican grazing land.

I am nevertheless free of financial cares
Nor, if more was my wish, would you refuse to give;
But I'd better expand limited revenue
    By contraction of my desires   40

Than were I to unite Alyattes' domain
With Mygdonia's plains. Those who are after much
Find much lacking. A man's lucky when God provides
    What's enough with a frugal hand.

17

Aelius, of ancient Lamus a noble sprig,
(For after him the earlier Lamiae
    Were named, we're told, and their descendants,
        Every branch in recorded memory,

Can trace their origin to that founder who   5
Reportedly was first to possess the walls
    Of Formiae and Liris' stream that
        Floods over shores of the Nymph Marica,

late tyrannus: — cras foliis nemus
multis et alga litus inutili   10
    demissa tempestas ab Euro
        sternet, aquae nisi fallit augur

annosa cornix. dum potes, aridum
compone lignum: cras genium mero
    curabis et porco bimenstri   15
        cum famulis operum solutis.

XVIII

Faune, Nympharum fugientum amator,
per meos finis et aprica rura
lenis incedas abeasque paruis
aequus alumnis,

si tener pleno cadit haedus anno   5
larga nec desunt Veneris sodali
uina craterae, uetus ara multo
fumat odore.

ludit herboso pecus omne campo,
cum tibi nonae redeunt Decembres;   10
festus in pratis uacat otioso
cum boue pagus;

inter audacis lupus errat agnos,
spargit agrestis tibi silua frondes,
gaudet inuisam pepulisse fossor   15
ter pede terram.

XIX

    Quantum distet ab Inacho
Codrus pro patria non timidus mori,
    narras et genus Aeaci
et pugnata sacro bella sub Ilio:
    quo Chium pretio cadum   5
mercemur, quis aquam temperet ignibus,

Wide-ruling king) tomorrow a storm sent down
From the east will strew the forest with many leaves   10
    And shore with unproductive seaweed
        Unless that prophet of rain the long-lived

Raven's mistaken. So, while you may, collect
Firewood that's dry; tomorrow together with
    Your servants, free of work, you'll treat your   15
        Genius to wine and a two-month-old pig.

18

Faunus, you the lover of fugitive Nymphs,
Enter my estate and its sunny acres
With your favour and, as you leave, be kindly
Toward the small nurslings,

If a tender kid, when the year's complete, falls   5
And the mixing-bowl, Aphrodite's comrade,
Holds abundant wine, and the ancient altar
Smokes with much fragrance.

All the flock disports on the grassy common
When for you the Nones of December come round.   10
Festive villagers in the fields are free, their
Oxen at leisure.

Midst intrepid lambkins the wolf is prowling
And for you the woodland is scattering wild leaves.
Overjoyed the digger can dance a three-step   15
On the clay he hates.

19

    How much later than Inachus
Was king Codrus who dared die for his fatherland,
    All the issue of Aeacus
You spell out, and the wars fought below sacred Troy.
    What we pay for a Chian jar,   5
Who's providing the house, heating the water up,

      quo praebente domum et quota
Paelignis caream frigoribus, taces. —
      da lunae propere nouae,
da noctis mediae, da, puer, auguris   10
      Murenae: tribus aut nouem
miscentor cyathis pocula commodis.
      qui Musas amat imparis,
ternos ter cyathos attonitus petet
      uates; tris prohibet supra   15
rixarum metuens tangere Gratia
      nudis iuncta sororibus.
insanire iuuat: cur Berecyntiae
      cessant flamina tibiae?
cur pendet tacita fistula cum lyra?   20
      parcentis ego dexteras
odi: sparge rosas. audiat inuidus
      dementem strepitum Lycus
et uicina seni non habilis Lyco.
      spissa te nitidum coma,   25
puro te similem, Telephe, Vespero
      tempestiua petit Rhode:
me lentus Glycerae torret amor meae.

XX

Non uides quanto moueas periclo,
Pyrrhe, Gaetulae catulos leaenae?
dura post paulo fugies inaudax
      proelia raptor,

cum per obstantis iuuenum cateruas   5
ibit insignem repetens Nearchum,
grande certamen, tibi praeda cedat,
      maior an illa.

interim, dum tu celeris sagittas
promis, haec dentis acuit timendos,   10
arbiter pugnae posuisse nudo
      sub pede palmam

At what hour I can rid myself
Of Pelignian cold, all this you leave unsaid. —
      Quickly pour to the new-born moon,
Pour to midnight and pour, boy, to the augurate   10
      Of Murena. With three or nine
Ladlefuls let the wine-cups be well mixed for us.
      Crazy bards who adore the odd-
numbered Muses will claim ladlefuls three times three,
      But to touch any more than three   15
Is forbidden by a Grace (for she's afraid of brawls),
      Joined in this by her naked kin.
But I mean to be mad. Why the delay to blow
      Berecynthian-reeded pipes?
Why hang silent the syrinx and the cithara?   20
      I abominate niggardly
Handouts. Scatter the rose petals. Let envious
      Lycus hear the demented din,
And the lady next door, ill-matched with old Lycus.
      You, so sleek with your mane of hair,   25
Counterpart of serene Vesper, O Telephus,
      Nubile Rhode is after you,
While I'm roasted by slow love for my Glycera.

20

Can't you see how dangerous it is to meddle,
Pyrrhus, with the Gáetulan lioness' cubs?
Very soon you'll run from the fierce encounter,
Timorous raider,

When, through gangs of young men who try to stop her,   5
She'll advance reclaiming superb Nearchus.
Then the epic fight: will the prize be yours or
Is she the stronger?

Meantime, while you're choosing your speediest arrows
And while she is sharpening her dread incisors,   10
You're informed that the arbiter of the contest
Has placed a bare foot

fertur et leni recreare uento
sparsum odoratis umerum capillis,
qualis aut Nireus fuit aut aquosa   15
raptus ab Ida.

XXI

O nata mecum consule Manlio,
seu tu querellas siue geris iocos
    seu rixam et insanos amores
        seu facilem, pia testa, somnum,

quocumque lectum nomine Massicum   5
seruas, moueri digna bono die,
    descende Coruino iubente
        promere languidiora uina.

non ille, quamquam Socraticis madet
sermonibus, te negleget horridus: 10
    narratur et prisci Catonis
        saepe mero caluisse uirtus.

tu lene tormentum ingenio admoues
plerumque duro, tu sapientium
    curas et arcanum iocoso   15
        consilium retegis Lyaeo,

tu spem reducis mentibus anxiis
uirisque et addis cornua pauperi
    post te neque iratos trementi
        regum apices neque militum arma.   20

te Liber et, si laeta aderit, Venus
segnesque nodum soluere Gratiae
    uiuaeque producent lucernae,
        dum rediens fugat astra Phoebus.

On the palm of victory and lets the soft breeze
Kiss his shoulders dappled with scented tresses,
Fair as Nireus was or the boy kidnapped from
Well-watered Ida.

21

O born with me in Manlius' consulship,
Whether you bring complaining or comedy
    Or brawling and erotic madness,
        Or, trusty wine-jar, untroubled slumber,

On what account soever you guard the choice   5
Massic, for broaching only on a special day,
    Come down, on Corvinus' instructions
        That there be served a more mellow vintage.

Although he's soaked in Socrates' dialogues
He'll never sneer at you as a Cynic might.   10
    We're told that even old Cato often
        Warmed up his 'virtue' with undilute wine.

You bring your gentle torture to bear on wits
Too often lifeless. You, thanks to humorous
    Lyaeus, can lay bare the worries   15
        And secret thoughts of philosophers too.

You bring back hope and strength to defeatist minds
And give the poor man horns of defiant pride,
    So after you he fears no angry
        Monarch's tiara or soldiers' weapons.   20

Liber, the Graces loth to unloose their knot,
And Venus if she's present in happy mood,
    And living lamps will make you last till
        Stars fly away from returning Phoebus.

XXII

Montium custos nemorumque, Virgo,
quae laborantis utero puellas
ter uocata audis adimisque leto,
diua triformis,

imminens uillae tua pinus esto, 5
quam per exactos ego laetus annos
uerris obliquum meditantis ictum
sanguine donem.

XXIII

Caelo supinas si tuleris manus
nascente Luna, rustica Phidyle,
    si ture placaris et horna
        fruge Lares auidaque porca,

nec pestilentem sentiet Africum 5
fecunda uitis nec sterilem seges
    robiginem aut dulces alumni
        pomifero graue tempus anno.

nam quae niuali pascitur Algido
deuota quercus inter et ilices 10
    aut crescit Albanis in herbis
        uictima, pontificum securis

ceruice tinget; te nihil attinet
temptare multa caede bidentium
    paruos coronantem marino 15
        rore deos fragilique myrto.

immunis aram si tetigit manus,
non sumptuosa blandior hostia,
    molliuit auersos Penatis
        farre pio et saliente mica. 20

22

Guardian of mountain and forest, Virgin
Who if thrice invoked will attend young women
During pains of childbirth and save them from death,
Goddess Trimorphic,

Yours the pinetree leaning above my farmhouse   5
And at each year's end I shall gladly give it
Blood of one boar-pig who is still perfecting
His oblique onslaught.

23

If, country-dweller Phidyle, you have raised
Your hands, upturned, to heaven when the moon is new,
    And if with incense, this year's corn and
        Ravenous pig you've appeased the Lares,

Then neither shall the plenteous vineyard feel   5
The pestilent south-westerly nor the crops
    Infertile mildew nor sweet nurslings
        Seasonal ills when the year is fruiting.

Let promised victims feeding among the oak-
And ilex-trees of snow-covered Algidus   10
    Or growing fat on Alban grasses
        Stain with their severed necks pontiff's axes.

It's no concern of yours to attempt to please
Your little Gods with multiple slaughtering
    Of young sheep, when you garland Them with   15
        Rosemary and easily broken myrtle.

A hand, if guiltless touching the altar-stone,
Given no more pull by sumptuous offerings,
    Can soften ill-disposed Penates
        With devout wheatmeal and leaping salt-grains.   20

XXIV

Intactis opulentior
thesauris Arabum et diuitis Indiae
    caementis licet occupes
terrenum omne tuis et mare publicum:
    si figit adamantinos   5
summis uerticibus dira Necessitas
    clauos, non animum metu,
non mortis laqueis expedies caput.
    campestres melius Scythae,
quorum plaustra uagas rite trahunt domos,   10
    uiuunt et rigidi Getae,
immetata quibus iugera liberas
    fruges et Cererem ferunt
nec cultura placet longior annua
    defunctumque laboribus   15
aequali recreat sorte uicarius.
    illic matre carentibus
priuignis mulier temperat innocens
    nec dotata regit uirum
coniunx nec nitido fidit adultero.   20
    dos est magna parentium
uirtus et metuens alterius uiri
    certo foedere castitas,
et peccare nefas, aut pretium est mori.

    o quisquis uolet impias   25
caedis et rabiem tollere ciuicam,
    si quaeret PATER VRBIVM
subscribi statuis, indomitam audeat
    refrenare licentiam,
clarus postgenitis, quatenus, heu nefas,   30
    uirtutem incolumem odimus,
sublatam ex oculis quaerimus inuidi.
    quid tristes querimoniae,
si non supplicio culpa reciditur,
    quid leges sine moribus   35
uanae proficiunt, si neque feruidis
    pars inclusa caloribus
mundi nec Boreae finitimum latus

24

   Richer far than the undespoiled
Treasure-chests of Arabia and of wealthy Ind,
   Though you seize for your building schemes
All the land and the sea owned by the commonwealth,
   Still if dire Necessity   5
Hammers into your rooftops adamantine nails,
   You will neither unfetter mind
From fear nor disengage head from the noose of Death.
   Scythians out on the open plains,
Whose traditional carts trundle nomadic homes   10
   Use life better, and strict Getae
For whom unmeasured-off acres of land produce
   Fruits and cereals free of charge.
Cultivation that lasts more than a year's unknown,
   And the man who has worked twelve months 15
Is relieved on the same terms by a substitute.
   There, stepmothers are innocent,
Treating kindly the stepchildren whose mother died,
   And no wife with a dowry rules
Over husband or trusts specious adulterer.   20
   A big dowry is parents' in-
tegrity, and the chaste lifestyle with promise kept
   That's afraid of a second man;
And unfaith is taboo, or its reward is death.

   O whoever may wish to end   25
Godless bloodshed and irrational civil strife,
   If he wants the inscription on
Statues of him to read FATHER OF CITIES, then
   He must rein in our lawlessness,
Winning fame in the age after his own because   30
   (Shame on us!) in our envy we
Hate live virtue but miss it when it disappears.
   What's the use of forlorn complaint
If transgression is not pruned back by punishment?
   Or of vacuous laws without   35
Public morals? If that part of the world enclosed
   By unbearable tropic heat,
And the region that lies nearest to Boreas

durataeque solo niues
mercatorem abigunt, horrida callidi   40
    uincunt aequora nauitae,
magnum pauperies opprobrium iubet
    quiduis et facere et pati
uirtutisque uiam deserit arduae?

    uel nos in Capitolium,   45
quo clamor uocat et turba fauentium,
    uel nos in mare proximum
gemmas et lapides aurum et inutile,
    summi materiem mali,
mittamus, scelerum si bene paenitet.   50
    eradenda cupidinis
praui sunt elementa et tenerae nimis
    mentes asperioribus
formandae studiis. nescit equo rudis
    haerere ingenuus puer   55
uenarique timet, ludere doctior,
    seu Graeco iubeas trocho
seu malis uetita legibus alea,
    cum periura patris fides
consortem socium fallat et hospites   60
    indignoque pecuniam
heredi properet. scilicet improbae
    crescunt diuitiae, tamen
curtae nescio quid semper abest rei.

XXV

    Quo me, Bacche, rapis tui
plenum? quae nemora aut quos agor in specus
    uelox mente noua? quibus
antris egregii Caesaris audiar
    aeternum meditans decus   5
stellis inserere et consilio Iouis?
    dicam insigne, recens, adhuc
indictum ore alio. non secus in iugis
    exsomnis stupet Euhias
Hebrum prospiciens et niue candidam   10

With snow hardened upon the ground,
Does not frighten away traders, and if astute   40
   Ships' captains can defeat rough seas,
And if poverty, great mark of disgrace, bids all
   Do and suffer no matter what
And abandons the steep path of integrity?

   Either, then, to the Capitol   45
Where the favouring crowd's noisy support invites,
   Or else into the nearest sea
Let's send jewels and stones, also our useless gold,
   Supreme evil's material cause,
If we really feel sorrow for our misdeeds.   50
   The alphabet of our crooked greed
Needs deletion; young minds overly sensitive
   Need the moulding of more severe
Occupations. The boy born of free parents now,
   Uninstructed, can't sit a horse   55
And is frightened to hunt, better prepared to play,
   Should you order, with Grecian hoop
Or maybe with the dice (though it's against the law);
   While his father's perfidious word
Defrauds partners in commerce and his visitors   60
   In his hurry to make a pile
For some unworthy heir. — Granted that ill-acquired
   Wealth accumulates, nonetheless
There is always a shortfall and a sense of lack.

25

   Bacchus, where are you rushing me
Full of you? To what woods, or to what caves am I
   Driven at speed with a mind renewed?
In what glens to be heard planning to introduce
   Peerless Caesar's immortal fame   5
Among stars in the sky, and to the council of Jove?
   Something singular, fresh, unspoken
Till now by other tongue, let me declare. Just as,
   Vigilant on the mountain heights,
Maenad gazing afar, over the Hebrus and   10

145

  Thracen ac pede barbaro
lustratam Rhodopen, ut mihi deuio
  ripas et uacuum nemus
mirari libet. o Naiadum potens
   Baccharumque ualentium   15
proceras manibus uertere fraxinos,
   nil paruum aut humili modo,
nil mortale loquar. dulce periculum est,
  o Lenaee, sequi deum
cingentem uiridi tempora pampino.   20

XXVI

Vixi puellis nuper idoneus
et militaui non sine gloria:
  nunc arma defunctumque bello
   barbiton hic paries habebit,

laeuum marinae qui Veneris latus   5
custodit. hic, hic ponite lucida
  funalia et uectis securesque
   oppositis foribus minacis.

o quae beatam diua tenes Cyprum et
Memphin carentem Sithonia niue,   10
  regina, sublimi flagello
   tange Chloen semel arrogantem.

XXVII

Impios parrae recinentis omen
ducat et praegnans canis aut ab agro
raua decurrens lupa Lanuuino
fetaque uulpes;

rumpat et serpens iter institutum,   5
si per obliquum similis sagittae
terruit mannos. ego cui timebo
prouidus auspex,

Snow-white Thracia and Rhodope
Trod by barbarous feet, marvels in silent awe,
    I too out in the wilds admire
River-banks and the grove's solitary appeal.
    Lord of Naiads and Bacchanals,   15
Strong enough with their bare bands to uproot tall trees,
    Nothing small or in humble style,
Nothing subject to death let me proclaim. The risk,
    O Lenaeus, is sweet — to attend
The God wearing a green wreath of the tendrilled vine.   20

26

I've lived till lately able to cope with girls
And not without distinction have soldiered there,
    But now this wall shall have my weapons
    And my demobilized barbitos too,

The wall protecting maritime Venus's   5
Left flank. Yes, here, just here put the luminous
    Hemp torches and crowbars and axes
    Threatening doors that were barred against them.

O Goddess who rule fortunate Cyprus and
Memphis that never suffers Sithonian snow,
    Queen Venus, raise your whip and touch up
    Chloe — once only — the high and mighty.

27

May an owl's monotonous hooting and a
Pregnant bitch or brownie-grey she-wolf trotting
Down from the Alban hills or a vixen with cubs
Lead on the wicked,

And a snake disrupt, once begun, their journey,   5
If it darts across like an arrow and scares the
Ponies. As for me, when I fear for someone,
A canny prophet

antequam stantis repetat paludes
imbrium diuina auis imminentum, 10
oscinem coruum prece suscitabo
solis ab ortu.

sis licet felix, ubicumque mauis,
et memor nostri, Galatea, uiuas
teque nec laeuus uetat ire picus 15
nec uaga cornix.

sed uides quanto trepidet tumultu
pronus Orion? ego quid sit ater
Hadriae noui sinus et quid albus
peccet Iapyx. 20

hostium uxores puerique caecos
sentiant motus orientis Austri et
aequoris nigri fremitum et trementis
uerbere ripas.

sic et Europe niueum doloso 25
credidit tauro latus et scatentem
beluis pontum mediasque fraudes
palluit audax.

nuper in pratis studiosa florum et
debitae Nymphis opifex coronae 30
nocte sublustri nihil astra praeter
uidit et undas.

quae simul centum tetigit potentem
oppidis Creten, 'pater o relictum
filiae nomen pietasque' dixit 35
'uicta furore!

unde quo ueni? leuis una mors est
uirginum culpae. uigilansne ploro
turpe commissum an uitiis carentem
ludit imago 40

uana, quae porta fugiens eburna
somnium ducit? meliusne fluctus
ire per longos fuit an recentis
carpere flores?

I shall raise by prayer a croaking raven
From the sunrise, well before that prophetic   10
Bird of threatening showers has flown again to
Its stagnant marshes.

Happiness, wherever you choose, be yours,
Galatea, and may you forget me never;
On the left no magpie or wandering crow   15
Bars your departure.

But you see how stormily now Orion
Hurries downward? I have experience of
The Adriatic Gulf when it's black, and how white
Japyx can play false.   20

May the wives and children of enemies feel
The unexpected onset of rising Auster
And the dark sea's roar and the shuddering of
Wave-lashed embankments.

It was thus Europa entrusted that false   25
Bull with her snow-white body, and at teeming
Ocean's monstrous creatures and perils round her
Paled in her daring.

Earlier in meadows in search of flowers and
Weaver of a garland she owed the Wood-Nymphs,   30
Then in night's faint light she could make out nothing
But stars and water.

When she reached Crete (strong in its hundred cities),
'Father' she exclaimed 'O the name your daughter
Disregarded! O filial obligation   35
Conquered by passion!

Why have I come here? For the virgins' crime one
Death is too light. Am I awake bewailing
Scandalous misconduct, or innocent, de-
ceived by an empty   40

Phantom which, escaping the Gate of Ivory,
Brings a dream? But was it a better choice to
Ride across long wearisome waves or gather
Newly-blown flowers?

siquis infamem mihi nunc iuuencum   45
dedat iratae, lacerare ferro et
frangere enitar modo multum amati
cornua monstri.

impudens liqui patrios penates;
impudens Orcum moror. o deorum   50
siquis haec audis, utinam inter errem
nuda leones!

antequam turpis macies decentis
occupet malas teneraeque sucus
defluat praedae, speciosa quaero   55
pascere tigris.

"uilis Europe," pater urget absens,
"quid mori cessas? potes hac ab orno
pendulum zona bene te secuta
laedere collum.   60

siue te rupes et acuta leto
saxa delectant, age te procellae
crede ueloci; nisi erile mauis
carpere pensum

regius sanguis dominaeque tradi   65
barbarae paelex." aderat querenti
perfidum ridens Venus et remisso
filius arcu.

mox ubi lusit satis, 'abstineto'
dixit 'irarum calidaeque rixae,   70
cum tibi inuisus laceranda reddet
cornua taurus.

uxor inuicti Iouis esse nescis.
mitte singultus; bene ferre magnam
disce fortunam: tua sectus orbis   75
nomina ducet.'

If that cursed bull were surrendered to me   45
In my present anger, I'd try to knife him
And to smash the horns of a monster whom I
Once loved so dearly.

Shamelessly I left my paternal Home-Gods,
Shameless I'm delaying my death. O if there's   50
Any God hears this, may he let me wander
Nude among lions!

Long before starvation emaciates my
Comely face and moisture has drained away from
Their soft-hearted prey, in my beauty make me   55
Fodder for tigers.

"Worthless Europa" (absent my father rates me)
"Why delay your death? From this rowan, hanging
By the belt you're luckily wearing, you can
Break your own neck-bone.   60

Or if precipices and deadly-sharp rocks
Tempt you more, then quickly commit yourself to
The headlong gale, unless you would rather spin weighed
Wool for a mistress

Though you're royal blood, and as concubine be   65
Given to some barbarian wife." ' — With sly smile
Venus and her son with his bowstring slackened
Witnessed her grieving.

Then, when she'd had sport enough, 'Time' she said 'to
Stop your tantrums and this impassioned brawling   70
Since the bull you hate will surrender you his
Horns to be shattered.

Unawares you're wife to unconquerable
Jupiter. Stop sobbing and learn to bear great
Fortune with distinction. A continent shall   75
Commemorate you.'

XXVIII

Festo quid potius die
Neptuni faciam? prome reconditum,
   Lyde, strenua Caecubum
munitaeque adhibe uim sapientiae.
      inclinare meridiem   5
sentis et, ueluti stet uolucris dies,
   parcis deripere horreo
cessantem Bibuli consulis amphoram.
      nos cantabimus inuicem
Neptunum et uiridis Nereidum comas: 10
   tu curua recines lyra
Latonam et celeris spicula Cynthiae;
      summo carmine, quae Cnidon
fulgentisque tenet Cycladas et Paphon
      iunctis uisit oloribus   15
dicetur, merita Nox quoque nenia.

XXIX

Tyrrhena regum progenies, tibi
non ante uerso lene merum cado
   cum flore, Maecenas, rosarum et
      pressa tuis balanus capillis

iamdudum apud me est: eripe te morae,   5
nec semper udum Tibur et Aefulae
   decliue contempleris aruum et
      Telegoni iuga parricidae.

fastidiosam desere copiam et
molem propinquam nubibus arduis: 10
   omitte mirari beatae
      fumum et opes strepitumque Romae.

plerumque gratae diuitibus uices
mundaeque paruo sub lare pauperum
   cenae sine aulaeis et ostro   15
      sollicitam explicuere frontem.

28

What more suitable thing to do
On the feast day of Neptune? At the double bring
    Out the Caecuban stored away,
Lyde, and batter the stronghold of Philosophy.
    You can see that the noon-day sun's   5
In descent, and as if hurrying Time stood still
    You are slow to abduct from store
Consul Bibulus' long-draughtdodging amphora.
    We'll both strike up a song in turn
Of Neptune and the green hair of the Nereids.   10
    Then you'll sing to your curving lyre
Of Latona and the swift arrows of Cynthia;
    And to finish you'll sing the Queen
Of Cnidos and the far-shimmering Cyclades,
    Bound for Paphos on harnessed swans,   15
Also Night with a well-merited lullaby.

29

Tyrrhenian descendant of kings, for you
From jar as yet untilted a mellow wine
    With bloom of roses, Maecenas, and
        Oil of the balm-nut pressed out for your hair

Have waited long here. So, tear yourself away.   5
Don't simply gaze at well-watered Tivoli
    And sloping fields of Aefulae and
        Heights of Telegonus, father-slayer.

Deny yourself the plenty that satiates,
The massive tower that neighbours the clouds' sublime.   10
    Forget your admiration for the
        Smoke and the wealth and the din of blest Rome.

It's mostly change that pleases the man of means,
And simple meals in poor people's modest homes
    (No tapestries or purple dyes) have   15
        Smoothed out the lines on a worried forehead.

iam clarus occultum Andromedae pater
ostendit ignem, iam Procyon furit
    et stella uesani Leonis
        sole dies referente siccos;   20

iam pastor umbras cum grege languido
riuumque fessus quaerit et horridi
    dumeta Siluani caretque
        ripa uagis taciturna uentis.

tu ciuitatem quis deceat status   25
curas et Vrbi sollicitus times
    quid Seres et regnata Cyro
        Bactra parent Tanaisque discors.

prudens futuri temporis exitum
caliginosa nocte premit deus   30
    ridetque si mortalis ultra
        fas trepidat. quod adest memento

componere aequus: cetera fluminis
ritu feruntur, nunc medio alueo
    cum pace delabentis Etruscum   35
        in mare, nunc lapides adesos

stirpisque raptas et pecus et domos
uoluentis una, non sine montium
    clamore uicinaeque siluae,
        cum fera diluuies quietos   40

irritat amnis. ille potens sui
laetusque deget cui licet in diem
    dixisse 'uixi. cras uel atra
        nube polum Pater occupato

uel sole puro; non tamen irritum   45
quodcumque retro est efficiet neque
    diffinget infectumque reddet
        quod fugiens semel hora uexit.'

Fortuna saeuo laeta negotio et
ludum insolentem ludere pertinax   50
    transmutat incertos honores,
        nunc mihi nunc alii benigna.

Andromeda's bright father now shows his fire
Till lately hidden, Prócyon rages now
    And frenzied Leo's constellation,
        While the Sun brings back the arid season.   20

The weary shepherd now with his listless flock
Looks out for shade and water and shaggy-haired
    Silvanus' thickets, while the silent
        River-bank misses inconstant breezes.

You worry, though, what system best suits the State   25
And in your care for Rome are afraid of what
    Chinese and Cyrus' Bactrian realm and
        Dissident Tanais may be plotting.

But God, who has foreknowledge, conceals in night
Impenetrable the outcome of future time   30
    And laughs if mortals are unduly
        Anxious. Remember to settle calmly

What's here and now. The rest's not unlike a stream
That's borne along at one time within its bed
    Serenely gliding towards the Etruscan   35
        Sea, at another chaotically

Whirling eroded rocks and uprooted trunks
And cattle and houses, not without echoing noise
    From mountains and the neighbouring forest
        As the ferocious flash-flood enrages   40

Quiescent rivers. He will have self-control
And happiness who's able at each day's end
    To say 'I've lived. Tomorrow whether
        Jupiter covers the sky with black cloud

Or radiant sunshine, still he will never make   45
Whatever's now behind me invalid, or
    Re-fashion and undo what once the
        Hurrying hour has carried with it.'

Fortune enjoys her business of cruelty
And obstinately playing her wanton game   50
    Re-distributes precarious honours,
        Now to me, now to another generous.

laudo manentem: si celeris quatit
pinnas, resigno quae dedit et mea
   uirtute me inuoluo probamque 55
      pauperiem sine dote quaero.

non est meum, si mugiat Africis
malus procellis, ad miseras preces
   decurrere et uotis pacisci
      ne Cypriae Tyriaeque merces 60

addant auaro diuitias mari.
tunc me biremis praesidio scaphae
   tutum per Aegaeos tumultus
      aura feret geminusque Pollux.

XXX

Exegi monumentum aere perennius
regalique situ pyramidum altius,
quod non imber edax, non Aquilo impotens
possit diruere aut innumerabilis
annorum series et fuga temporum. 5
non omnis moriar multaque pars mei
uitabit Libitinam: usque ego postera
crescam laude recens, dum Capitolium
scandet cum tacita uirgine pontifex:
dicar, qua uiolens obstrepit Aufidus 10
et qua pauper aquae Daunus agrestium
regnauit populorum, ex humili potens
princeps Aeolium carmen ad Italos
deduxisse modos. sume superbiam
quaesitam meritis et mihi Delphica 15
lauro cinge uolens, Melpomene, comam.

I praise her staying, but, if she shakes swift wings,
Resign what she has given and wrap myself
    In my own virtue, to go courting   55
        Trustworthy Poverty minus dowry.

It isn't my way, if the ship's mast should groan
In African storm-winds, to have weak recourse
    To wretched prayers, employing vows to
        Bargain that cargo from Tyre and Cyprus   60

Should not increase the wealth of the greedy sea.
Me then in safety over Aegean surge
    Protected by the two-oared dinghy
        Breezes and Pollux the twin will carry.

30

I've achieved a memorial that will outlive bronze,
Higher-class than the royal rubble of the Pyramids,
Which no blustering north wind, no eroding rain
Will have power to destroy, nor the innumerable
Succession of the years and the swift flight of times.   5
I shan't totally die, but a large part of me
Will escape Libitina. I shall be growing still
Fresh in future acclaim, so long as Pontifex
Shall with Vesta's mute Maid climb the Capitoline.
I'll be famed where berserk Aufidus loudly objects   10
And where Daunus the ill-watered was sovereign
Over pastoral tribes, risen from low birth to power
As the first to adapt fine-spun Aeolic song
To Italian rhythms. Take to yourself the pride
That your merit has earned, Melpomene, and with   15
Apollonian bay graciously wreathe my locks.

CARMINVM LIBER QVARTVS

I

Intermissa, Venus, diu
rursus bella moues? parce precor, precor.
    non sum qualis eram bonae
sub regno Cinarae. desine, dulcium
      mater saeua Cupidinum,   5
circa lustra decem flectere mollibus
    iam durum imperiis; abi
quo blandae iuuenum te reuocant preces.
    tempestiuius in domum
Pauli purpureis ales oloribus   10
    comissabere Maximi,
si torrere iecur quaeris idoneum.
    namque et nobilis et decens
et pro sollicitis non tacitus reis
      et centum puer artium   15
late signa feret militiae tuae,
    et quandoque potentior
largi muneribus riserit aemuli,
    Albanos prope te lacus
ponet marmoream sub trabe citrea.   20
    illic plurima naribus
duces tura, lyraeque et Berecyntiae
    delectabere tibiae
mixtis carminibus non sine fistula;
    illic bis pueri die   25
numen cum teneris uirginibus tuum
    laudantes pede candido
in morem Salium ter quatient humum.
    me nec femina nec puer
iam nec spes animi credula mutui   30
    nec certare iuuat mero
nec uincire nouis tempora floribus.
    sed cur heu, Ligurine, cur
manat rara meas lacrima per genas?

ODES, BOOK FOUR

1

        Venus, after long armistice
Is it war once again? Pity me, please, oh please!
        I am not as I was beneath
Kindly Cínara's rule. After some fifty years,
        Cruel Mother of sweet Desires,   5
Cease attempting to move one now impervious
        To your sensual commands. Be off
With you where the galant prayers of young men invite.
        You will revel more seasonably
Taking flight on your bright swans to the house where lives   10
        Paullus Fabius Maximus,
If to kindle a well-qualified heart's your aim.
        For he's noble and handsome too,
Not tongue-tied in distressed prisoners' defence at law;
        As a youth of a hundred arts   15
He will carry the ensign of your warfare far.
        And when, winning the day, he laughs
At the extravagant gifts made by his rival in love,
        Not far off from the Alban Lakes
He will place you in marble under a citron roof.   20
        There you'll breathe, in profusion, rich
Frankincense and delight in the sweet consonance
        Of the lyre accompanying
Berecynthian flute, not without pipes of Pan.
        There twice every day shall boys,   25
Praising loud with unwed girls your divinity,
        Beat the ground with their naked feet
In the Salian style dancing in triple time.
        Me nor woman nor boy today
Can delight nor naïve hope of a mutual love   30
        Nor competitive drinking bouts
Nor to wear on my head garlands of fresh-cut flowers. —
        Yet why, ah, Ligurinus, why
Brims and flows the rare tear over and down my cheeks?

cur facunda parum decoro   35
inter uerba cadit lingua silentio?
    nocturnis ego somniis
iam captum teneo, iam uolucrem sequor
    te per gramina Martii
Campi, te per aquas, dure, uolubilis.   40

II

Pindarum quisquis studet aemulari,
Iulle, ceratis ope Daedalea
nititur pennis, uitreo daturus
nomina ponto.

monte decurrens uelut amnis, imbres   5
quem super notas aluere ripas,
feruet immensusque ruit profundo
Pindarus ore,

laurea donandus Apollinari,
seu per audacis noua dithyrambos   10
uerba deuoluit numerisque fertur
lege solutis,

seu deos regesque canit, deorum
sanguinem, per quos cecidere iusta
morte Centauri, cecidit tremendae   15
flamma Chimaerae,

siue quos Elea domum reducit
palma caelestis pugilemue equumue
dicit et centum potiore signis
munere donat,   20

flebili sponsae iuuenemue raptum
plorat et uiris animumque moresque
aureos educit in astra nigroque
inuidet Orco.

multa Dircaeum leuat aura cycnum,   25
tendit, Antoni, quotiens in altos
nubium tractus: ego apis Matinae
more modoque,

Why while speaking should eloquent   35
Tongue fall silent with unseemly embarrassment?
There are times in my dreams at night
When I'm holding you close, times when I'm following you
While you race on the Field of Mars,
Or, hard heart, as you swim past in the fluent stream.   40

2

Anyone who strives to compete with Pindar,
Iullus, trusts in pinions by Daedalean
Expertise wax-joined and is doomed to name some
Glassy-clear ocean.

Like a mountain stream rushing down, which heavy
Rain has swollen over its recognised banks,
Pindar seethes and unconfined races on with
Deep-thundering voice,

Winner of the crown of Apolline laurel
Whether he rolls down in adventurous dithy-   10
rambs his new-coined words and is borne along by
Free-flowing rhythms,

Or he sings of Gods and of kings, by blood the
Sons of Gods, whose hands laid the Centaurs low in
Well-deserved death, laid low the terrifying   15
Fiery Chimaera,

Or he tells of those the Elean palm brings
Home again as godlike, of charioteer or
Boxer, giving them a more precious gift than
One hundred statues,   20

Or he mourns the fate of young husband torn from
Weeping bride and lauds to the Stars his golden
Character and spirit and strength, begrudging
These to black Orcus.

Strong the air-stream lifting the Swan of Dirce   25
Every time, Antonius, he soars aloft to
Spacious cloudland. I, as a Matine bee in
Manner and method,

grata carpentis thyma per laborem
plurimum, circa nemus uuidique   30
Tiburis ripas operosa paruus
carmina fingo.

concines maiore poeta plectro
Caesarem, quandoque trahet ferocis
per sacrum cliuum merita decorus   35
fronde Sygambros,

quo nihil maius meliusue terris
fata donauere bonique diui
nec dabunt, quamuis redeant in aurum
tempora priscum.   40

concines laetosque dies et Vrbis
publicum ludum super impetrato
fortis Augusti reditu forumque
litibus orbum.

tum meae, si quid loquar audiendum,   45
uocis accedet bona pars et 'o sol
pulcher, o laudande' canam recepto
Caesare felix.

isque dum procedit, io Triumphe,
non semel dicemus, io Triumphe,   50
ciuitas omnis dabimusque diuis
tura benignis.

te decem tauri totidemque uaccae,
me tener soluet uitulus, relicta
matre qui largis iuuenescit herbis   55
in mea uota,

fronte curuatos imitatus ignis
tertium lunae referentis ortum,
qua notam duxit, niueus uideri,
cetera fuluus.   60

Harvesting sweet thyme with intensive labour
Round the woodland glades and the river-banks of   30
Watered Tibur, small-scale I fabricate my
Painstaking lyrics.

You shall sing as poet with grander plectrum
Caesar when, adorned with a well-earned crown of
Laurel leaf, he drags up the Via Sacra   35
Savage Sygambri;

Fate and gracious Gods have not given nor will
Ever give this earth any greater thing than
Him or better, even though Time return to
Primordial gold.   40

You shall sing of holidays and the City's
Public Games, and Forum bereft of lawsuits,
Honouring return of the brave Augustus
Granted to our prayers.

Then, if I can utter what's worth the hearing,   45
I'll take part in good voice and 'O the lovely
Sun! O praise him!' I'll sing, in happiness for
Caesar's homecoming.

And, as he processes, *Io Triumphe!*
More than once we'll all say, *Io Triumphe!*   50
All the citizens, and to merciful Gods
We'll offer incense.

You shall pay ten bulls and as many milch kine,
Me a young bull-calf shall release, who's left his
Mother and grows up on lush meadow grass as   55
My votive offering.

Who with forehead horned imitates the young moon's
Fiery crescent now for the third time rising;
Where his markings are he's snow-white to look at,
Otherwise tawny.   60

III

      Quem tu, Melpomene, semel
nascentem placido lumine uideris,
      illum non labor Isthmius
clarabit pugilem, non equus impiger
         curru ducet Achaico   5
uictorem, neque res bellica Deliis
      ornatum foliis ducem,
quod regum tumidas contuderit minas,
      ostendet Capitolio:
sed quae Tibur aquae fertile praefluunt   10
      et spissae nemorum comae
fingent Aeolio carmine nobilem.
      Romae, principis urbium,
dignatur suboles inter amabilis
      uatum ponere me choros,   15
et iam dente minus mordeor inuido.
      o testudinis aureae
dulcem quae strepitum, Pieri, temperas,
      o mutis quoque piscibus
donatura cycni, si libeat, sonum,   20
      totum muneris hoc tui est,
quod monstror digito praetereuntium
      Romanae fidicen lyrae;
quod spiro et placeo, si placeo, tuum est.

IV

Qualem ministrum fulminis alitem,
cui rex deorum regnum in auis uagas
      permisit expertus fidelem
         Iuppiter in Ganymede flauo,

olim iuuentas et patrius uigor   5
nido laborum propulit inscium
      uernique iam nimbis remotis
         insolitos docuere nisus

3

When you, Melpomene, have once
Looked with favouring eye on anyone at birth,
    Then no Isthmian toil shall make
Him a pugilist well-known, no impetuous steed
        Pull him on in Achaean car   5
As the winner, nor war's business display him crowned
    With a Delian wreath of bay
On the Capitoline Hill as a general
    Who crushed the arrogant threats of kings.
But the waters that flow past fertile Tivoli   10
    And the forest's thick foliage
Form him famous for Aeolian poetry.
    At Rome, queen of the world's cities,
Her sons deign to include me in the lovable
    Choral company of the bards,   15
And today I am less bitten by Envy's tooth.
    O Pierian who modulate
Golden turtleshell's sweet resonance, who could give,
    Should your pleasure be such, to dumb
Fishes also the voice of the poetic swan,   20
    It is wholly of your gift
That the finger of those passing by points me out
    Soloist of the Roman lyre;
My inspiration and success, if I succeed, is yours.

4

Like thunderbolt's wing'd bearer whom Jupiter,
Heaven's sovereign, has given the sovranty
    Of all itinerant birds for proving
        Trustworthy over blond Ganymedes —

At first his youth and natural energy   5
Ejected him from the eyrie unaware of strife,
    And vernal winds, now storms were over,
        Taught his timidity unaccustomed

uenti pauentem, mox in ouilia
demisit hostem uiuidus impetus,   10
   nunc in reluctantis dracones
      egit amor dapis atque pugnae,

qualemue laetis caprea pascuis
intenta fuluae matris ab ubere
   iam lacte depulsum leonem   15
      dente nouo peritura uidit:

uidere Raetis bella sub Alpibus
Drusum gerentem Vindelici (quibus
   mos unde deductus per omne
      tempus Amazonia securi   20

dextras obarmet, quaerere distuli,
nec scire fas est omnia); sed diu
   lateque uictrices cateruae
      consiliis iuuenis reuictae

sensere quid mens rite, quid indoles   25
nutrita faustis sub penetralibus
   posset, quid Augusti paternus
      in pueros animus Nerones.

fortes creantur fortibus et bonis;
est in iuuencis, est in equis patrum   30
   uirtus neque imbellem feroces
      progenerant aquilae columbam.

doctrina sed uim promouet insitam
rectique cultus pectora roborant;
   utcumque defecere mores,   35
      indecorant bene nata culpae.

quid debeas, o Roma, Neronibus,
testis Metaurum flumen et Hasdrubal
   deuictus et pulcher fugatis
      ille dies Latio tenebris   40

qui primus alma risit adorea,
dirus per urbis Afer ut Italas
   ceu flamma per taedas uel Eurus
      per Siculas equitauit undas.

Wing-movements, so that soon on the folded sheep
As foe he plummets down in a lightning swoop,   10
    Next, love of feasting and of battle
        Drive him to master the writhing serpent —

Or as a roe, on flourishing pasturage
Intent, can see a lion-cub, lately driven
    From tawny mother's milky udder,   15
        And will fall prey to his newly-grown teeth,

So Vindelicians saw under Rhaetian Alps
The warrior Drusus marching (I now postpone
    Enquiry whence the custom came that
        Time out of mind has equipped their right hands   20

With Amazonian battle-axe, for to know
All the answers is not fitting), but their brigades,
    For long and everywhere victorious,
        Conquered in turn by a young man's tactics,

Soon realized what judgement and character   25
Could do when nurtured well under favouring
    Domestic Gods, and what Augustus'
        Fatherly care for the youthful Neros.

The brave are born of brave and good parentage.
There is in stallions, there is in bulls their sires'   30
    Potential, and ferocious eagles
        Never engender unmilitant doves.

It's training, though, develops the inborn flair,
And right behaviour strengthens the character.
    Whenever principles are lacking   35
        Vice will contaminate natural goodness.

O Rome, how much you owe the Neronians
Metaurus stream bears witness and Hasdrubal's
    Defeat and that most glorious day which
        Scattering the darkness that covered Latium   40

First smiled on her with bounteous victory,
Since through Italian cities the African
    Destroyer rode like flame in pinewoods
        Or the east wind on Sicilian billows.

post hoc secundis usque laboribus 45
Romana pubes creuit et impio
    uastata Poenorum tumultu
        fana deos habuere rectos,

dixitque tandem perfidus Hannibal:
'cerui, luporum praeda rapacium, 50
    sectamur ultro quos opimus
        fallere et effugere est triumphus.

gens, quae cremato fortis ab Ilio
iactata Tuscis aequoribus sacra
    natosque maturosque patres 55
        pertulit Ausonias ad urbis,

duris ut ilex tonsa bipennibus
nigrae feraci frondis in Algido,
    per damna, per caedis ab ipso
        ducit opes animumque ferro. 60

non hydra secto corpore firmior
uinci dolentem creuit in Herculem
    monstrumue submisere Colchi
        maius Echioniaeue Thebae.

merses profundo, pulchrior euenit; 65
luctere, multa proruet integrum
    cum laude uictorem geretque
        proelia coniugibus loquenda.

Carthagini iam non ego nuntios
mittam superbos: occidit, occidit 70
    spes omnis et fortuna nostri
        nominis Hasdrubale interempto.'

nil Claudiae non perficient manus,
quas et benigno numine Iuppiter
    defendit et curae sagaces 75
        expediunt per acuta belli.

Thereafter through campaigns ever prosperous   45
Our Roman youth grew strong and in all the shrines
    Laid waste by impious Punic turmoil
        Overturned Gods were again set upright.

At last there spoke up treacherous Hannibal:
'We're stags, the natural prey of rapacious wolves,   50
    But keep pursuing those it would be
        Glorious triumph to trick and run from.

The race that after Ilium's burning braved
Being tossed on Tuscan waters to emigrate
    With Household Deities, and sons and   55
        Elderly sires to Ausonian cities,

Like evergreen oak lopped by a two-edged axe
On Algidus abounding in dark-hued leaves,
    In spite of loss and slaughter gathers
        From steel itself renewed heart and vigour.   60

No hydra's chopped flesh grew more persistently
To Hercules' frustration at his defeat,
    Nor Colchis nor Echion's Thebes gave
        Magical birth to a greater monster.

Sink them without trace: finer, they re-appear.   65
When wrestled with, they floor to prolonged applause
    An undefeated victor and fight
        Battles for wives to expatiate on.

No more shall I be sending to Carthage town
Proud messages now. Overthrown, overthrown   70
    Is every hope and all our famous
        Fortune with Hasdrubal's fatal ending.' —

There's nothing Claudian hands cannot bring to pass;
For Jupiter protects them with favouring
    Divinity, and prescient counsels   75
        Carry them safely through war's ordeals.

V

Diuis orte bonis, optime Romulae
custos gentis, abes iam nimium diu:
maturum reditum pollicitus patrum
    sancto concilio, redi.

lucem redde tuae, dux bone, patriae.   5
instar ueris enim uultus ubi tuus
affulsit populo, gratior it dies
    et soles melius nitent.

ut mater iuuenem, quem Notus inuido
flatu Carpathii trans maris aequora   10
cunctantem spatio longius annuo
    dulci distinet a domo,

uotis ominibusque et precibus uocat
curuo nec faciem litore dimouet,
sic desideriis icta fidelibus   15
    quaerit patria Caesarem.

tutus bos etenim rura perambulat,
nutrit rura Ceres almaque Faustitas,
pacatum uolitant per mare nauitae,
    culpari metuit fides,   20

nullis polluitur casta domus stupris,
mos et lex maculosum edomuit nefas,
laudantur simili prole puerperae,
    culpam poena premit comes.

quis Parthum paueat, quis gelidum Scythen,   25
quis Germania quos horrida parturit
fetus, incolumi Caesare? quis ferae
    bellum curet Hiberiae?

condit quisque diem collibus in suis
et uitem uiduas ducit ad arbores;   30
hinc ad uina redit laetus et alteris
    te mensis adhibet deum.

5

Good Gods' progeny, best guardian of Romulus'
People, you've been away now for too long a time.
Having promised the grave Fathers in conference
    Your return would be soon, return!

Bring, good leader, the light back to your fatherland,   5
For whenever your face dawns like the spring upon
Roman people the day passes more gratefully
    And the sun has a better shine.

As a mother with vows, omens, and prayers invokes
Her young son whom the south wind with its envious   10
Breath far over the width of the Carpathian Sea
    (Where he's been for a year and more)

Separates from his sweet home while his mother there
Keeps her gaze every day fixed on the curving shore,
So too, smitten by deep longing, most loyally   15
    His own country for Caesar yearns.

For in safety the ox plods up and down the fields.
Ceres nurtures the fields and kindly Plenteousness.
Over pacified seas mariners wing their way.
    Good Faith dreads to be found at fault.   20

Homes are chaste, undefiled by immorality.
Law and custom have stamped out the corruption of vice.
Child and sire look alike, bringing the mother praise.
    Crime's close partner is Punishment.

Who'd fear Parthians? Who'd fear the frost-bitten Scyth   25
Or those hordes that uncouth Germany brings to birth,
While our Caesar is safe? Who'd be concerned at war
    With barbaric Iberia?

Each man closes the day on his own vineyard slopes
At the marriage of grape-vines to unwedded trees,   30
Then returns for his wine, happily, and invites
    You as God to the second course.

te multa prece, te prosequitur mero
defuso pateris, et Laribus tuum
miscet numen, uti Graecia Castoris   35
    et magni memor Herculis.

'longas o utinam, dux bone, ferias
praestes Hesperiae' dicimus integro
sicci mane die, dicimus uuidi,
    cum sol Oceano subest.   40

VI

Diue, quem proles Niobea magnae
uindicem linguae Tityosque raptor
sensit et Troiae prope uictor altae
Pthius Achilles,

ceteris maior, tibi miles impar,   5
filius quamuis Thetidis marinae
Dardanas turris quateret tremenda
cuspide pugnax —

ille, mordaci uelut icta ferro
pinus aut impulsa cupressus Euro,   10
procidit late posuitque collum in
puluere Teucro;

ille non inclusus equo Mineruae
sacra mentito male feriatos
Troas et laetam Priami choreis   15
falleret aulam,

sed palam captis grauis, heu nefas, heu
nescios fari pueros Achiuis
ureret flammis, etiam latentem
matris in aluo,   20

ni tuis uictus Venerisque gratae
uocibus diuom pater adnuisset
rebus Aeneae potiore ductos
alite muros —

You with many a prayer, you he salutes with un-
mixed wine poured from the bowl, joining your deity
With the Lares, as Greece honours the memory   35
    Of the Twins and great Hercules.

'Grant, good leader, O grant peace and long holidays
To Hesperia!' So say we at dawn when dry
Ere the day has begun. So too we say when soaked
    While the sun is below the sea.   40

6

God that punished Niobe's sons and daughters
For her boastful language, and Tityos the
Rapist, and, near-captor of lofty Ilium,
Phthian Achilles,

Greater than the rest but as soldier no match   5
For yourself, though son of the Sea-Nymph Thetis
And a fighter shaking Dardanian towers with
Murderous spear-point —

Like a pinetree toppled by biting axe-blade
Or a cypress blown to the ground by Eurus   10
He was felled and sprawling in Teucrian dust
Pillowed his neck there.

He would not have hidden in the Horse, Minerva's
Specious sacrifice, nor deceived the Trojans
Wrongly holidaying and Priam's courtiers   15
Joyfully dancing,

But, to captives openly merciless (ah,
Horror!) he'd have burnt in Achaean fire
Infant children, even the babe still hiding
In mother's belly,   20

If the Father of Gods, overcome by your and
Gracious Venus' voices, had not accorded
To Aeneas' destiny walls constructed
With better omen —

doctor argutae fidicen Thaliae, 25
Phoebe, qui Xantho lauis amne crinis,
Dauniae defende decus Camenae,
leuis Agyieu.

spiritum Phoebus mihi, Phoebus artem
carminis nomenque dedit poetae: 30
uirginum primae puerique claris
patribus orti,

Deliae tutela deae, fugacis
lyncas et ceruos cohibentis arcu,
Lesbium seruate pedem meique 35
pollicis ictum,

rite Latonae puerum canentes,
rite crescentem face Noctilucam,
prosperam frugum celeremque pronos
uoluere mensis. 40

nupta iam dices 'ego dis amicum,
saeculo festas referente luces,
reddidi carmen docilis modorum
uatis Horati.'

VII

Diffugere niues, redeunt iam gramina campis
      arboribusque comae;
mutat terra uices, et decrescentia ripas
      flumina praetereunt.
Gratia cum Nymphis geminisque sororibus audet 5
      ducere nuda choros.
immortalia ne speres, monet annus et almum
      quae rapit hora diem.
frigora mitescunt Zephyris, Ver proterit Aestas,
      interitura simul 10
pomifer Autumnus fruges effuderit, et mox
      Bruma recurrit iners.
damna tamen celeres reparant caelestia lunae:
      nos ubi decidimus

Musical Thalia's lyre-playing teacher,   25
Phoebus, who in Xanthus' stream wash your long hair,
Vindicate the Daunian Muse's honour,
Smooth-cheeked Agyieus.

I'm inspired by Phoebus and Phoebus gave me
The art of lyric song and the name of poet. —   30
First among the maidens, and boys that spring from
Eminent fathers,

By the Delian Goddess protected, whose bow
Disciplines wild deer and elusive lynxes,
Keep the Lesbian foot and the metric beat as   35
Given by my thumb-stroke,

Duly celebrating the son of Leto,   .
Duly Noctiluca with crescent lantern,
She who prospers crops, quickly rolling onward
The impermanent months.   40

Soon, as bride, you'll say 'When the century brought
Round again its festival, I performed a
Hymn to please the Gods by that skilled metrician
The poet Horace.'

7

Snows have melted away. Now grasses return to the meadows
        And leafy tresses to trees.
Earth is renewing her changes, and swollen rivers, subsiding,
        Flow past confined by their banks.
Joining the Nymphs and her own twin sisters a Grace has the courage
        Naked to lead off the dance.   5
'Hope not for life everlasting' the year forewarns and the hour that
        Robs us of genial day.
West winds temper the cold. Then Spring's trampled under by Summer,
        Destined to perish herself   10
Soon as fruit-bearing Autumn has poured out his harvest. Thereafter
        Winter's inertia returns.
Swiftly, however, the moons make good their celestial losses:
        We, having gone down to join

175

quo pius Aeneas, quo diues Tullus et Ancus,   15
    puluis et umbra sumus.
quis scit an adiciant hodiernae crastina summae
    tempora di superi?
cuncta manus auidas fugient heredis, amico
    quae dederis animo.   20
cum semel occideris et de te splendida Minos
    fecerit arbitria,
non, Torquate, genus, non te facundia, non te
    restituet pietas.
infernis neque enim tenebris Diana pudicum   25
    liberat Hippolytum
nec Lethaea ualet Theseus abrumpere caro
    uincula Pirithoo.

VIII

Donarem pateras grataque commodus,
Censorine, meis aera sodalibus,
donarem tripodas, praemia fortium
Graiorum, neque tu pessima munerum
ferres, diuite me scilicet artium   5
quas aut Parrhasius protulit aut Scopas,
hic saxo, liquidis ille coloribus
sollers nunc hominem ponere, nunc deum.
sed non haec mihi uis, nec tibi talium
res est aut animus deliciarum egens: 10
gaudes carminibus; carmina possumus
donare, et pretium dicere muneri.
non incisa notis marmora publicis,
per quae spiritus et uita redit bonis
post mortem ducibus, non celeres fugae   15
reiectaeque retrorsum Hannibalis minae
non incendia Karthaginis impiae
eius qui domita nomen ab Africa
lucratus rediit clarius indicant
laudes quam Calabrae Pierides, neque   20
si chartae sileant quod bene feceris,
mercedem tuleris. quid foret Iliae
Mauortisque puer, si taciturnitas

Aeneas the true-hearted and millionaire Tullus and Ancus,   15
  Then are but dust and a shade.
Who can know if the Gods above will add a tomorrow
  On to our total today?
Everything you have given your own dear soul will escape the
  Covetous grasp of an heir.   20
When once you have departed and on you has Minos delivered
  Prestigious arbitrament,
No high birth, Torquatus, no eloquence, and no religion
  Ever restores you to life.
For not even Diana can free from the darkness of Hades   25
  Virginal Hippolytus,
Nor has Theseus the power to strike those Lethean chains off
  Pirithous the belov'd.

8

I would gladly present sought-after works in bronze,
Censorinus, and wine-bowls to my closest friends.
Tripods I would present, trophies of disciplined
Grecians, neither would *you* pick up the worst of gifts
Were I, that is to say, rich in those *objets d'art*   5
Which Parrhasius or Scopas contributed,
One in marble and one expert in liquid hues
At portraying a God, perhaps, or perhaps a man.
But I have not the power, nor does your property
Or mentality want that kind of luxury.   10
Your delight is in song, and it is song that I
Can give and can bestow value upon the gift.
Neither marble engraved as public document
By which spirit and life come back again to good
Leaders after their death, nor Hannibal's swift flight   15
Nor the threatenings that rebounded upon himself,
Nor the fires that laid impious Carthage low
Place in clearer relief than the Calabrian Muse
That man's praises who came back from North Africa's
Subjugation enriched with but a splendid name.   20
Nor if parchment withheld mention of your good deeds
Would you reap their reward. What would the son of Mars
And of Ilia be, if taciturnity

obstaret meritis inuida Romuli?
ereptum Stygiis fluctibus Aeacum   25
uirtus et fauor et lingua potentium
uatum diuitibus consecrat insulis.
dignum laude uirum Musa uetat mori:
caelo Musa beat. sic Iouis interest
optatis epulis impiger Hercules,   30
clarum Tyndaridae sidus ab infimis
quassas eripiunt aequoribus ratis,
ornatus uiridi tempora pampino
Liber uota bonos ducit ad exitus.

IX

Ne forte credas interitura quae
longe sonantem natus ad Aufidum
    non ante uulgatas per artis
        uerba loquor socianda chordis:

non, si priores Maeonius tenet   5
sedes Homerus, Pindaricae latent
    Ceaeque et Alcaei minaces
        Stesichoriue graues Camenae,

nec, siquid olim lusit Anacreon,
deleuit aetas; spirat adhuc amor   10
    uiuuntque commissi calores
        Aeoliae fidibus puellae.

non sola comptos arsit adulteri
crinis et aurum uestibus illitum
    mirata regalisque cultus   15
        et comites Helene Lacaena,

primusue Teucer tela Cydonio
direxit arcu; non semel Ilios
    uexata; non pugnauit ingens
        Idomeneus Sthenelusue solus   20

Out of envy suppressed Romulus' just deserts?
Virtue, favour, and fine language of powerful   25
Bards from Stygian waves have redeemed Aeacus,
In the Fortunate Isles hallowing him a place.
The Muse vetoes the death of a man worthy of praise.
The Muse blesses with heaven. Hardworking Hercules
Thus can share the ideal banquets of Jupiter,   30
Thus the Tyndarids' star shining among the clouds
Rescues storm-beaten ships out of the deepest seas,
And, his forehead adorned with the green-tendrilled vine,
Liber sees that our vows lead to a happy end.

9

Lest you perhaps suppose that the words will die
Which, near to booming Aufidus born, I speak
    By arts not hitherto made public
        For combination with lyre music,

Reflect that though Maeonian Homer takes   5
First place, Pindaric Muses are not unknown
    Nor Cean, neither those of stately
        Stesichorus nor Alcaeus the rebel.

Nor have the years destroyed what Anacreon
Once lightly sang, and still today breathes the love   10
    And lives the passion entrusted to her
        Barbitos by that Aeolian girl.

Not Spartan Helen only was set alight
In admiration of an adulterer's
    Neat hair and gold-embroidered cloak and   15
        Princely behaviour and train of followers,

Nor Teucer first to shoot from Cydonian bow
His arrows; not once only was Ilios
    Beleaguered, nor alone did mighty
        Idomeneüs or Sthenelus have   20

dicenda Musis proelia; non ferox
Hector uel acer Deiphobus grauis
    excepit ictus pro pudicis
        coniugibus puerisque primus.

uixere fortes ante Agamemnona   25
multi; sed omnes illacrimabiles
    urgentur ignotique longa
        nocte, carent quia uate sacro.

paulum sepultae distat inertiae
celata uirtus. non ego te meis   30
    chartis inornatum sileri
        totue tuos patiar labores

impune, Lolli, carpere liuidas
obliuiones: est animus tibi
    rerumque prudens et secundis   35
        temporibus dubiisque rectus,

uindex auarae fraudis et abstinens
ducentis ad se cuncta pecuniae,
    consulque non unius anni,
        sed quotiens bonus atque fidus   40

iudex honestum praetulit utili,
reiecit alto dona nocentium
    uultu, per obstantis cateruas
        explicuit sua uictor arma.

non possidentem multa uocaueris   45
recte beatum; rectius occupat
    nomen beati qui deorum
        muneribus sapienter uti

duramque callet pauperiem pati
peiusque leto flagitium timet,   50
    non ille pro caris amicis
        aut patria timidus perire.

Fights fit for Muses telling; and Hector fierce
And energetic Deiphobus were not
    The first to suffer heavy blows while
        Guarding their virtuous wives and children.

Brave men there were before Agamemnon's time,   25
A multitude, but buried in endless night
    They lie unwept and unremembered,
        All for the lack of a sacred poet.

Small difference exists between cowardice
Entombed and hidden courage. I'll not allow   30
    My page to leave your praise unspoken
        Or the iniquity of oblivion

To prey on your life's labours, O Lollius,
Without resistance. You have a mind of wise
    Experience in affairs, of upright   35
        Judgement in perilous times and prosperous.

Chastising greed and fraud it remains untouched
By the universal magnet of ready cash,
    Its consulate not one year only
        But whensoever as good and true judge   40

It favours honour over expediency,
Rejects the bribes of criminals with a look
    Of high disdain and through opposing
        Factions deploys its victorious weapons.

The man of great possessions you'd not be right   45
To label happy. This one more rightly earns
    The name of happy who is skilled at
        Using the gifts of the Gods with wisdom

And bearing all the hardships of poverty,
Who's more afraid of infamy than of death,   50
    No laggard he to give his own life
        For his dear friends or his native country.

X

O crudelis adhuc et Veneris muneribus potens,
insperata tuae cum ueniet bruma superbiae
et quae nunc umeris inuolitant, deciderint comae,
nunc et qui color est puniceae flore prior rosae,
mutatus, Ligurine, in faciem uerterit hispidam,   5
dices 'heu', quotiens te speculo uideris alterum,
'quae mens est hodie, cur eadem non puero fuit,
uel cur his animis incolumes non redeunt genae?'

XI

Est mihi nonum superantis annum
plenus Albani cadus, est in horto,
Phylli, nectendis apium coronis,
est hederae uis

multa, qua crinis religata fulges;   5
ridet argento domus, ara castis
uincta uerbenis auet immolato
spargier agno;

cuncta festinat manus, huc et illuc
cursitant mixtae pueris puellae,   10
sordidum flammae trepidant rotantes
uertice fumum.

ut tamen noris quibus aduoceris
gaudiis, Idus tibi sunt agendae,
qui dies mensem Veneris marinae   15
findit Aprilem,

iure sollemnis mihi sanctiorque
paene natali proprio, quod ex hac
luce Maecenas meus adfluentis
ordinat annos.   20

Telephum, quem tu petis, occupauit
non tuae sortis iuuenem puella
diues et lasciua tenetque grata
compede uinctum.

10

O still cruel and still master of all Venus's potent gifts,
When the winter for your pride shall arrive taking you by surprise
And the tresses that now float on your shoulders are cut off and fall
And the colour that now betters the flower even of the crimson rose
Suffers change, Ligurinus, and is turned into a bristly sight,   5
Then whenever you see your second self there in the glass you'll ask
'Why, alas, as a boy were not my thoughts those that I have today?
Or why cannot my cheeks come back unaged matching my feelings now?'

11

I've a wine-jar brimming with vintage Alban
Nine and more years old. In my kitchen garden
There is parsley, Phyllis, for twining garlands
And lots of ivy

You can use to tie back your hair and dazzle us.   5
Beams the house with silver. The altar bound with
Sacred foliage longs to be sprinkled from a
Lamb's immolation.

All the hands are hurrying. Hither and thither
Boys and girls are rushing, in ordered muddle.   10
Even the flames are worked up, rotating wreaths of
Eddying black smoke.

But, that you may know to what entertainment
You're invited, it's to a celebration
Of the Ides dividing the month of Venus   15
Sea-born in April,

Rightly a Feast for me and more sacred almost
Than my own birthday, for it is from this same
Dawn that my Maecenas enumerates the
Increase of his years.   20

Telephus your favourite's a youth of higher
Class than you and caught by another girl who's
Both well-off and sexy and holds him fast in
Comfortable fetters.

terret ambustus Phaethon auaras   25
spes et exemplum graue praebet ales
Pegasus terrenum equitem grauatus
Bellerophontem,

semper ut te digna sequare et ultra
quam licet sperare nefas putando   30
disparem uites. age iam, meorum
finis amorum -

non enim posthac alia calebo
femina — condisce modos amanda
uoce quos reddas: minuentur atrae   35
carmine curae.

XII

Iam ueris comites, quae mare temperant,
impellunt animae lintea Thraciae,
iam nec prata rigent nec fluuii strepunt
      hiberna niue turgidi.

nidum ponit Ityn flebiliter gemens   5
infelix auis et Cecropiae domus
aeternum opprobrium, quod male barbaras
      regum est ulta libidines.

dicunt in tenero gramine pinguium
custodes ouium carmina fistula   10
delectantque deum cui pecus et nigri
      colles Arcadiae placent.

adduxere sitim tempora, Vergili.
sed pressum Calibus ducere Liberum
si gestis, iuuenum nobilium cliens,   15
      nardo uina merebere.

nardi paruus onyx eliciet cadum
qui nunc Sulpiciis accubat horreis,
spes donare nouas largus amaraque
      curarum eluere efficax.   20

Phaëthon's cremation deters ambitious   25
Hopes, and wingèd Pegasus gives a weighty
Warning by refusing his mortal rider
Bellerophon's weight:

You should always aim at what suits your station,
Thinking hopes beyond what is right forbidden,   30
Shunning paired disparity. Come away, then,
Last of all my loves —

For I'll never warm to another woman
After this — come, join me and learn some tunes to
Render with your lovable voice. Song lessens   35
Black disappointment.

12

Now the attendants of Spring who pacify the sea,
Gentle breezes from Thrace, power the canvas sails.
Now no meadows are frozen, nor do the rivers roar
    Overflowing with winter snow.

Procne's building her nest, grieving for Itylus   5
Inconsolably, poor bird, everlasting shame
Of the family of Cecrops, for her cruel revenge
    On the barbarous lust of kings.

In the tender young grass keepers of fattening
Sheep play tunes on the pan-pipes and repeat their songs,   10
Entertaining the God pleased by Arcadia's
    Pine-dark mountains, its flocks and herds.

Springtime, Vergilius, comes with a thirst as well.
But if drinking a wine pressed in Campania
Takes your fancy, as young noblemen's protégé,   15
    You must earn it from me with nard.

One small onyx of nard lures out an amphora
Which at present reclines down in Sulpicius' store,
Generous donor of new hopes, that can wash away
    The sour taste of anxiety.   20

ad quae si properas gaudia, cum tua
uelox merce ueni: non ego te meis
    immunem meditor tingere poculis,
        plena diues ut in domo.

uerum pone moras et studium lucri   25
nigrorumque memor, dum licet, ignium
    misce stultitiam consiliis breuem:
        dulce est desipere in loco.

XIII

Audiuere, Lyce, di mea uota, di
audiuere, Lyce: fis anus; et tamen
    uis formosa uideri
        ludisque et bibis impudens

et cantu tremulo pota Cupidinem   5
lentum sollicitas: ille uirentis et
    doctae psallere Chiae
        pulchris excubat in genis.

importunus enim transuolat aridas
quercus et refugit te, quia luridi   10
    dentes, te quia rugae
        turpant et capitis niues.

nec Coae referunt iam tibi purpurae
nec cari lapides tempora quae semel
    notis condita fastis   15
        inclusit uolucris dies.

quo fugit uenus, heu, quoue color? decens
quo motus? quid habes illius, illius,
    quae spirabat amores,
        quae me surpuerat mihi,   20

felix post Cinaram notaque et artium
gratarum facies? sed Cinarae breuis
    annos fata dederunt,
        seruatura diu parem

If you're eager for such joys you must come at once
Bringing with you the goods. I don't propose to allow
    You to soak in my wine-cups absolutely free,
        Not being rich with a well-stocked house.

No, but banish delay and the pursuit of gain,   25
And, remembering the black funeral fires, mix
    With your plans and advice brief folly while you may;
        Unwisdom in its place is sweet.

13

The Gods, Lyce, have heard — Lyce, the Gods have heard
My prayers: you're middle-aged, soon to be old, and yet
    You still wish to look lovely,
        Unashamedly drink and play

And, whenever you're drunk, seek to resuscitate   5
With shrill-quavering song Cupid's lethargic lust.
    He camps out on the fair cheeks
        Of green Chia the kitharist.

For he ruthlessly flies past desiccated oaks
And takes care to avoid you because yellowing   10
    Front teeth, you because wrinkles
        And your snowy thatch turn him off.

Purple dresses from Cos, jewels of highest price
Can't bring back to you now years that are once for all
    Stored in traceable records,   15
        Open prisoners of flying Time.

Where O where is your charm and your complexion fled?
Where the beautiful poise? What now remains of her,
    Of her who used to breathe love,
        Who stole me from myself, the one   20

Next to Cínara successful, a vision famed
For her glamorous arts? Cinara, though, was given
    Few short years by the Fates, who
        Saved up Lyce for many moons

cornicis uetulae temporibus Lycen,   25
possent ut iuuenes uisere feruidi
    multo non sine risu
        dilapsam in cineres facem.

XIV

Quae cura Patrum quaeue Quiritium
plenis honorum muneribus tuas,
    Auguste, uirtutes in aeuum
        per titulos memoresque fastus

aeternet, o qua sol habitabilis   5
illustrat oras, maxime principum?
    quem legis expertes Latinae
        Vindelici didicere nuper,

quid Marte posses. milite nam tuo
Drusus Genaunos, implacidum genus,   10
    Breunosque uelocis et arces
        Alpibus impositas tremendis

deiecit acer plus uice simplici.
maior Neronum mox graue proelium
    commisit immanisque Raetos   15
        auspiciis pepulit secundis,

spectandus in certamine Martio
deuota morti pectora liberae
    quantis fatigaret ruinis,
        indomitas prope qualis undas   20

exercet Auster Pleiadum choro
scindente nubis, impiger hostium
    uexare turmas et frementem
        mittere equum medios per ignis.

sic tauriformis uoluitur Aufidus,   25
qui regna Dauni praefluit Apuli,
    cum saeuit horrendamque cultis
        diluuiem minitatur agris,

As a match for the longevity of a crow,   25
So that passionate young men could go visiting
    With much laughter the old torch
        Fallen now to a heap of ash.

14

What act of Roman Senate or Citizens,
Augustus, could immortalize your deserts
    With adequate reward of honours
        Using inscriptions and written records,

O mightiest of Princes wherever sun
Illuminates inhabited continents?
    Your power in war Vindelici have
        Recently learnt, though before not under

Our Latin rule; for Drusus with troops of yours
Laid low Genauni, turbulent warrior tribe,   10
    And agile Breuni and their strongholds
        Perched on vertiginous Alpine summits,

Retaliating with double punishment.
The elder Nero brother thereafter joined
    Ferocious battle, and, with happy   15
        Auspices, routed the cruel Rhaetians,

Conspicuous as fighter on Mars's field
With sheer destruction breaking the foes' morale
    Who'd sworn to meet their death as free men,
        Much as when Auster whips up the untamed   20

Sea-waves (the band of Pleiades in their dance
Cleaving the cloudrack), eagerly would he charge
    The hostile squadrons and would ride his
        Whinnying steed through the conflagration.

As tauromorphic Aufidus surges on   25
(Bounding the realm of Daunus the Apulian)
    When he is furious and threatens
        Ruinous flood to the well-tilled farmland,

ut barbarorum Claudius agmina
ferrata uasto diruit impetu   30
    primosque et extremos metendo
        strauit humum sine clade uictor,

te copias, te consilium et tuos
praebente diuos. nam tibi quo die
    portus Alexandrea supplex   35
        et uacuam patefecit aulam,

Fortuna lustro prospera tertio
belli secundos reddidit exitus
    laudemque et optatum peractis
        imperiis decus arrogauit.   40

te Cantaber non ante domabilis
Medusque et Indus, te profugus Scythes
    miratur, o tutela praesens
        Italiae dominaeque Romae.

te fontium qui celat origines   45
Nilusque et Hister, te rapidus Tigris,
    te beluosus qui remotis
        obstrepit Oceanus Britannis,

te non pauentis funera Galliae
duraeque tellus audit Hiberiae,   50
    te caede gaudentes Sygambri
        compositis uenerantur armis.

XV

Phoebus uolentem proelia me loqui
uictas et urbis increpuit lyra,
    ne parua Tyrrhenum per aequor
        uela darem. tua, Caesar, aetas

fruges et agris rettulit uberes   5
et signa nostro restituit Ioui
    derepta Parthorum superbis
        postibus et uacuum duellis

So Claudius, with indomitable assault,
Destroyed the iron-clad hordes of barbarians   30
    And mowing down both first and last ranks
        Strewed all the ground, without loss in victory,

With you providing forces and strategy
And favouring Gods. For, on the very day
    That suppliant Alexandria opened   35
        To you her harbours and empty palace,

Propitious Fortune fifteen years afterwards
Afforded you a prosperous end to war,
    Assigning praise and long-sought glory
        For the accomplishment of your orders.   40

By you Cantabrians never before subdued
And Medes and Indians and the nomadic Scyths
    Are awe-struck, O most sure defence of
        Italy and the world's mistress Roma.

To you the Nile who hides the beginnings of   45
His stream, to you both Hister and Tigris swift,
    To you the beast-infested seas that
        Roar in the ears of the distant Britons,

To you the land of Gaul that despises death
Pays homage and the stubborn Iberian.   50
    Even slaughter-relishing Sygambri,
        Weapons discarded, bow down before you.

15

When I would tell of battles and conquered towns,
Phoebus with jangling lyre reprimanded me –
    Not over Tyrrhene seas to hoist my
        Miniature mainsail. — Your era, Caesar,

Has brought back lavish crops to the countryside   5
And, tearing down from arrogant Parthian doors
    Our captured standards, has restored them
        To Roman Jupiter, and has closed up

Ianum Quirini clausit et ordinem
rectum euaganti frena licentiae   10
    iniecit emouitque culpas
        et ueteres reuocauit artis,

per quas Latinum nomen et Italae
creuere uires famaque et imperi
    porrecta maiestas ad ortus   15
        solis ab Hesperio cubili.

custode rerum Caesare non furor
ciuilis aut uis exiget otium,
    non ira, quae procudit ensis
        et miseras inimicat urbis.   20

non qui profundum Danuuium bibunt
edicta rumpent Iulia, non Getae,
    non Seres infidique Persae,
        non Tanain prope flumen orti.

nosque et profestis lucibus et sacris   25
inter iocosi munera Liberi
    cum prole matronisque nostris
        rite deos prius apprecati

uirtute functos more patrum duces
Lydis remixto carmine tibiis   30
    Troiamque et Anchisen et almae
        progeniem Veneris canemus.

Quirinus' Janus, free of hostilities
And placed a curb upon the permissiveness   10
    That strays from ordered right, and banished
        Crime, and recovered the ancient life-style

By which the Latin name and Italian
Predominance has grown and the Empire's fame
    And majesty now stretches from the   15
        Far western bed of the Sun to his rising.

While Caesar guards us, no civic madness or
Armed violence can drive out established peace,
    No angry pride that forges swordblades
        And sets at enmity wretched cities.   20

Not they who drink the Danube's deep-flowing stream
Shall disobey the Julian decrees, not Goths
    Not Chinese or perfidious Persians,
        Not those near Tanais river nurtured.

And we, on ordinary and sacred days,   25
Amid the gifts of Liber the humorist
    Together with our wives and children,
        Having first prayed to the Gods in due form,

We then shall hymn, to strains of the Lydian pipe
(As did our fathers), leaders courageous proved   30
    And Ilium and Anchises and
        Lifegiving Venus's famous offspring.

CARMEN SAECVLARE

Phoebe siluarumque potens Diana,
lucidum caeli decus, o colendi
semper et culti, date quae precamur
tempore sacro,

quo Sibyllini monuere uersus   5
uirgines lectas puerosque castos
dis, quibus septem placuere colles,
dicere carmen.

alme Sol, curru nitido diem qui
promis et celas aliusque et idem   10
nasceris, possis nihil urbe Roma
uisere maius.

Rite maturos aperire partus
lenis, Ilithyia, tuere matres,
siue tu Lucina probas uocari   15
seu Genitalis.

diua, producas subolem patrumque
prosperes decreta super iugandis
feminis prolisque nouae feraci
lege marita,   20

certus undenos deciens per annos
orbis ut cantus referatque ludos
ter die claro totiensque grata
nocte frequentis.

Vosque, ueraces cecinisse Parcae,   25
quod semel dictum stabilis per aeuum
terminus seruet, bona iam peractis
iungite fata.

fertilis frugum pecorisque Tellus
spicea donet Cererem corona;   30
nutriant fetus et aquae salubres
et Iouis aurae.

CARMEN SAECULARE

Phoebus and Diana, the Queen of forests,
Radiant glory of heaven, O worshipful and
Ever worshipped, grant the requests we make at
This holy season,

When Sibylline verses have given command that   5
Chosen unmarried girls and unblemished boys should
Sing a hymn in honour of Gods who favour
The Seven Hilltops.

Nurturing Sun, who with your brilliant chariot
Bring and hide the day and are born the same yet   10
Other, may you never see anything more
Great than Rome city.

As is right, be gentle, enable timely
Childbirth, guard our mothers, O Ilithyia,
Or Lucina, if you approve that title,   15
Or Genitalis.

Goddess, rear us offspring and cause to prosper
Rulings of the Fathers on female yokemates
And the marriage law that's designed to increase
Our population,   20

So that every ten times eleven years a
Regular rotation may bring back public
Games and music thrice in bright daylight and thrice
In grateful darkness.

And may you, Parcae, ever truly singing   25
That which, once pronounced, an unalterable
Mark preserves eternally, add good fates to
Those now completed.

Bountiful in crops and in cattle may Earth
Make a gift to Ceres of wheaten garland.   30
May young life be nourished by Jove's fresh air and
Health-giving waters.

condito mitis placidusque telo
supplices audi pueros, Apollo;
siderum regina bicornis, audi,   35
Luna, puellas.

Roma si uestrum est opus Iliaeque
litus Etruscum tenuere turmae,
iussa pars mutare lares et urbem
sospite cursu,   40

cui per ardentem sine fraude Troiam
castus Aeneas patriae superstes
liberum muniuit iter, daturus
plura relictis:

di, probos mores docili iuuentae,   45
di, senectuti placidae quietem,
Romulae genti date remque prolemque
et decus omne.

Quaeque uos bobus ueneratur albis
clarus Anchisae Venerisque sanguis,   50
impetret, bellante prior, iacentem
lenis in hostem.

iam mari terraque manus potentis
Medus Albanasque timet securis,
iam Scythae responsa petunt, superbi   55
nuper et Indi.

iam Fides et Pax et Honos Pudorque
priscus et neglecta redire Virtus
audet apparetque beata pleno
Copia cornu.   60

Augur et fulgente decorus arcu
Phoebus acceptusque nouem Camenis,
qui salutari leuat arte fessos
corporis artus.

si Palatinas uidet aequus aras,   65
remque Romanam Latiumque felix
alterum in lustrum meliusque semper
prorogat aeuum,

Weapon laid aside, pacified and gentle
Hear the supplicatory boys, Apollo.
Sovereign twy-horned of the constellations,   35
Moon, hear the maidens.

If your work is Rome and if Trojan squadrons
Gained and held the Etrurian coast, a remnant
Bidden change their home and their city by a
Voyage of salvation,   40

Those for whom unscathed from out burning Ilium
Virtuous Aeneas, survivor of his
Country, built a high road to freedom, giving
More than had been lost:

Gods, to willing youth give a sense of duty,   45
Give to uncomplaining old age contentment,
To the race of Romulus wealth and offspring
And every honour.

What the glorious blood of Anchises and of
Venus asks with white bulls in veneration   50
Let him gain, victorious in war but generous
To the defeated.

Now by sea and land our effective power and
Alba Longa's axes alarm the Parthians.
Now the Scyths and Indians, lately so proud,   55
Ask us for rulings.

Now Good Faith and Peace and old-fashioned Shame and
Honour dare return and neglected Virtue.
Blessed Plenty makes her appearance now with
Horn overflowing.   60

Augur and majestic with glittering bow,
Phoebus, welcome friend to the nine Camenae,
He whose healing art can relieve the weary
Limbs of the body,

If he looks on Palatine altars justly,   65
He prolongs Rome's power and Latium's welfare
Into a second cycle and an ever better
Age in the future;

quaeque Auentinum tenet Algidumque,
quindecim Diana preces uirorum 70
curat et uotis puerorum amicas
applicat auris.

Haec Iouem sentire deosque cunctos
spem bonam certamque domum reporto,
doctus et Phoebi chorus et Dianae 75
dicere laudes.

And Diana, keeper of Aventine and
Algidus, fulfils the requests the Fifteen   70
Men propose and lends a kind ear to prayers
Made by the children.

That the will of Jove and of all the Gods is
Such I take home good and assured hope, having
Learnt to sing in chorus the praise of Phoebus   75
And of Diana.

Differences from Garrod's revision of Wickham's Oxford Classical Text

Minor differences of spelling, capitalization, punctuation etc are not recorded. The OCT reading is given second. With readings not found in any MS the emender's name is given.

BOOK ONE

2.39	Marsi *Faber* : Mauri
6.3	qua : quam
7.7	decerptae frondi *Erasmus* : decerptam fronti
17	perpetuos : perpetuo
27	auspice Teucro : auspice : Teucri
8.2	te deos oro : hoc deos uere
12.20	honores : honores.
31	quod : †quia
57	latum : laetum
15.20	crines : cultus
16.8	si : sic
20.10	uides *Munro* : bibes
25.20	Euro *editio Aldina 1501* : Hebro
26.9	Pimplei *Bentley* : Piplei
31.9	Calena : Calenam *Porphyrio*
18	et *Lambinus* : at
32.1	Poscimus : Poscimur
35.17	saeua : serua
19	aenos *Campbell* aena
22	sed *Peerlkamp* : nec
38.6	cura *Bentley* : curo

BOOK TWO

5.16	petet : petit
10.18	citharae : cithara
11.23–4	incomptam ... comam ... nodo *Bentley* : in comptum ... comas ...
13.15	Thynus *Lachmann* : Poenus
16.19	mutamus patriae? : mutamus? patriae
18.30	sede : fine

BOOK THREE

3.12	bibet : bibit
34	discere : ducere
4.4	citharaque : citharaue
10	limina Pulliae : limen Apuliae
5.15	trahenti : trahentis
8.27	horae : horae ac

TEXTUAL DIFFERENCES

14.11	expectate *J.Gow* : expertae
14	exiget : eximet
17.5	ducit *D.Heinsius* : ducis
19.12	miscentor *Rutgers* : miscentur
20.8	illa *Peerlkamp* : illi
24.4	terrenum *Lachmann* … publicum : Tyrrhenum … Apulicum
26.7	securesque *Bentley* : et arcus
27.15	uetat : uetet
28.12	Cynthiae; : Cynthiae,
15	oloribus : oloribus;
16	dicetur, : dicetur

BOOK FOUR

2.49	isque dum procedit, *Bentley* : terque, dum procedis,
4.6	propulit : protulit
17	Raetis : Raeti
7.15	pius : pater
10.2	bruma *Bentley* : †pluma
5	Ligurine : Ligurinum
14.28	minitatur : meditatur

CARMEN SAECULARE

26	dictum stabilis per aeuum *Bentley* : dictum est stabilisque rerum
36	puellas. : puellas:

NOTES

BOOK ONE

1

This first poem in effect dedicates the collected edition of the Odes (Books 1–3) to Horace's patron Maecenas. Horace contrasts his own ambition to be recognized as a lyric poet with the ambition or lifestyle of athletes, politicians, landowners, small farmers, merchants, hedonists, soldiers and huntsmen, providing vivid action-shots of each.

Metre: First Asclepiad

Added: 20 large, 22 perhaps.

1   Gaius Maecenas, a wealthy and sybaritic Roman knight who claimed descent from the ancient kings of Etruria but refused public office, was Octavian/Augustus' close friend and adviser. An amateur author himself, he was a famous patron of literature.

3   **Olympic dust**: in the Olympic Games held every four years at Elis in NW Peloponnese.

6   **Lords ... ours**: ambiguous like the Latin and could refer to *Gods* or *them*.

7   *hunc*: understand *iuuat* from 4.

8   **honours three**: the *cursus honorum* of quaestor, praetor and consul.

9   *illum*: understand *iuuat* again.

10   Libya was a main source of the Roman corn supply.

13   **Myrtoan**: SW Aegean between Peloponnese and Cyclades.

     Attalic terms: i.e. the most generous terms. Attalus III of Pergamum (d. 133 BC) left his kingdom and great wealth to the Romans, who made it the province of Asia, their richest province.

14   **Cypriot**: Cyprus was famous for its woods and shipbuilding.

15   **Africus**: SW wind.

     Icarian: in E Aegean around the Sporades where Icarus fell into the sea on his flight from Crete with his father Daedalus.

17   *ratis: -is*, the older form of the plural *-es* in *-i* stems (nouns and adjectives making genitive plural in *-ium*), is common in Horace, e.g. 1.2.5 *gentis*, 8 *montis*, 21 *ciuis*, 29 *partis*, 31 *candentis*.

19   **Massic**: from Mt Massicus in S Latium on the Campanian border.

28   **Marsian**: the Marsi lived in central Italy, E of Rome, near the Fucine Lake.

29   **poetic**: lit. 'learned, well trained.'

31   **choruses**: also 'dances.' He sees them in imagination (2.19.1–4)

32–3   **Euterpe ... Polyhymnia**: here the Muses of lyric poetry — choral and solo respectively, as their instruments prove.

34   **barbitos**: a large seven-stringed lyre of Asiatic origin used by the Lesbian poets
     Alcaeus and Sappho (6th century BC).
35   Alexandrian scholarship recognized nine lyric poets: Pindar, Bacchylides,
     Sappho, Anacreon, Stesichorus, Simonides, Ibycus, Alcaeus and Alcman (*Greek
     Anthology* 9.184).
     uatibus: uates, an old Latin word for 'seer' who delivered his utterances in verse
     had been used by Virgil as a grander synonym for the Greek *poeta*. Here its
     combination with the Greek *lyricus* implies that the canon could be extended to
     include a Latin poet.

2

It is generally agreed that this ambitious ode in honour of Octavian/Augustus owes much
to Virgil *Georgics* 1.466–514 and was written some time after Octavian's defeat of
Antony at Actium in 31 BC. It falls into two main sections: 1–24 the Father God's anger
with the Roman people for their sinful civil wars; 25–52 which of the Olympians should
the people invoke to put things right?

Metre: Sapphics.

Added: 24 one another, 25 all.

3   **sacred summits**: probably the twin summits of the Capitoline — the Arx and that
     on which stood the great temple of Jupiter Capitolinus, which must have been hit
     by lightning.
5   *gentis:* see 1.1.17 n.
6   **Age of Pyrrha**: a reference to the great flood of which Deucalion (the Greek
     Noah) and his wife Pyrrha were the sole survivors.
7   **Proteus**: the old sea-god who shepherded Neptune's seals.
13–16 This flood may be the one dated by Dio Cassius (53.20.1) to January 27 BC
     immediately after Octavian received the name Augustus, having resigned his
     extraordinary powers.
15–16 refer to the Regia (official residence of the Pontifex Maximus), the Atrium Vestae
     (where the Vestal Virgins lived), and the temple of Vesta; all these were built by
     King Numa.
17   Ilia, daughter of Aeneas and mother by Mars of Romulus and Remus, was thrown
     into the Tiber for breaking her Vestal vows, but Tiber rescued her and made her
     his wife. She was here complaining about the murder of her descendant Julius
     Caesar and about the civil war that followed.
     nimium: OLD 2 'very much, greatly;' with *querenti* perhaps a quotation from an
     earlier poet.
23   **Persians**: the Parthians, a military aristocracy whose empire extended from
     Euphrates to Indus (former empire of the Medes and Persians). In 53 BC with
     10,000 mounted archers and knights in chainmail they defeated Crassus and his
     numerically superior force at Carrhae in N Mesopotamia, killing him and
     capturing the Roman standards. See *OCD*[3] Parthia; Licinius Crassus (1); Surenas.
30   **our crime**: the civil war.
32   **Apollo**: god of medicine, poetry and prophecy whose most famous shrine was at
     Delphi.
33   **Erycina**: cult-title of Venus who had a famous temple on Mt Eryx in NW Sicily.
     Understand 'come' *(uenias)* from line 30.
35   **sire**: Mars the war-god, cf. 17 n. Again understand 'come.'

39   **Marsian**: see 1.1.28 n. The name *Marsi* is related to Mars; they were a very warlike tribe.

41–44 A most remarkable stanza suggesting that Octavian ('the young man,' born in 63 BC) is the incarnation of the god Mercury (son of Jupiter and Atlas' daughter Maia). N–H on line 43 compare Hellenistic ruler-cult: Alexander dressed as Hermes, Ptolemy III wearing Hermes' headgear and Ptolemy V likened to the Egyptian Hermes. Fraenkel 249 refers to Homer *Iliad* 24.347 where Hermes takes the shape of a young ruler. N–H sum up: 'This range of ideas belongs to the East, and Horace's words show blurred traces of the eastern belief in a divine saviour.'

46   **Quirinus**: the name of Romulus after his deification; he was swept up into heaven by a whirlwind, or in Mars' chariot.

49   Possibly a reference to Octavian's great triple triumph in 29 BC.

51   **Medes**: cf. 22 n.

52   **Caesar**: Octavian is named at last.

3

A propempticon or 'send-off' poem for Horace's friend the poet Virgil, who is making a voyage to Athens. He is given the honour of coming third addressee after Maecenas and Octavian.

Metre: Fourth Asclepiad.

Added: 2 twin, 7 there, 36 sad.

1–8   *Sic ... sic:* not the usual *quid pro quo* construction (*OLD* 8) but consecutive *sic* (*OLD* 3) with following *ut* omitted: *sic te regat ut reddas ...* .

1   Venus is called 'the Cyprian' in Homer, having famous temples at Paphos and Amathus in Cyprus.

2   Helen's brothers Castor and Pollux, the Gemini of the Zodiac, are appealed to with Venus as gods of the sea and also as constellations used in navigation. But some take *lucida sidera* here as referring to the electrical phenomenon of St Elmo's fire.

3   **Father of Winds**: Aeolus.

4   **Iapyx**: the wind blowing WNW from the Iapygian promontory (the heel of Italy), favourable for the crossing to Greece.

12   **Africus**: see 1.1.15 n.

13   **Aquilo**: the NE wind.

14   *tristis:* for this form of the acc. pl. see 1.1.17 n. and cf. *infamis* in 20 below.
       Hyades: the Rainers, a group of stars in the constellation Taurus.
       Notus: the S wind.

15   **Adria**: the Adriatic.

17   **he**: the inventor of ships.

20   **Acroceraunians**: dangerous cliffs on the coast of Epirus.

24   **untouchable**: here 'that ought not to be touched.'

27   **son of Iapetus**: Prometheus.
       'Daring' is not repeated, in order to bring out the bad meaning of *audax* in line 27.

32–33 In the Latin 'laggard' goes with 'necessity' and 'far-distant' with 'death.'

34   **Daedalus**: when escaping from Minos' Crete with his son Icarus.

36   Hercules' last labour was to bring back the dog Cerberus from the Underworld.

38   Truer today than in Horace's time.

4

A spring song in the tradition of those at the start of the tenth book of the *Greek Anthology*. The addressee is probably Lucius Sestius who succeeded Augustus as consul in the second half of 23 BC, although, like Horace, he had fought on the side of Brutus in the civil war. The ode is to be compared with 4.7 in a similar epodic metre.

Metre: Third Archilochian.

Added: 2 down the shore.

2   The sailing season has begun again.

5   **Cytherean**: the island of Cythera SW of Cape Malea in the Peloponnese was sacred to Venus because on her birth from the sea she was believed to have stepped ashore there.

6   **Graces**: 'Charites' in Greek; three daughters of Venus named Aglaia, Thalia, and Euphrosyne.

7   *grauis:* for this form of the acc. pl. see 1.1.17 n. and in this ode 14 *turris.*

8   The workshops of the Cyclopes were under volcanoes (named after the fire-god Vulcan).

9   **glistening**: with oil or unguent.
    myrtle: sacred to Venus.

11   **Faunus**: a Latin rustic god, identified with the Greek Pan.

12   *agna ... haedo:* for this ablative see *OLD immolare* 2b.

13   **Death**: the connexion with Faunus was first seen by Dr William Barr, who pointed out that Faunus' festival on the Ides (13th) of February was immediately followed in the Roman calendar by the Parentalia or festival of the dead.

16   *fabulae:* the noun is used as an adjective, cf. Persius 6.74 *popa uenter* 'Priest belly.'

17   **intangible**: *OLD exilis* 3, though this passage is quoted under 2 'ill-provided, poor;' one cannot get both in English.

18   *talis:* lit. 'knucklebones.'
    king of drinking: = the *arbiter bibendi* at a symposium, who decided the proportions in which wine and water should be mixed.

5

The most famous of all Horace's odes. Milton's unrhymed version of it is well known and in line 9 pushes English syntax to its limit:

Who now enjoyes thee credulous all Gold,

where 'credulous' refers to 'Who' (the boy) and 'all Gold' to 'thee' (Pyrrha). Sir Ronald Storrs made a collection of several hundred versions in different languages. A selection from this entitled *Ad Pyrrham* was published in 1959.

Metre: Third Asclepiad.

1   **in a large wreath of rose**: more often taken as 'lying on rose-petals.' 'Under the spreading rose' is also possible.

2   **Pyrrha**: the Greek name refers to the colour of her hair.

8   **unruffled**: see *OLD aequor* 3 'The sea, esp. considered as calm and flat.'

13–16 Here again, as in the first stanza, the Latin interweaving of nouns and adjectives cannot be represented in English. Literally 'Me a sacred wall with votive tablet indicates to have hung up drenched garments to powerful sea-god.' Survivors of a shipwreck would often put up an inscribed (and sometimes illustrated) plaque in the temple of the god they regarded as their saviour; they might also hang up a memento of their misadventure.

16   **a**: because 'the' would refer to Neptune. For the masculine referring to Venus cf. Calvus *pollentemque deum Venerem*, quoted by Servius on *Aeneid* 2.632 *ducente deo* (also Venus).

6

An ode in honour of Agrippa and Varius (for whom see the notes below) in the form of a 'recusatio' or demurrer, politely refusing an invitation to write epic verse celebrating the victories of Caesar and Agrippa.

Metre: Second Asclepiad.

1   **Varius**: Lucius Varius Rufus, a famous epic and tragic poet, who seconded Virgil in introducing Horace to his patron Maecenas and who later, with Plotius Tucca, supervised the posthumous publication of Virgil's *Aeneid*.

2   *Maeonii*: Homeric and therefore epic; Homer was thought to have been a native of Maeonia (Lydia).

5   **Agrippa**: Marcus Vipsanius Agrippa, Augustus' loyal adviser and most distinguished commander, defeated Sextus Pompey at Naulochus in 36 BC and Antony at Actium in 31 BC. He paid for many public works in Rome and married Augustus' daughter Julia.

6   *stomachum*: ironic for Achilles' 'wrath,' the subject of the *Iliad*.

7   Ironic reference to Odysseus and his wanderings in the *Odyssey*.

8   **Pelops' ... family**: Tantalus his father, his sons Atreus and Thyestes, his grandsons Agamemnon and Menelaus, and his great-grandchildren Electra and Orestes were frequent subjects of tragedy. Varius' *Thyestes* was famous and won him a million sesterces from Octavian.

12   Scan 'glorificaysh nand yours.'

14   **Meriones**: charioteer of the Cretan king Idomeneus in *Iliad* 15. He appears again with Diomedes at 1.15.26–28.

15   **Tydides**: Diomedes the son of Tydeus. In *Iliad* 5, egged on by Pallas Athene, he fights Ares (the Latin Mars) and Aphrodite (Venus), wounding them both.

16   Perhaps *quis* is 'which' (Horace or Varius) here, for *uter* 'which (of two); in any case the implied answer is probably 'only a Varius.' N–H suggest that Varius may have been 'contemplating a *Diomedeia*.'

18   *sectis*: possibly 'cut to a point;' it is not clear whether they have been cut back so as not to scratch or cut to a point to be able to scratch.

19   *siue*: *uel si*.

      if the heat is on: i.e. 'if I'm in Love.'

20   *non praeter*: = *secundum* 'according to.'

7

Lines 1–14 are similar in construction to the first ode in this Book: there various lifestyles are contrasted with that of the lyric poet; here various famous Greek cities, about which Hellenistic poets had written and were writing, are contrasted with the attractions of Tibur (modern Tivoli), where Maecenas had given Horace a small estate.

The second half, in the manner of Pindar, gives advice to the distinguished Plancus, a native of that place, and ends with an example from mythology to support the advice.

Lucius Munatius Plancus had been consul with Brutus in 42 BC, the year of Philippi, and in 41 joined Mark Antony in Asia. In 32 he switched allegiance to Octavian and in 27 was the senator who proposed that Octavian be given the cognomen Augustus.

Metre: First Archilochian.

Added: 11 a chord in my heart, 12 cascades, 20–21 now ... later, 26 There.

1   **far-famed**: the Latin *claram* can also mean 'bright' and refer to the sunshine of Rhodes.

3   Bacchus' mother Semele was daughter of Cadmus, founder of Thebes.

4   **Tempe**: a famous beauty spot where the river Peneios flows between Mts Ossa and Olympus.

6   **Pallas' city**: Athens.

8   **Juno**: Jupiter's wife, goddess of marriage. Identified with Hera, the wife of Zeus, who was specially worshipped in the Argolid and at Samos.

9   **ideal for horses**: because of its grassy plain. In Homer the formulaic epithet for Argos is 'horse-feeding,' *hippoboton*.

11   **Larissa**: in Thessaly.

12   **Albunea**: the Sibyl of Tibur.

13   **Tiburnus**: a founder of Tibur.

14   **changeable**: 'the water can be directed now into one channel, now into another' N–H.

15   **white**: because it clears the sky of clouds; the phrase translates the Greek *leukonotos*. The ordinary S wind (*notos*) brought rain. Ennius calls the sun *albus*.

19   **eagles**: the legionary standards.

21–32   Teucer was half-brother of the Homeric hero Ajax. When he returned home his father Telamon exiled him for not having avenged the death and disgrace of Ajax. Teucer sailed off to Cyprus and founded another Salamis there. This was the subject of Pacuvius' tragedy *Teucer*. Plancus' brother was proscribed and killed in 42 BC.

23   **Lyaeus**: 'the loosener,' cult title of Bacchus, here used for wine.

       poplar: sacred to Hercules, patron of wanderers; he had a special cult at Tibur.

8

The topic of heterosexual love as inimical to manly pursuits occurs in Greek and Roman comedy. Horace uses it here, where Sybaris is a young Roman who suddenly shirks the athletic and military sports that the sons of senators and knights practised for some two years after their assumption of the *toga uirilis*. Clearly Horace, or, if you prefer, the speaker takes a great interest in the boy, is presumably in love with him and blames Lydia for stealing him. The exaggeration of *properes amando perdere ... oderit ... timet Tiberim tangere ... sanguine uiperino cautius uitat* and the nickname 'the Sybarite' suggest frustrated emotion. The romantic comparison with Achilles at the end is helped by the hidden reference in 5–7 to the *Lusus Troiae* that connects Augustan Rome with heroic Troy.

Metre: Greater Sapphics.

Added: 12 or discus.

1   **Lydia**: a Greek courtesan who reappears in 1.13 and 25, and 3.9.

4   The Campus Martius was Rome's recreation ground.

5-7   The boys' equestrian training included the complicated and dangerous *lusus Troiae* described by Virgil (*Aeneid* 5.545–603) and revived by Augustus (Suetonius *Augustus* 43).

7   Gaul provided the best cavalry horses.

    wolf's-bit: a bit with jagged teeth.

10   **olive oil**: used by athletes to anoint themselves.

    display ... armour: or 'have forearms that are bruised by weapons.' Wooden foils were used for practice. One might get bruises on the shield-arm or the sword-arm.

14   **Thetis' son**: Achilles, son of the sea-nymph Thetis and the Greek hero Peleus. Knowing that he would die if he went to Troy, Thetis sent Achilles to Lycomedes king of Scyros, who dressed him in women's clothes and hid him in the women's apartments.

16   The Lycians were the Trojans' chief allies against the Greeks.

    cultus: OLD 5 and 8.

9

The first two stanzas are based on an ode of Alcaeus in the same metre, of which six lines (Fragment 338) are preserved by Athenaeus (*floruit* c. AD 200):

> Zeus is raining and from heaven comes a great
> Storm, and frozen are the streams of waters ...
>
> Defeat the storm by making up
> The fire and mixing unstintingly the wine
> Honey-sweet, but round your forehead
> Put a soft woollen band.

In Horace we are at a symposium *à deux*. 'Thaliarchus' is a genuine Greek name, whose etymology is probably 'lord of the feast.' It occurs on a 5th-century BC Athenian box as the name of a beautiful boy, and West reads the poem as 'the lover-poet consoling his beloved for the onset of puberty when he will no longer be attractive to men.' Horace combines Greek and Italian motifs, unworried by apparent inconsistencies, hinting at possible symbolism, displaying especially in the last stanza his mastery of linguistic mosaic.

Metre: Alcaics.

Added: 11 there, 22 heard.

1   **See**: lit. 'You see' (singular).

2   *Soracte:* in Etruria some 25 miles N of Rome.

7-8   The mixture of Greek and Latin is striking and perhaps symbolic of the Horatian ode. A Sabine *diota* (Greek for a 'two-eared' jar) would contain Sabine wine , which was inexpensive (presumably we are in Sabine country). — Quinn takes 'Thaliarchus' as jocular: 'Horace ... expects the *puer* to wait upon him ... dignifying him with a title absurdly out of keeping with the unpretentious wine he is to serve.'

18   **Campus**: see 1.8.4; it was also a place where lovers met.

21-24   Alternatively one can take *gratus puellae risus* and *pignus* as further subjects of *repetantur*.

10

A hymn in praise of Mercury/Hermes exhibiting the formal features of the genre: invocation of the god, his ancestry, relative clause introducing his main achievements, followed by his other attributes with a reference to legends about him and with anaphora (*te* 5 and 9, *tu* 17). Alcaeus had written a hymn to Hermes, of which the first stanza survives (Fragment 308b) — in Sapphics, which is also Horace's metre here:

> Lord of Mt Cyllene, all hail. For I've a
> Mind to sing of thee, whom among the high peaks
> Maia bore, pregnant by the son of Cronos,
> Ruler of all things.

Metre: Sapphics.

1   Bentley's punctuation *Mercuri, facunde nepos* ... is better but makes difficulties for the translator into Sapphics.
    grandson: see 1.2.41–44 n.
3   *uoce:* as god of eloquence.
4   *palaestrae:* wrestling, or the wrestling school. Hyginus *Fabulae* 277 *Mercurius et palaestram mortales primus docuit* 'Mercury was also the first to teach mankind wrestling.'
6   Mercury's invention of the lyre on the day of his birth is told in the Homeric *Hymn to Hermes* 24ff., as is the theft of Apollo's cattle but not of his quiver. He made the sounding-board of the lyre out of tortoise- or turtle-shell.
9–12 Alcaeus' hymn told of the theft of the cattle and presumably also of the quiver. Apollo must have felt for an arrow in order to give Hermes a fright, only to find that the quiver had been stolen while he was talking.
13–16 This famous incident occurs in *Iliad* 24 where the Trojan king Priam goes with rich presents into the Thessalian camp to ask Achilles for his son Hector's dead body.
14 **Atridae**: Agamemnon and Menelaus, sons (or grandsons) of Atreus.
17–20 Mercury as psychopomp or conductor of the souls of the dead to the Underworld makes a beautiful ending to the ode.
17–18 *laetis ... sedibus:* the Elysian Fields.

11

An offbeat love-poem (cf. 1.9). Lines 2b–3 and 6–8 are characteristically Epicurean, but the Master did not believe that gods had any interest in humans. West is especially good on this ode.

Metre: Greater Asclepiad.

2–3 **Leuconoe:** presumably an hetaera. The name is likely to have some bearing on the meaning of the poem, but what bearing is an open question. The literal etymology is 'white-mind.' Some take this to mean naïvety, others clear-headedness.
    Babylonios ... numeros: the calculations involved in casting a horoscope. Astrology began in Babylonia and in Horace's time was taken seriously by many of the well educated, notably the Stoics. The Epicureans rejected its claims.
5   The Latin is a fine example of rhythmic onomatopoeia.
6   *uina liques:* perhaps implies 'Take trouble with life's pleasures, so as to make the most of them.'

12

Pindar's second *Olympian Ode* begins 'Hymns that rule the lyre, what God, what hero, and what man shall we celebrate?' Horace addresses the same questions in reverse order to Clio, later the Muse of history. In constructing an ode to answer them he avoids as usual the obvious and clear-cut. Three stanzas (13–24) deal with gods, two (25–32) with Greek heroes (demi-gods), four (33–48) with a Roman hero (demi-god) and Roman men, three (49–60) return to Jupiter and introduce his vicegerent Caesar *diui filius*.

Metre: Sapphics

Added: 20 Surely, 25 twin, 30 Stormy, 36 the Younger, 48 Sky's.

5–6   These mountains, Helicon in Boeotia, Pindus in Thessaly, Haemus in Thrace were famous as haunts of the Muses.

9   Orpheus' mother was the Muse Calliope.

14   **Parent**: Jupiter/Zeus (in Homer 'Father of men and gods.'). The rhapsodes who recited Homeric poetry always began with Zeus. So Aratus (*Phaenomena* 1) says 'From Zeus let us begin,' cf. Virgil *Eclogue* 3.60 *ab Ioue principium*. See 3.1.5–8 n.

19   **Pallas**: Zeus' first wife was Metis ('Counsel'), daughter of Tethys and Oceanus. When she became pregnant Zeus swallowed her for fear she would produce a child wiser than himself. In due course Pallas Athena (= the Roman Minerva) was born fully armed from his head.

22   **Liber**: 'Free,' a cult title of Bacchus, god of wine, the son of Jupiter by Semele.
    the Virgin: Diana/Artemis, daughter of Jupiter and Latona, and sister of Phoebus Apollo.

25   The heroes come now, i.e. the sons of gods by mortal mothers: Hercules, son of Jupiter and Alcmena ('Alcides' because grandson of Alceus), and Castor and Pollux, for whom see 1.3.2 n. Castor was the horseman, Pollux the boxer.

34   **Romulus**: Rome's founder; though a demi-god (son of Mars by Ilia) he heads the list of famous Roman men.
    Pompilius: Numa, founder of Roman religion, succeeded Romulus as king of Rome.

35   **Collatine**: the Latin has Tarquinius, who is clearly not Tarquin the Proud or Tarquinius Priscus, but can be taken as Tarquinius Collatinus, the first consul and founder with Brutus of the Roman republic. His rods are consular rods and 'proud' to distinguish him from Superbus. Horace cannot mention Brutus because of the tyrannicide and the word Collatinus is awkward in Sapphics; for him see *OCD*[3] Tarquinius Collatinus.

36   **Cato the Younger**: Horace's contemporary, who fought against Julius Caesar and committed suicide at Utica in 46 BC. He was a famous Stoic whose death could mark the end of the Roman republic.

37   **Regulus**: see 3.5.13ff. n.
    Scauri: Marcus Aemilius Scaurus, consul 115 BC, and his son who committed suicide after fleeing from the Cimbri in 102 BC rather than face his father; alternatively Marcus Aurelius Scaurus, consul 108 BC, captured by the Cimbri and killed for advising them that there was no point in their crossing the Alps — the Romans were invincible. See N–H.
    Paullus: Lucius Aemilius Paullus, consul 216 BC, chose to die at Cannae rather than escape as he might have done without dishonour.

39   **with Camena's glory**: i.e. with Italian poetic glory, Camena being the native Latin Muse.

40   **Fabricius**: Gaius Fabricius Luscinus, consul 282 BC, famous for his in-
        corruptibility in the war against Pyrrhus.
41   **Dentatus**: Marcus Curius Dentatus, consul 275 BC, another incorruptible hero of
        the war against Pyrrhus.
        Camillus: Marcus Furius Camillus, whom Livy calls 'saviour of his country and
        second founder of Rome', describing how as Dictator he saved Rome from the
        Gauls after the Roman defeat at the Allia in 390 BC (*Histories* 5.49.7–10).
46   **Marcellus**: the most famous was Marcus Claudius, conqueror of Syracuse in 212
        BC, but the Roman reader would be reminded of Augustus' nephew Marcus
        Claudius, who married Augustus' daughter Julia in 25 BC but died young in 23
        BC.
47   **Julian star**: the reader would think of the comet that appeared at Julius Caesar's
        funeral games in 44 BC, but probably also of Augustus, Caesar's adopted son.
52   **Seconding**: there is no inconsistency with line 18 where it is a question of power,
        but here it is a question of support, though of course the other meaning cannot be
        excluded.
53   **Parthians**: see 1.2.22 n.
60   **lightnings**: strictly 'thunderbolts.'

13

Horace here declares an interest in Lydia that did not surface in 1.8. She has found
another toy boy, and Horace presents the reader with a physiological description of angry
and jealous love to set against the ideal pictured in the last four lines. The translation is
freer than usual. See Introduction p. xv.

Metre: Fourth Asclepiad.

Added: 2 And ... and, 3 yuk. I can feel it, 4 and oedematous, 6 Shaken out of, 10
Fuelled, 12 lower, 18 mutual.

1   **Telephus**: recurs in 3.19 and 4.11.
2   *cerea:* refers to pallor as well as smoothness.
4–8   The liver in antiquity was thought to be the seat of the violent emotions; cf.
        Horace *Satires* 1.9.66 *meum iecur urere bilis* 'bile was burning my liver,' i.e. he
        was furious. — One is reminded of the totally different symptoms in Catullus 51.
16   **The quintessence ... nectar**: lit. 'the fifth part of her own nectar.' West has
        shown how this can be taken as referring to the Aristotelian 'fifth essence' or
        (loosely) 'finest part' of anything.

14

We are lucky enough to have Quintilian's explanation of this ode. In his *Institutio
Oratoria* 8.6.44 (published c. AD 95) he says that it is an allegory of the type that con-
sists of an extended metaphor: the ship is the Roman republic, the storms civil wars, the
harbour peace and concord. This interpretation is generally accepted, especially as
Alcaeus had used the same allegory in two of his poems (Fragments 6 and 208) and it is
probable that Horace has taken over the idea from him. But one should not press the
allegory here too far and demand explanations of 'mast,' 'yard-arms,' 'ropes' etc. —
There is no agreement about its likely date, but one possibility is the time of Odes 1.2.

Metre: Third Asclepiad.

Added: 7 to gird it.

5   *celeri ... Africo:* lit. 'Swift Africus,' the SW wind of 1.1.15 and 1.3.12.

11   *Pontica pinus:* Pontus, especially Bithynia, was famous for timber and ship-building. The phrase would have point if referring to Aeneas' fleet, made with timber from the Propontis area, when he sailed from Troy to begin the foundation of Rome.

17–18   *nuper ... nunc:* lately during the civil war and now when it could break out again.

20   **glistening**: 'the reader should visualize not white-washed villages but (imaginary) marble cliffs. Cf. 3.28.14 *fulgentis ... Cycladas* [gleaming Cyclades], Virg. *Aen.* 3.126 *niueamque Parum* [and snow-white Paros], Ov. *Epist.* 21.82 *candida Delos* [white Delos]' N–H.

    Cyclades: 'the Cyclades are and were notorious for their winds' N–H.

15

Porphyrio tells us that in this ode Horace imitates Bacchylides who makes Cassandra prophesy the future of the Trojan war. Bacchylides was a 5th-century BC Greek choral lyric poet. Horace's imitation cannot have been close, because he puts the prophecy in the mouth of the sea-god Nereus, while Paris is sailing back with Helen from Sparta to Troy. Perhaps Horace wanted to try his hand at dealing with an epic theme in the metre of solo lyric (monody). Paris and Helen may well have reminded his contemporary readers of Antony and Cleopatra, but there is no allegory here.

Metre: Second Asclepiad.

Added: 28 great, 36 all.

1   *Pastor:* can mean 'herdsman' as well as 'shepherd.' Paris as an infant was exposed on Mt Ida, found by shepherds and brought up among them.

2   *Idaeis:* because built of timber from Ida.

7   **match**: marriage to Helen, promised him by Venus when he awarded her the beauty prize in preference to Juno and Minerva. — Virgil places the swearing of the oath at Aulis, and at *Aeneid* 4.425–426 makes Dido say: *non ego cum Danais Troianam exscindere gentem/ Aulide iuraui classemue ad Pergama misi* 'It was not I who swore with the Greeks at Aulis to destroy the Trojan race nor I who sent the fleet to Troy.'

10   **Dardan**: Troy was founded by Dardanus, Priam's great-great-great-grandfather.

11   **aegis**: a shield covered with goat-skin, fringed with snakes, and at its centre Medusa's frightful head.

15   *carmina diuides:* the precise meaning of this is disputed.

17   **Cnossian**: Cnossus was the capital of Crete, and Cretans were famous as archers.

18   **Ajax**: not the great Ajax but the son of Oileus, called 'swift' at *Iliad* 14.520.

19   **powdering**: lit. 'smearing,' with dust instead of unguent, as he lies on the ground dying.

21   **Laertiades**: Ulysses, son of Laertes, was responsible for the wooden horse that caused Troy's capture (*Odyssey* 8.494).

22   **Nestor**: the wise old counsellor from Pylos.

24   **Teucer**: 1.7.21 n.

    Sthenelus: charioteer of Diomedes.

26   **Meriones**: 1.6.14 n.

27   **Diomed**: an older English spelling of Diomedes, son of Tydeus. Tydeus was one of the 'Seven against Thebes,' his son one of the greatest heroes after Achilles.

16

In this ode Horace addresses an anonymous female whom he has earlier satirized and to whom he now hands over his copy of the libellous verses. He tries to placate her anger with a lengthy and amusingly pompous diatribe on anger's origin, effects and perils. He too in his young days when he wrote the offending verses had fallen a victim to it, but now wishes to be friends with her again.

Metre: Alcaics.

Added: 21 flattened, 27 all.

1   Perhaps translated from a Greek line originally referring to Helen of Troy, daughter of Leda by Jupiter in the form of a swan.

3   **Iambics**: from Archilochus (c.700 BC) onwards the iambic trimeter was used as the metre for invective verse, so that the word *iambi* can mean invective verse in other metres too.

5   **Dindymene**: the Phrygian Goddess Cybele whose native cult place was Mt Dindymus. Her orgiastic priests, the Galli, made themselves eunuchs.
    Pythian: Apollo. Python was the old name for Delphi, his best known oracular shrine where the priestess went into a trance and prophesied.

7   **Liber**: 1.12.22 n.
    Corybantes: young male priests whose orgiastic music and dances were associated with Cybele, Bacchus, and Rhea.

9   **Norican**: an area comprising the Austrian Alps, famous for its steel.

12   **hurtling**: has to be three syllables here.

13   There was a legend that Prometheus (literally 'Forethinker') created the first man and woman out of clay. In Horace's version he appears to have no human qualities available to add to this but is forced to use animal ones.

17   The anger is that of Atreus against his brother Thyestes for seducing his wife. Varius (1.6.1 n.) had recently produced his tragedy *Thyestes*.

18   **cities**: such as Carthage whose walls were totally destroyed by the Romans in 146 BC and their site ploughed over.

27   **recanted**: the word *recantatis* is coined here by Horace to refer to the famous 'recantation' (Greek *palinodia*) of Stesichorus (6th century BC) who was said to have been blinded when he criticized Helen of Troy in a poem but regained his sight when he wrote a palinode.

28   ***animum ... reddas:*** understand *meum* (*OLD reddo* 1c) and *tuum* (*OLD animus* 9c).

17

An invitation to a girl to leave the city and join Horace on his Sabine farm, which is under the protection of the god Faunus (the Latin Pan), for an idyllic musical drinking party.

The identity of metre and the name Tyndaris (originally used of Helen of Troy, step-daughter of Tyndareus, cf. 1.16.1 n.) suggested to Porphyrio that Tyndaris is also the anonymous addressee of 1.16.

Metre: Alcaics.

Added: 4 of winter, 9 Roman, 19 two.

1   *Lucretilem:* according to Porphyrio a mountain in Sabine country, perhaps the modern Monte Gennaro.

2	*Lycaeo:* a mountain sacred to Pan in Arcadia.
4	The Latin simply has 'and rainy winds.'
6	**elusive**: with both nouns in the Latin, cf. 1.31.6 n.
7	**husband**: the he-goat.
9	**sacred to ... Mars**: a she-wolf suckled Romulus and Remus, twin sons of Mars, the Roman god of war.
10	*fistula:* the pan-pipe. Is Faunus playing, or a shepherd, or even Tyndaris?
12	**Ustica**: another Sabine mountain (Porphyrio).
13	*di:* also used of great men, cf. *Satires* 2.6.52 *deos quoniam propius contingis* 'since you are more closely connected with the gods.' The double meaning avoids smugness and compliments Maecenas.
16	*ruris honorum:* corn, fruit, vegetables, and flowers.
	into your lap: lit. 'for you.'
17	*Caniculae:* the Dogstar (Sirius) whose rising in July brings on the dog days, hottest time of the year in the Mediterranean area.
18	**Teian strings**: the lyre of Anacreon of Teos, 6th-century BC Greek poet of love and wine.
19	**one man**: Ulysses.
20	**brittle**: lit. 'glassy,' 'glittering.' Publilius Syrus (1st century BC) has *Fortuna vitrea est; tum cum splendet frangitur* 'Fortune is brittle; when she shines she breaks.' It is not clear why Circe is so called. She was not a sea-goddess, but perhaps needed careful handling. Porphyrio is puzzled: *'uitream' parum decore mihi uidetur dixisse pro 'candidam.'* 'I feel that he has put "glassy" inappropriately for "white" .'
22–23	**Semeleian / Thyoneus**: cult titles of Bacchus, son of Semele who was also called Thyone.

18

Nothing is known for certain about the Varus to whom this ode is addressed except that he has an estate near Tibur.

Horace begins by translating a line of Alcaeus (Fragment 342) in the same metre:

> There is no other tree you are to plant earlier than the vine.

He goes on to sing the praises of wine in moderation. He is supported by the findings of six Danish doctors (*British Medical Journal* for 6 May 1995 p.1165) who conclude that drinking up to five glasses of wine a day halves one's chances of dying of heart disease!

Metre: Greater Asclepiad.

Added: 13 Therefore.

2	**Catilus**: a founder of Tibur and brother of Tiburnus (1.7.13 n.).
3	**the God**: Bacchus.
4	**any other way**: than by wine-drinking.
7	**Liber**: 1.12.22 n.
8	**brawl**: the famous fight begun by the Centaurs at the wedding of Pirithous, king of the Lapithae, and Hippodamia. The fight was represented on the Parthenon metopes, now in the British Museum.
9	**Sithonians**: a Thracian tribe. Sithonia was the middle and wildest of the three Chalcidean peninsulas. The English metre requires a strong break in the word: Si-thonians.
	Euhius: cult title of Bacchus. This story is otherwise unknown.

10–11 'When in their eagerness for lust they separate right and wrong by a narrow line'
N–H.
Bassareus: another cult title of Bacchus.
11–12 must refer to profanation of the Bacchic mysteries. The orgia or mystic emblems
of the god were concealed under leaves in a sacred casket, the *cista mystica*.
14–15 **camp-followers**: because drunkenness encourages self-centred boasting and
betrayal of secrets.
Berecynthian: a bass horn used in the worship of Bacchus (Catullus 64.263) and
of Cybele, who had a shrine on Mt Berecynthus in Phrygia.
plus nimio: 'more than what is too much, i.e. far too much, to excess' (*OLD
nimium*[1] 1c).

19

Horace represents himself as love's victim yet again, though he had thought he was
through with loving. Glycera (the Greek name means 'Sweetie') is the trouble and he
prepares to sacrifice to Venus in the hope of mercy. The theme comes from early Greek
lyric and later occurs in the *Greek Anthology* (see N–H).

Metre: Fourth Asclepiad.

Added: 1 sweet, 3 All, 4 I thought.

1   **cruel Mother of sweet Desires**: Venus; 'sweet' has been added from 4.1.4–5.
2   **Semele's boy**: Bacchus.
3   **All as one**: replaces the 'ands' connecting the preceding nouns.
6   **white ... stone**: lit. 'marble.' The marble quarried on Paros was famous for its
brilliant whiteness.
10   **Cyprus**: 1.3.1 n.
11   The Scythians and the Parthians provided subjects for contemporary epic poetry.
The former, a nomadic people, occupied an area north of the Black Sea from the
Carpathians to the Don; for the Parthians see 1.2.22 n.

20

Why does Horace offer his patron cheap Sabine wine, when at 1.17.21 he offers Tyndaris
'innocuous Lesbian' and at 4.11.2 Phyllis a nine-year-old Alban, both classy wines? Why
was this Sabine wine stored in a Greek jar? We are half-way through Book 1; the
twentieth ode is first in the second group of 19 odes and like the first ode in the first
group of 19 celebrates Maecenas. It pictures the easy man-to-man relationship between
poet and patron. Contrast Philodemus' invitation to Piso in the *Greek Anthology*, 11.44,
with its fawning final couplet. We are probably to imagine Horace talking to Maecenas
who has visited him on his Sabine farm by invitation or even unexpectedly. The wine is
Sabine because Maecenas has given Horace the farm there. It is stored in a Greek jar
because in the literal meaning the jar, having contained better wine, would improve the
taste of the local wine, and in the metaphorical because the form of Horace's odes is
Greek. Catullus in poem 27 had used wine as a symbol of poetry. In that case the last
stanza here would refer to grander and more generally accepted types of poetry, such as
that of Varius and Virgil, if not to Maecenas' own 'precious' and extravagant literary
productions.

Metre: Sapphics.

Added: 3 that year, 5 Tiber, 8 doubly.

2	***cantharis***: *cantharus* was a Greek two-handled wine-cup.
3	Cf. 2.17.22–26; Maecenas had recovered from a serious illness.
5	***care Maecenas***: cf. 2.20.7 *dilecte Maecenas*. Some later MSS read *clare*, which Bentley and Housman support as going with *eques*; but the point is that *eques* has no adjective here, mirroring Maecenas' determination to be nothing more.
6	**paternal river**: the Tiber rises in the district of Arezzo, Maecenas' home town (N–H).
9	**Caecuban ... Calenian**: high-class wines from Latium and Campania respectively.
10	**you provide**: Munro's *uides* (*OLD* 19) for the awkward *bibes* of the MSS. These wines are what Maecenas provides for his guests at home. Keeping *tu bibes* one translates 'you can quaff' taking the future as at 1.7.1 *Laudabunt alii* 'Others can praise ....'
11–12	**Falernian ... Formian**: choice wines from Campania and Latium respectively.

21

A hymn supposedly for a double choir of girls and boys in honour of Diana and Apollo and their mother Latona, ending with a prayer. The ode invites comparison with Catullus 34, also for a double choir of girls and boys and in a related metre. The main difference is that Catullus 34 is a real hymn, in which the chorus refer to themselves as 'we,' whereas in Horace the poet (or is it the two choir leaders?) refers to the choir as 'you' and tells them what to do.

Metre: Third Asclepiad.

Added: 1 in honour, (*tenerae* omitted), 8 Lycian, 10 island, 12 full, 16 to action.

2	**Cynthius**: Apollo was born on Mt Cynthus on Delos; similarly Diana is Cynthia.
5	**girls**: lit. 'you.'
	leaves: lit. 'tresses.'
6	**Algidus**: a peak in the Alban hills near Tusculum in Latium SE of Rome. The adjective *gelido* refers to the meaning of the name. The temple of Diana Nemorensis was not far off.
7–8	**Erymanthine ... Cragus**: Erymanthus is a mountain in Arcadia: Cragus was one in Lycia.
9	**Tempe**: 1.7.4 n.
12	**brother's lyre**: because it was invented by Mercury, Apollo's half-brother (see 1.10.6).

22

One of the Seven Sages of Greece, Bias of Priene, is reported to have said that 'a good conscience' (*orthē syneidesis*) is 'fearless' (*aphobon*). Horace starts with an extension of this thought (1–8), and supports it with a personal experience (9–10), drawing from this a surprise ending (17–24) which undercuts the apparent seriousness of the opening.

Metre: Sapphics.

Added: 8 stream, 10 unafraid.

4	**Aristius**: added from *Satires* 1.9.61, where we gather that he is a close friend with a sense of humour.
5–8	Cf. Catullus 11.5–8, also in Sapphics.
6	**Syrtes**: here = the Libyan desert.

217

8   **Hydaspes**: the furthest river reached by Alexander — in NW India and now called the Jhelum.

9   **Lalage**: the Greek name means 'Chatterbox;' so 24 *dulce loquentem*.

11   **Sabellian**: Horace refers to himself as *Sabellus* at *Epistles* 1.16.49 in the context of his Sabine farm, and Servius on Virgil *Georgics* 3.255 explains *Sabellicus* as *Sabinus*.
            wolf: 'during the exceptional cold spell of February 1956 a postman was attacked and eaten by wolves near the village of Mandela, in the immediate neighbourhood of Horace's farm' Fraenkel 186 n. 3.

14   **Land of Daunus**: Apulia, colonized by the legendary Illyrian king Daunus, cf. 3.30.11.

15   **Juba**: Juba II king of Mauretania, a learned man and a prolific writer.

23–24 Cf Tibullus 1.2.27–28 *quisquis amore tenetur eat tutusque sacerque/ qualibet; insidias non timuisse decet* 'The love-possessed are sacred, safe to wander where they will;/ To fear no ambush is their privilege.'

23   *dulce ridentem*: cf. Catullus 51.5, also in Sapphics.

23

The idea of this ode may have come from Anacreon (see 1.17.18 n.), author of the following fragment (408):

> Gently as fawn, new-born,
> Unweaned, which trembles when left
> In a wood by its horned mother.

Metre: Third Asclepiad

Added: 4 fitful.

1   **You are running away**: lit. 'You avoid me.'
            Chloe: the name means 'fresh, green shoot.'

5–6   *ueris ... aduentus*: this is the reading of the MSS, but many editors accept the emendation *uepris ... ad uentum* 'a thorn-bush with fluttering leaves shivers in the wind;' such a bush would have to have bigger leaves on longer stalks than our hawthorn.

9   **Gaetulan**: the Gaetuli were a Mauretanian (Moroccan) tribe.

24

An epicedium or funeral ode, addressed to the poet Virgil on the death of a common friend, Quintilius Varus of Cremona (Porphyrio), instanced by Horace at *Ars Poetica* 438ff. as a model literary critic.

Metre: Second Asclepiad.

Added: 14 forest, 17 our human, 18 of ghosts.

1–2a   Paraphrase; literally 'What shame or limit could there be to longing for so dear a head.' Paraphrased by Pater even more freely: 'What thought of others' thoughts about one could there be with the regret for "so dear a head" fresh at one's heart?' (*Marius* Part 1 *ad fin.*)

3   **Melpomene**: appealed to as the Muse of lyric verse, cf. 3.30.16 and 4.3.1, etymologically from Greek *melpomai* 'I sing and dance;' later she became the Muse of Tragedy.

11 **pius**: one thinks of *pius Aeneas*, but the *Aeneid* was not yet published, though Virgil could have given readings from it to friends.

12 **in their keeping on other terms**: the Latin has 'entrusted on other terms,' not making it clear whether Quintilius was entrusted to the gods or to Virgil. If the second, read 'Only lent you on other terms.'

17 **Not disposed**: in the Latin goes with Mercury.

18 See 1.10.17–19.

20 Closer 'What it's wicked to seek to mend.' But *corrigere* is a word that Quintilius as literary critic must have used a good deal, cf. *Ars Poetica* 438–9 *Quintilio si quid recitares, 'corrige, sodes,/ hoc' aiebat 'et hoc,'* 'If you recited anything to Quintilius, "Correct this, please, and this" was his response' and it must come in the translation.

25

A variant of the paraclausithyron, or song at the closed door; cf. 3.10. Lydia has already appeared twice: at 1.8 as leading Sybaris astray and at 1.13 as in love with Telephus and making Horace jealous. She will appear again at 3.9 in a delightful love duet, but in this ode Horace gets his own back, pleased by the decline in her clientele and prophesying for her a nymphomaniac old age. 4.13 makes an interesting comparison.

Metre: Sapphics.

Added: 1 they come, 2 gravel, 6 the cry.

3–4 **amatque/ ianua limen**: the door does not open but hugs the threshold as lovers are so few.

7–8 The excluded lover's complaint in the past.

10 **leuis**: OLD 12 and 13 'powerless' and 'insignificant,' because in her heyday she had been 'fickle' (*OLD* 15).

11–12 The dark time between the old moon and the new was thought to bring bad weather.

14 Cf. Virgil *Georgics* 3.266 *scilicet ante omnis furor est insignis equarum* 'Certainly the mad lust of mares above all is remarkable.'

15 **liver**: 1.13.4 n.

18 **ivy and ... myrtle**: presumably represent blonde and brunette. Ivy is Bacchus' plant and myrtle that of Venus.

26

The Lamia of this ode is presumably the Lamia of 1.36.7 and the Aelius Lamia of 3.17. He must have been interested in literature for Horace to dedicate this early poem in Alcaics to him, and the scholiast on *Ars Poetica* 288 records an Aelius Lamia as writer of plays on Roman themes. The words *fontibus integris* (6) and *fidibus nouis* (10) combined with the unique break between words in line 11 after the fourth syllable suggest that this may well have been Horace's first attempt at Alcaics. He is feeling overjoyed at having naturalized this Lesbian metre in Latin.

Metre: Alcaics.

Added: 12 eight.

3–4 may refer to Cotiso, king of the Dacians, a warlike people north of the Danube in modern Romania who moved south and threatened the Roman frontier; cf. 3.8.18.

5   Tiridates made himself king of Parthia about the time of Actium but was defeated by Phraates in 30 BC and fled to Octavian. He won the kingship again in 26 but was again ejected by Phraates in 25; cf. 3.8.19–20.

6   *fontibus integris:* literary sources previously untapped; here Alcaeus. Cf. Lucretius 1.927–8 *iuuat integros accedere fontis/ atque haurire, iuuatque nouos decerpere flores* ... 'it's a joy to go to unpolluted springs and drink, it's a joy to pick fresh flowers ....'

7   *flores:* verses.

8   *coronam:* presumably the garland is this poem, unless it includes the next ode, which is also in Alcaics.

9   *Pimplei:* vocative of *Pimpleis* 'Lady of Pimpla.' Pimpla or Pimplea was a place and a spring near Mt Olympus associated with Orpheus and the Muses, who are sometimes called *Pimpleides.*

10   *fidibus nouis:* new lyric verse.

11   *Lesbio... plectro:* in a Lesbian metre.

27

Porphyrio reports that the idea for this ode came from Anacreon Book 3, and there are two Anacreontic fragments that must have been part of the poem in question. In Fragment 356a the poet calls for a bowl mixed with two parts of water to one of wine; 356b reads (roughly):

> Come again, let us no longer
> With banging and with shouting
> Go in for Scythian drinking
> Of wine, but drink to beauti-
> ful songs in moderation.

Quinn calls the ode 'the most animated of H.'s dramatic monologues.' It has three sections: 1–8, 9–18, 18–24.

Metre: Alcaics. (Horace does not use Anacreontics.)

Added: 2 downright, 6–7 please/ Just, 17 And so, 20 far, 23 Why.

1–8   The poet intervenes, pleading for moderation in drinking.

2   The Thracians were well known as heavy drinkers.

3   *uerecundumque Bacchum*: cf. 1.18.7 *modici ... Liberi.*

5   *acinaces*: 'a long straight dagger used by the Persians and Scyths' N–H. The word occurs in Fragment 465 of Anacreon.

9–12   The poet is invited to take part and agrees provided that a young Greek drinker reveals his love.

10   **Falernian**: 1.20.11 n.
        Opuntian: from Opus, a town in Locris, north of Lake Copais in Boeotia. 'The implication is that Megylla is better known to H's audience than her brother (and herself present)' Quinn.

13–18   The poet encourages the reluctant boy to speak out.

14   **Venus**: 'charmer' J. Gow. Cf. 1.33.13.

18–24   He hears the whispered secret and comments on it.

19   **Charybdis**: the monster opposite Scylla in the straits of Messina, used here of a voracious hetaera.

22   **Thessaly**: famous for witchcraft.

24 **Chimaera**: a monster with lion's head, serpent tail and goatish middle (*Iliad* 6.181), killed by Bellerophon mounted on Pegasus, the winged horse, but representing here a combination of quick temper, deceitfulness, and lust.

28

It is not until lines 21–22 that the reader of this remarkable ode realizes that the speaker of lines 1–20 is not Horace but the ghost of a drowned man (23–24). The ghost begins by addressing the famous Pythagorean mathematician Archytas of Tarentum near whose tomb he is standing, and then at line 23 turns to address a passing sailor and to beg for burial.

Metre: First Archilochian (only here and in *Epode* 12, suggesting that the ode is an early experiment, combining and expanding two types of Greek funerary epigram).

Added: 4 now, 11 he had lived in, 12 then, 13 the Goddesses, 28 lap, 34 ever, 36 over me.

3 The precise whereabouts of the Matine shore are obscure — somewhere on the coast of Calabria or Apulia.
 exiguous dust: the amount of earth required to bury Archytas was as nothing compared to the total of sandgrains in the world.
5 **aerial houses**: perhaps in the astrological sense of Signs of the Zodiac.
7 **Pelops' father**: Tantalus, a son of Jupiter, the Gods' favourite mortal and later the great sinner, whose sin is variously reported.
8 **Tithonus**: Priam's brother, carried up to heaven by Aurora, goddess of the dawn. She obtained immortality for him from Zeus but forgot to ask for eternal youth, so he grew ever older and more decrepit until finally the goddess turned him into a cicada. If the text is right Horace must be counting this metamorphosis as a death, cf. 2.16.30.
9 **Minos**: the Cretan king, son of Jupiter and Europa, and Jupiter's confidant.
10 **Panthoides**: the Homeric hero Euphorbus, son of Panthus. His shield hung in the temple of Hera at Argos and the philosopher Pythagoras by recognizing it proved that in a previous life he had been Euphorbus; so the patronymic here refers to Pythagoras.
 Orcus: Pluto, king of the Underworld.
15 **nature and truth**: 'almost a hendiadys for "the truth about nature" ' J. Gow.
16 *semel*: 'once only' need not contradict *iterum* (10); Euphorbus died once, Pythagoras also died once. Others take it as a flat denial of the truth of Pythagoras' claim to reincarnation.
17 I.e. some die in the madness of war.
20 **Proserpina**: wife of Pluto; she cut off a lock of hair from those about to die (Virgil *Aeneid* 4. 698).
21 *me quoque*: need not imply that Archytas was drowned; the speaker may simply mean that he like other sailors drowned or like others is dead.
 Illyrian waves: the Adriatic.
 Notus: 1.3.14 n.
22 **setting Orion**: in November when stormy weather sets in.
24 *capiti inhumato*: the hiatus is surprising.
25 **Eurus**: 1.25.20.
26 **Hesperian**: Italy was named poetically *Hesperia* 'the western land.'
 Venusia: in Apulia, Horace's birthplace.
28 **to your lap**: lit. 'to you.'

29   Neptune was father of Taras the legendary founder of Tarentum.

30   *neglegis*.: *OLD* 1b.

35–36 For ritual burial it was enough to cast earth three times on the corpse.
      run: or 'sail' (*OLD curro* 3a).

29

Iccius, who reappears in *Epistles* 1.12 as manager of Agrippa's Sicilian estates, is about to join the staff of the prefect of Egypt, Aelius Gallus, in an expedition against Arabia Felix (25 BC — see *Res Gestae* 26.5). He had previously been studying philosophy, perhaps at Athens, and Horace teases him about his supposed volte-face.

Metre: Alcaics.

Added: 6 in battle.

4   **Sheba**: the Sabaei inhabited the south-western corner of the Arabian peninsula, today's Yemen; a rich trading nation, they chiefly dealt in spices of all kinds (see Strabo 16.780).

5   **Parthian**: lit. 'Mede,' cf. 1.2.22 and 51 n. Horace exaggerates intentionally, pretending that the expedition will later attack Parthia.

     tibi: not only the object of *seruiet* but dative of the agent with *necato*. Horace jokingly turns Iccius into an Achilles, who had killed the husband of Briseis before making her his concubine (*Iliad* 19.295ff. and cf. 2.4.2 n.).

9   **Serican**: more exaggeration; China will be attacked after Parthia.

13   **Panaetius**: the famous 2nd-century BC Stoic philosopher who joined the circle of Scipio Aemilianus at Rome in 144 BC and was head of the Stoic school at Athens from 129–109. His best-known work was *Peri tou kathekontos* 'On Duty,' which Cicero used for his *De Officiis*.

     nobilis: for this accusative plural see 1.1.17 n.; or it could be taken as genitive singular with *Panaeti*.

15   **Socrates' household**: probably the Stoics, who claimed descent from Socrates.

     Spanish: Spanish steel was famous. For 'breastplates' one could read 'chain-mail.'

16   **in spite of ... promise**: ironic. 'You are a disappointment. We all expected better of you.'

30

Glycera reappears from 1.19. The ode is a development of a cletic (i.e. invocatory) hymn, in the form of a Hellenistic epigram. Glycera is a courtesan; the shrine her house, and Horace elegantly hopes that her attractions will bring her many young lovers to civilize and a good income (Mercury being the god of gain). This ingenious advertisement would put Glycera in Horace's debt. West takes the ode differently — as a sequel to 1.19.9–16: 'Stripped of its theology, that is to say violated and diminished, 1.30 means that Horace wishes to find Glycera passionate, uninhibited, gracious, and joyous, and that he himself longs for the return of his vitality, charm, and youthfulness.'

Metre: Sapphics.

1–2   Cnidos in Caria and Paphos in Cyprus were cult centres of Aphrodite/Venus.

5   **passionate Boy**: Cupid.

31

The temple on the Palatine that Octavian had vowed to Apollo to celebrate the defeat of Sextus Pompey at Mylae in 36 BC and of Antony and Cleopatra at Actium in 31 BC was finally dedicated on 9 October 28 BC. Two days later came the annual festival of the Meditrinalia (from *meditrina* probably = *medicina*, one of Apollo's concerns) when libations of the year's new wine were poured in expectation of good health. Lines 2–3 imply that it is at this festival Horace addresses his prayer to Apollo.

Metre: Alcaics.

Added: 2 the year's (to make clear the reference to Meditrinalia), 16 Olives and.

6   **Indian**: in the Latin goes with 'gold' as well, the so-called *apo koinou* ('in common') construction.
7   **Liris**: 'a river entering the Tyrrhenian sea near Minturnae, now the Garigliano' (*OLD*).
10   **Calene**: 1.20.9 n.
13   **Gods' favourite too**: i.e. not only fortune's.
17   **Latoan**: son of Leto/Latona, see 1.21 introduction.
20   **lyric**: lit. 'the cithara' for music and lyric poetry. The statue of Palatine Apollo represented him as playing the lyre and singing (Propertius 2.31.5–6).

32

A prayer to the Lesbian lyre for a Latin ode in the tradition of Alcaeus. This poem itself may be the ode requested, cf. 1.26 which is probably the garland to be woven for Lamia. Indeed, if 1.26 represents the first poem in Alcaics that Horace wrote, perhaps this is the first one in Sapphics. In that case the earlier verses he refers to would be in Asclepiads, a metre used by Alcaeus, who of course also used Sapphics.

Metre: Sapphics.

1   *Poscimus*: picks up 1.31.1 *poscit*, connecting the two poems.
     I: lit. 'we;' the Latin plural is easier to handle in this metre.
     barbitos: 1.1.34 n.
2   *quod*: Bentley takes *Latinum ... carmen* (3–4) as the antecedent. Most editors refer it to *quid* (1); in that case translate the first stanza:

> I beseech you, barbitos, if at leisure
> In the shade I've ever produced with you light
> Verse to live for this year and more, come voice a
> Lyric in Latin.

5   *Lesbio ... ciui*: the description of Alcaeus as 'a citizen of Lesbos' reminds the reader of his party-political verse *(stasiotika)*.
7   *udo*: 'in the tideless Mediterranean wet sand suggests that there has been a storm' N–H. Mr Anthony Bowen supposes that the beach is wet because this is where a spring spreads out down into the sea and the boat would be moored or beached near fresh water.
10   *puerum*: Cupid.
11   **Lycus**: the name means 'wolf.' — *Fortis uir in sua re publica cognitus quae de iuuenum amore scribit Alcaeus!* 'Well known in his own country as a brave man, such things Alcaeus writes on loving youths!' Cicero *Tusculans* 4.71.
13   **Turtleshell**: 1.10.6 n.
15   *cumque*: presents a puzzle. Porphyrio takes it as *quandocumque* 'whenever.'

salue: saluus sis 'be all right' *mihi* 'for me;' one has to push it a bit to arrive at 'be gracious to me.' — Scan the first three words of the English line as 'Consolaysh nin trouble.'

33

An ode addressed to Horace's friend the elegiac poet Albius Tibullus (ten or more years his junior and also the addressee of *Epistles* 1.4) chaffing him for his apparent vulnerability in love.

Metre: Second Asclepiad.

Added: 15 By name ... even.

1   *plus nimio:* 1.18.15 n.
2   **Glycera:** see 1.19 introduction. The name does not in fact occur in the extant verse of Tibullus.
     miserabilis: best taken as accusative plural, though the lover is regularly *miser.* It was believed that the elegiac metre originated as a lament and love elegy is often a lament. Horace uses the adjective here in two senses: 'pathetic' and 'contemptible.'
6   **Cyrus:** 1.17.25.
7   **sharp-tongued:** or perhaps 'the prude.'
     Pholoe: 2.5.17 and Tibullus 1.8.69.
11   There seems to be an intentional conflation here of the yoke that joins lovers together and the yoke under which the defeated were made to pass by the victors: *OLD iugum* 2b and 5.
13   *ipsum me:* the personal reminiscence comes in the last stanza, as at 1.5.13–16.

34

In the Epicurean gospel of Lucretius Book 6 verses 400–401 we read:

> *denique cur numquam caelo iacit undique puro*
> *Iuppiter in terras fulmen sonitusque profundit?*

> Again, why does Jupiter never hurl his bolt
> at the earth or produce noise from a perfectly clear sky?

According to Epicurus thunder was caused by clouds clashing together, a material cause with which the gods had nothing to do. The gods, like human beings, were a product of natural evolution. They existed in perfect happiness and would not destroy that by interfering in this faulty world of ours. Horace, however, claims that personal experience of thunder from a clear sky has shaken his belief in Epicureanism and caused him to return to his earlier conventional belief in (and fear of?) unpredictable divine intervention in human affairs. The last stanza with its description of Fortuna leads into the following ode in the same metre and some scholars have argued that the two are in fact one poem.

Metre: Alcaics.

Added: 15 head.

1   *infrequens:* Epicurus taught that the philosopher should take part in the conventional religious ceremonies of his city.
5   *Diespiter:* archaic 'Day's-father' = Jupiter.

10 **Styx**: the river surrounding the Underworld; Virgil *Georgics* 4.480 *nouies Styx interfusa coercet* (sc. *inferos*) 'Styx winding nine-fold round confines [the dead].'

Taenarus: here stands for the Underworld, because on Cape Tainaron, the southernmost point of the Peloponnese, there was a cave believed to be an entrance to Hades, like Avernus in Italy.

11 *Atlanteus … finis:* probably the western end of the Atlas mountain range or the Atlantic Ocean.

35

A hymn in honour of the goddess Fortuna (following on from 1.34.14–16), ending with a prayer that she will protect Augustus in his projected campaigns against Britain and the east, and with gloomy reflections on the recent civil war.

Metre: Alcaics

Added: 8 merchant, 18 dowel-pins, 32 coastline, 33 blood.

1   There was a famous temple of Fortuna at Anzio, on the west coast of Italy some 80 kilometres south of Rome.

6   *ruris:* understand *dominam*; it is otiose with *colonus* (N–H).

7   **Carpathian**: the sea round the island of Carpathos between Rhodes and Crete was proverbially stormy.

8   **Thynian**: Bithynia produced good timber and was famous for ship-building.

9   **Scyths**: 1.19.11 n.

    Dacians: 1.26.3–4 n.

14 **standing pillar**: cf. Milton *Paradise Lost* 2.300–302, of Satan:

> with grave
> Aspect he rose, and in his rising seem'd
> A Pillar of State.

17 **Necessity**: the Greek Anangke walks ahead of Fortuna as lictors precede a Roman magistrate.

18–19 A translator has room to spare here, so *cuneos* has been split into its two meanings 'dowel-pins' and 'wedges.' Necessity builds an immovable structure. Or are these accessories instruments of torture as West argues?

21–22 *colit … abnegat:* the singular verb treats *Spes* and *Fides* as a hendiadys.

22 The MSS read *nec comitem abnegat:* 'nor do they refuse companionship,' but this puts *Spes* and *Fides* on the same level as *uulgus* and *meretrix*, who are fair-weather friends. *sed* is Peerlkamp's correction. Bentley suggested *uertis* for *linquis* (24), which gives

> White-clad, nor do they cease their companionship
> Whenever in changed garb you over-
> throw as an enemy great men's houses.

29–30 There was talk of an invasion of Britain in 26 BC (Dio Cassius 53.22) and this would fit with Aelius Gallus' Arabian expedition (1.29).

40 **Massagetae**: a nomadic Scythian tribe east of the Caspian sea, in modern Kazakhstan.

36

A drinking party, following a thank-offering to the gods, to celebrate the safe return of a young officer from the war in Spain. Catullus 9 makes an interesting contrast.

Metre: Fourth Asclepiad.

Added: 12 dance, 14 the contest.

3   **Numida**: otherwise unknown.

4   **far Hesperia**: Spain as opposed to Hesperia = Italy (1.28.26 n.). The war in Spain lasted ten years, from 28 to 19 BC; Augustus was there in person from 26 to 24. Lucius Aelius Lamia, perhaps the father of this Lamia, was legate in charge of Hispania Citerior when Augustus left.

7   **Lamia**: 1.26 n.

8   **king**: Lamia was the leader of his group, cf. *Epistles* 1.1.59–60: *at pueri ludentes 'rex eris' aiunt/ 'si recte facies'* 'but boys at play say "you will be ruler if you keep the rules".'

9   A boy usually put on the *toga virilis*, indicating the end of childhood, between the ages of 15 and 17.

10   **Cretan mark**: lucky days were apparently marked in the calendar with white chalk (*creta*). Isidore *Origines* 16.1.6 *creta ab insula Creta vocata ubi melior est* 'chalk is so called from the island of Crete where it is of better quality.'

12   **Salii**: priests of Mars who performed ritual dances; the name derives fron *salire* 'to jump.'

13   **Damalis**: = 'heifer;' the Greek name of a hetaera.

14   **Bassus**: Ovid in *Tristia* 4.10 mentions an iambic poet of that name and Propertius 1.4 addresses him.

       Thracian: 1.27.2 n.

       amystide: Greek *amystis* is a long draught without taking breath.

15–16 The plants were used for garlands.

19   Lit. 'be torn away from her new adulterer' — presumably Numida.

20   *ambitiosior:* the implications are untranslatable; Damalis has determined designs on this well-off adulterer.

37

This ode celebrates the defeat (at Actium in September 31 BC) and suicide (at Alexandria in August 30 BC) of Cleopatra. It balances 1.2 and is a sequel to *Epode* 9 about Actium, but in neither poem is Mark Antony mentioned; he killed himself a few days before Cleopatra's suicide. Horace begins by quoting a translation of the first three words of a poem by Alcaeus in the same metre celebrating the death of the tyrant Myrsilus c. 600 BC: *nūn chrē methusthēn* 'now one must get drunk' (Fragment 332).

Metre: Alcaics.

Added: 2 in dances, 8 an end to, 13 consuming, 17 galleys, 19 timid, 30 And.

1   **unfettered**: lit. 'free' — from the danger of enslavement to a foreign queen.

3–4   refer to a *lectisternium* or festival of thanksgiving, when images of the gods were laid outside on couches and offered a banquet in celebration of a victory.

       Saliarian: 1.36.12 n.

6   **Caecuban**: 1.20.9 n. and *Epode* 9.1–4.

       the queen: Cleopatra.

9   **pervert company**: eunuchs.

       disease: refers here to sexual perversion, cf. Catullus 57.6 *morbosi pariter* 'diseased alike' of Caesar and Mamurra.

11   Cleopatra had been Julius Caesar's mistress and was married to Mark Antony.

13   **a single ship**: exaggerated propaganda. 'In fact Cleopatra escaped with sixty ships ... most of Antony's fleet surrendered intact' N–H.

15   **Mareotic**: a sweet wine from the district of Lake Mareotis near Alexandria.
17   **oared galleys**: lit. 'oars.'
30   **Liburnians**: fast war-galleys.
32   **Triumph**: when Octavian celebrated his triple triumph in 29 BC the procession included an image of Cleopatra and the snakes — Propertius 3.11.53 *bracchia spectaui sacris admorsa colubris* 'I saw your forearms bitten by the sacred snakes.'

38

Horace issues instructions to his slave on preparations for a little drinking-session (*à deux*?): no elaborate garlands, simple myrtle. It is hard not to take the poem as symbolic of Horace's life-style and, despite the contrast with the complication of the previous ode, of his unpretentious, though self-conscious, poetry.

Metre: Sapphics.

1   ***apparatus***: luxurious preparations. Persian luxury was proverbial: 3.9.4 *Persarum ... rege beatior*. — One is also reminded of Callimachus' rejection of 'the Persian chain' (= length) as a criterion of poetry
5   ***myrto***: 1.4.9 n.
6   ***cura***: Bentley's emendation of the MSS *curo*, which is weak after *odi* and *mitte*, makes *sedulus* ambiguous, and could be due to the attraction of *myrto* immediately above.
7   ***arta***: OLD *artus* 9 '(of crowds, etc.) Close-packed, dense; (of vegetation) dense, thick.' To achieve this the vine (probably on a trellis or pergola) would need to be pruned.

BOOK TWO

There is less metrical variety in Book 2. Of its twenty odes twelve are in Alcaics and six in Sapphics. The first eleven odes are alternately in Alcaics and Sapphics and the five Sapphic odes here are all twenty-four lines long.

1

The first ode is addressed to Gaius Asinius Pollio, born 76 BC, consul in 40, friend of Catullus and his circle, patron of Virgil and Horace. A poet famous for his tragedies, he was also a major orator, but his great work was the history of the Civil Wars starting in 60 BC. He built the first public library in Rome and instituted the practice of public readings of poetry and prose (*recitationes*). He died in AD 4.

Metre: Alcaics.

Added: 30 many, 36 quarter or ... spilt.

1   **Celer's consulship**: Quintus Metellus Celer, consul in 60 BC, the year of the first triumvirate of Caesar, Pompey and Crassus. 'This capture of the constitution may fairly be designated as the end of the Free State. From a triumvirate it was a short step to dictatorship' R. Syme *Roman Revolution* (1939) p.36.

12   *Cecropio ... cothurno:* Cecrops was the first king of Athens, and the cothurnus a thick-soled boot worn by actors in tragedy to increase their height.

16   Pollio celebrated his Dalmatian triumph in 39 or 38 BC. He devoted the spoils to the foundation of his public library.

17–24   Horace is thinking of Pharsalus in Thessaly where Caesar defeated Pompey in 48 BC, of Thapsus in Africa where he defeated the younger Cato in 46, and perhaps too of Philippi in Macedonia where Antony defeated Brutus and Cassius in 42. The suicide of the Stoic Cato at Utica soon after his defeat turned him into a martyr for the Republic. Lucan's epigram is famous: *uictrix causa deis placuit sed uicta Catoni* (1.128), 'the gods approved the victorious cause, Cato the vanquished.'

21   **hear ... generals**: speaking to their troops. Then in line 23 the construction has to change. To avoid this one could read 'hear of' instead of 'hear the' in 21, but this is tame after the vigour of 17–20.

25   For Juno's love of Africans and hatred of Trojans and therefore of Romans see the beginning of Virgil's *Aeneid*.

28   Jugurtha nearly succeeded in liberating Numidia from the Roman yoke, but was treacherously surrendered to the Romans by his father-in-law King Bocchus of Mauretania and strangled in the Tullianum at Rome in 104 BC.

32   **Medes**: 1.29.5 n.
       Hesperia: 1.28.26 n.

34   **Daunian**: strictly 'Apulian' (see 1.22.14 n.) but here by metonymy ('part for whole') = 'Italian.' — He is thinking of the war at sea against Sextus Pompey.

37–40   Horace ironically suggests that his light Muse should stick to poems of love and wine and not attempt to introduce the Simonidean dirge into Latin poetry.

38   **Cean**: Simonides of Ceos (c. 557–467 BC) was famous for his *threnoi*, 'dirges.'

39   **Dionean**: Dione was the mother of Venus but sometimes identified with her by Hellenistic and Latin poets.
40   Strictly *leuiore plectro* goes with *quaere*.

2

Stoic thoughts on the right use of money, on greed as a disease, and on the true kingdom of Reason (Virtue).

Metre: Sapphics.

Added: 18 King, 23 of treasure can pass.

1   **Silver**: or 'Money,' cf. French *argent*.
2   **Miser's subsoil**: lit. 'miserly earth.'
      Gaius Sallustius Crispus, great nephew and adopted son of the historian Sallust, whose wealth he inherited, succeeded Maecenas as Augustus' confidant, like Maecenas remaining a knight.
3   **plate**: or 'cash.'
5   **Proculeius**: friend of Augustus, brother of Varro Murena and of Terentia, the wife of Maecenas. He was given the task of arresting Cleopatra (Plutarch *Antony* 79).
9   **you**: like our generalizing use = 'one.'
10   **Gades**: modern Cadiz.
11   *uterque Poenus:* the Carthaginians in Africa and those in Spain (Nova Karthago).
13–16 Avarice is like dropsy.
17   **Reason**: a possible translation of the Stoic *uirtus* — Greek *aretē*, which Cicero at *Tusculans* 4.15.34 defines as *recta ratio*.
18–19 See 1.26.5 n.
      happy men: cf. 3.9.4 *Persarum ... rege beatior*. For the Stoics, of course, only the wise man was king.
      Cyrus: the Great, descendant of Achaemenes who founded the Achaemenid dynasty in the 6th century BC, from which the Parthian monarchy claimed descent.
22   **seeing**: lit. 'sees.'

3

An epicurean contrast to the preceding ode, less gloomy than its later congener 2.14. A genuine Epicurean would not have written line 24 or 27–28, implying fear of death. See also Introduction pp. xvi–xviii.

Metre: Alcaics.

Added: 23 You'll fall.

4   **Dellius**: Quintus Dellius, a clever diplomat, labelled by Messalla as *desultor bellorum ciuilium* 'circus-rider of the civil wars,' for changing sides so often. He deserted Antony before Actium and became, like Sallustius Crispus, a trusted confidant of Augustus. The advice that Horace appears to be giving him has probably been followed by Dellius throughout his life.
8   **Falernian**: 1.20.11 n.

      interiore nota: lit. 'of inner quality.' The amphorae were marked with the name of the consul of the year and stored away; the oldest wines would be furthest back in the store.

13   *breuis:* accusative plural, 1.1.17 n.

16   **Sisterly Three:** the three Fates, Clotho, Lachesis, and Atropos, who respectively spin, draw out, and cut the thread of every life.

18   **yellow Tiberinus:** 1.8.8.

21   **Inachus:** the mythical first king of Argos stands here for ancient aristocratic lineage.

24   *uictima:* of an animal sacrifice; not a dead metaphor in the Latin.
          Orcus: 1.28.10 n.

26–28 The metaphor changes. Fate has an urn in which everyone's name, written on a small wooden tablet, is shaken about until it jumps out.

27–28 *aeternum/ exsilium ....:* the elided hypermetric syllable in 27 must be a calculated effect in this context, so too the elision of the *-um* of *exsilium.*
        in: OLD 21.
        cumbae: the usual word for the boat in which Charon ferries the souls of the dead across the river Styx in the Underworld; the word here is dative, governed by *impositura.* The future participles pick up *moriture* (4) and help to unify the ode.

4

Young men in Roman Comedy fall in love with slave-girls, though their fathers disapprove. Horace humorously takes a more broad-minded view, appealing to heroic precedent, pretending that the girl may be of royal birth, and praising her good points, with an ironical disclaimer.

Metre: Alcaics.

Added: 9 Troy's, 10 great, 22 please.

2   **Xanthias:** the Greek name occurs only here in Horace and nothing more is known about the young man, who comes from Phocis, a small area in central Greece on the western border of Boeotia, containing Delphi.
       Briseis: Achilles' slave and concubine, of whom Agamemnon deprived him, arousing the wrath of Achilles and causing his withdrawal from the fighting in front of Troy.

5   **Tecmessa:** daughter of the Phrygian king Teuthras, slave and concubine of the great Ajax (1.15.18 n.).

7   **Atrides:** Agamemnon (1.10.14 n.) who fell in love with Cassandra, the prophetess daughter of King Priam of Troy.

10   **Thessaly's great victor:** Achilles, who came from Phthia in Thessaly and eventually killed Priam's son Hector on whom the safety of Troy depended.

11   **Pergama:** the citadel of Troy.

15   **of royal birth:** like Tecmessa and Cassandra.

16   **Penates:** household gods; 'unfair' because they allowed her to be enslaved.

17   **your sweetheart:** lit. 'she.'

23–24 Horace was born on 8 December 65 BC, so this ode was perhaps written in 24 BC.

5

E.A. Schmidt sums up the subject as 'Love that can wait because it loves.' But the ode has problems. Is Horace talking to himself like Catullus in Poem 8? Or giving advice to a friend? Is the friend already married to the girl, as *tuae ... iuuencae* (5–6) and *maritum* (16) could possibly imply? It seems easiest to take the ode as self-address and sequel to 1.22, in which case *maritum* is used loosely for 'lover.'

Metre: Alcaics.

1   *iugum:* in Latin marriage is *con-iugium.*
5   **heifer**: N–H quote a six-line fragment of Anacreon (Fragment 417) in which the poet addresses a girl in an extended metaphor as 'Thracian filly' frisking in the meadows, as yet unmounted.
9–12   The sudden change of metaphor is surprising, as he returns to the original one in the next stanza.
16   *petet:* has double meaning 'will seek' (*OLD* 10) and 'will butt' (*OLD* 2).
      Lalage: 1.22.9 n.
17   **Pholoe**: 1.33.7.
18   **Chloris**: at 3.15.7–8 a Chloris is Pholoe's mother.
20   **Cnidian**: 1.30.1 n.
23   **difference**: could also be 'decision.'

6

Horace here expresses in lyric form preferences that he still has when he publishes the *Epistles* in his forty-fifth year:

> *mihi iam non regia Roma*
> *sed uacuum Tibur placet aut imbelle Tarentum*

> Not royal Rome but empty Tibur
> Pleases me today or pacifist Tarentum. (*Epistles* 1.7.44–45)

Metre: Sapphics.

1–6   Cf. Catullus 11.1–12, but the situation is probably reversed here as a joke; Horace pretends that Septimius is wanting to take him to the war in Spain.
1   **Septimius**: a close friend but younger, as we can gather from stanzas 1 and 6. He may well be the Septimius whom Horace recommends to Tiberius in *Epistles* 1.9 and who was later a confidant of Augustus (see *Vita Horati*).
2   The Cantabrians, a warlike coastal and mountain tribe in Spain, were defeated in 29, 26 and 25 BC and finally subdued by Agrippa in 19 BC.
3   **Syrtes**: sandbanks off the Libyan coast.
      Moroccan: loosely for 'Libyan;' a recognized figure of speech, Greek *katakhresis*, Latin *abusio*.
5   **Tibur**: 1.18.2 n.
6   **retirement**: lit. 'old age.'
10   **Galaesus**: a river near Tarentum. Varro (*Res Rusticae* 2.2.18) records that the sheep around Tarentum were clad in skins to keep their fine fleeces from the dirt.
12   **Phalanthus**: founded Tarentum at the end of the 8th century BC; the name means 'Balding.'
15   **Hymettus**: the mountain near Athens famous for its honey and marble (2.18.3).
16   **Venafrum**: on the Via Latina in northern Campania, famous for its olive groves.
18   **Aulon**: in Greek is used of a hollow between hills, so here probably refers to a fertile valley near Tarentum.
19   Porphyrio has a perceptive note *inuidet enim tantum qui inferior est* 'only an inferior envies.'

20   **Falernum**: strictly this name for the district does not exist; it was *Falernus ager*. For the wine from there cf. 1.20.11.
21   The translation assumes that *locus, postulant*, and *arces* are military language here.
22   *ibi*: 'emphatic, *there*, and not in Spain' J. Gow.
24   **lyrist**: strictly 'bard,' a grander word than poet.

7

An ode celebrating the safe return to Italy of a former close comrade-in-arms. He had fought on the Republican side at Philippi in 42 BC, but on the death of Brutus had continued to serve against Octavian until some time after Actium when he must have succeeded in obtaining a pardon from the victor. In *Res Gestae* 3 Augustus writes: *uictorque omnibus ueniam petentibus ciuibus peperci* 'and as victor I spared the lives of all citizens who asked for mercy.'

Metre: Alcaics.

3   **Who ...?**: the answer must be Octavian, and the question a subtle form of compliment.
5   **Pompeius**: otherwise unknown.
6   **a boring day**: Brutus and his legions were in Asia during the summer of 43 BC, and in war soldiers are often more occupied in killing time than in killing the enemy.
8   **malobathrum**: the main ingredient was probably cinnamon, according to *Oxford English Dictionary*[2].
10   **dumped**: Horace is in good poetical company: Archilochus, Alcaeus and Anacreon all confess to leaving behind their shields (a military disgrace).
11   **Virtue**: Brutus was a convinced Stoic, for whom virtue was the *summum bonum*. Before killing himself he quoted a Greek tragedian: 'O Wretched Virtue, so you were a sham./ I took you seriously but you are Fortune's slave.'
13–14 A light-hearted Homeric rescue by the god whom Horace elsewhere claims as his protector, see 2.17.29 and *Satires* 2.6.5.
       epic mist: lit. 'thick air.'
15–16 The marine metaphor may hint that Pompeius served in the naval campaign of his namesake Sextus Pompey until his defeat at Naulochus in September 36 BC.
17   *Ioui:* possibly a reference to Augustus as Wilkinson suggests, cf. *Epistles* 1.19.43.
22   **tulip glasses**: paraphrase *ciboria* which were drinking cups 'shaped like the flower of the Egyptian bean' (*OLD*). The Egyptian local colour probably implies that Pompeius had served there. — *smooth* because not embossed.
25   **Venus**: the Venus throw at dice or knucklebones, cf. 1.4.18.
27   **Edonians**: not only were they a Thracian tribe and therefore hard drinkers (1.27.2 n.), but Philippi was in their territory.

8

A variation on the theme *Iuppiter ex alto periuria ridet amantum* 'Jupiter from on high laughs at lovers' perjuries,' a proverb which goes back to Hesiod recording how Zeus lied to Hera about Io. Horace accepts the amorality of beauty.

Metre: Sapphics.

Added: 9 Yes, 14 youngster, 21 ignorant.

2   **Barine**: lit. 'the girl from Bari;' the name suggests a Greek freedwoman.
3   **discoloured**: *nigro* also goes with *ungui* and *uno* with *dente*; the so-called *apo koinou* ('in common') construction.
13–14 Cf. 1.2.33–34.
       Even Venus: she ought to protect Barine's lovers.
       Nymphs: cf. 1.30.6.
21   **cubs**: lit. 'calves.'
24   *aura*: OLD 6 'fragrance,' 7b 'radiation,' and maybe 3a 'breath (of favour etc.).' The metaphor is clearer at 1.5.11–12 *nescius aurae/ fallacis*.

9

Advice to an elegiac poet-friend: 'Give up elegy and write epic panegyric in honour of Augustus.' 1.33 to Tibullus is comparable, but does not forbid him to continue writing elegiac verse.

Metre: Sapphics.

Added: 6 twelve, 20 Victory.

5   Gaius Valgius Rufus, a versatile poet and literary man, belonged like Virgil and Horace to the circle of Maecenas, and was appointed a suffect consul in 12 BC.
7   **Garganus**: Monte Gargano forming a promontory on the Adriatic coast of Apulia.
8   *orni*: '*ornus* is the manna-ash which takes the place of our ash on the hillsides of southern Europe' Mynors on Virgil *Georgics* 2.71.
10–12 Cf. Virgil *Georgics* 4.466 *te ueniente die, te decedente canebat* 'Of you at dawn of day, of you at dusk he sang.' Horace also imitates the repeated long *e*.
       loss of Mystes: presumably the death of a favourite Greek slave-boy. The name means 'The initiate.' For *ademptum* cf. Catullus 101.6 *heu miser indigne frater adempte mihi* 'Alas poor brother, unfairly taken from me.'
       Vespero: the evening star; six times in Virgil's *Georgics*.
13   **the ancient**: the Homeric hero Nestor, oldest of the Greeks at Troy, who lost his son Antilochus in the fighting there.
15   **parents**: Priam and Hecuba whose son Troilus was killed by Achilles.
20   The date of these events is uncertain.
       Niphates: a mountain in Armenia; Greek *niphas* = 'snow.'
21   *Medumque flumen:* Euphrates. For *Parthian* see 1.2.22 and 51.
23   **Geloni**: a Scythian tribe.

10

An ode recommending the Golden Mean and a state of mind prepared for changes of Fortune, a development of Apollo's commandment *mēden agan* 'nothing in excess.'

Metre: Sapphics.

1   *Licini:* one important group of Horatian MSS states that this is Licinius Murena, and it is generally held that he is the Licinius Murena adopted by Aulus Terentius Varro and thereafter known as Terentius Murena (see 2.2.5 n.). According to Dio (54.3) he conspired with Fannius Caepio against Augustus and was executed in 22 BC. This identification requires the publication of Horace's *Odes* before the conspiracy was discovered.
5   **Golden Mean**: 'Although it is now a cliché, the expression ... represents for its time an innovative attempt to render the abstraction not only concrete but also

emotionally compelling' Santirocco p.94. It derives from Aristotle's teaching that virtue is intermediate between two vicious extremes. The word *mediocritas* was coined by Cicero to represent the Greek *mesotēs* 'middleness.'

7   ***sordibus****: OLD sordes* 1 'dirt' 4 'meanness.'

9   ***saepius****:* if the variant *saeuius* is accepted read 'harder' for 'oftener.'

13   ***infestis ... secundis****:* to parallel the ablative of neuter plural *infesta* and *secunda* Heinze quotes Tacitus *Annals* 2.14 *pauidos aduersis, inter secunda non diuini non humani iuris memores* 'Panicky in adversity, when things went well neglectful of both divine and human law.'

11

A dramatic monologue advising a rich friend to take time off and enjoy life. The setting is a garden.

Metre: Alcaics.

Added: 22 here.

1   **Cantabri**: 2.6.2 n. *Scythians*: 1.19.11 n.

3   **Quinctius**: probably the Quinctius addressed in *Epistles* 1.16 where he is called 'well off' (*beatus*). The Hirpini were a Samnite tribe.

4   *trepides in: OLD trepido* 4a 'be anxious;' *in* 17 'with regard to.'

14   *sic*: lit. 'as we are.'

16   'The exotic form *Assyria* [for *Syria*] increases the impression of luxury' N–H.
       nard: an expensive oil, the spikenard of Mark 14.3.

17   **Euhius**: 1.18.9 n. — Rudd (1993) p.69 points out that a true Epicurean would not have written this, for care is banished not by wine but by Epicurus' doctrine.

21   **Lyde**: a variant of Lydia, 'the Lydian girl.'

12

A variant of the so-called recusatio, to be compared with 1.6 (see its introduction) and in the same metre; but in this case the poetry Horace is inspired to write is in praise of Licymnia and not love poetry in general.

Metre: Second Asclepiad (marking the end of the alternation of Alcaics and Sapphics in 2.1–11).

Added: 3 for such harsh themes, 15 tender, 19 supple.

1   **Numantia**: a strategic Celtiberian town on the upper Douro, which resisted Roman domination for many years until sacked by Scipio Aemilianus in 133 BC.

2   **The Sicilian sea**: a reference to the Roman victories at Mylae (260 BC) and the Aegatian Islands (241) in the first Punic war.

5   **Lapiths and Hylaeus**: 1.18.8 n. Hylaeus was one of the Centaurs.

6–8   The Giants tried to reach Olympus but the gods could not defeat them without the help of a mortal, so Jove appealed to Hercules.

7–9   Lit. 'at the danger from whom ... Saturn's house trembled.'

10–12 Lit. 'fights of Caesar and menacing kings' necks led through the streets.'

14   **Licymnia**: certain scholia state that this is a pseudonym for Maecenas' wife Terentia. They may go back to the 2nd-century AD Horatian commentator Helenius Acro and look like good ancient evidence. As usual the pseudonym is metrically equivalent to the real name, cf. Lesbia for Clodia, Delia for Plania; in that case 'my lady' here is respectful and does not mean 'my mistress.'

20   **sacred day**: 13 August. Diana's temple was on the Aventine.

21   **Achaemenes**: first of the Persian kings and founder of the Achaemenid dynasty.

22   **Mygdonian**: Mygdon was a legendary king of Phrygia.

26   *facili saeuitia*: Porphyrio is puzzled: *Quid est 'facilis saeuitia'? Utrum quae facile nascitur an quae facile mollitur?* 'What is "easy cruelty"? Is it easily aroused, or easily mollified?' — see *OLD facilis* 9a.

13

Horace mentions in this ode and three others (2.17, 3.4 and 8) that he was nearly killed by a falling tree. Here he treats the event in serio-comic fashion. He begins by describing the criminal character of the tree's planter, continues with a variation on the theme 'in the midst of life we are in death,' and ends by imagining how he could have heard Sappho and especially Alcaeus charming the Underworld with their singing. In fact the last four stanzas are a panegyric of Alcaeus' political and war poetry (his *stasiotika*), whereas 1.32 praises his love-poetry.

Metre: Alcaics.

Added: 6 Poor, 10 The brute, 31 deposed and, 39 then.

8   **Colchis**: Medea's homeland, associated with magic and potions.

15   **Thynian**: *Thynus* is Lachmann's correction of the manusripts' *Poenus* 'Punic.' 'The Bithynians were great sailors and merchants ... and lived on the Bosphorus. In Horace's time there were no Carthaginian sailors and, if there had been, it would have been absurd to select the Bosphorus as the only danger they feared' J. Gow.

18   **Parthians**: 1.2.22 n.

22   **Aeacus**: with Minos and Rhadamanthus one of the judges of the dead.

24   *Aeoliis*: the Lesbian lyric poets Sappho and Alcaeus wrote in their native Aeolic dialect; see also 1.1.34 n.

33   **beast**: Cerberus, the monstrous dog guarding the Underworld, here intentionally grotesque, being given a hundred heads instead of the usual three.

36   **Eumenides**: 'the kindly ones,' euphemistic name for the Furies.

37   **Prometheus**: here punished in Hades for his theft of fire from the gods.
       Pelops' father: 1.28.7 n.

39   **Orion**: the giant hunter punished in Hades for assaulting Diana.

14

A famous *memento mori* in the same metre as the preceding ode. Horace enlarges on death's inevitability and leaves Postumus to draw his own conclusions about how to live; contrast 2.3 and the advice there given to Dellius. — Perhaps one of the repeated names in line 1 (*Postume, Postume*) can be thought of as an adjective 'last-born' and this can be taken as 'You do not yet know how to live,' or as the superlative of *post, posterior* 'behindhand.' Cf. Martial 5.58:

> cras uiues? hodie iam uiuere, Postume, serum est.
> ille sapit quisquis, Postume, uixit heri.

> You'll live tomorrow, Postumus? But today's already too late.
> The wise man, Postumus, lived yesterday.

Metre: Alcaics.

1   **Postumus**: unknown; possibly the Postumus of Propertius 3.12. For the repetition (*geminatio*) at this place in the line cf. 2.17.10 *ibimus, ibimus*, 3.3.18 *Ilion, Ilion*, 4.4.70 *occidit, occidit*.

6   *illacrimabilem*: unable to weep.

7   Alternative: 'Unweeping Pluto who imprisons ....' For Pluto see 1.4.17 n.

8   **Tityos**: a giant who assaulted Leto, was shot by her children Apollo and Artemis, and was punished in Tartarus.

        Geryon: a three-headed, three-bodied giant killed by Hercules.

9   **gloomy water**: the Styx, see 1.34.10 n.

17   **Cocytus**: 'the river of wailing' in the Underworld.

18   **Danaus' ... brood**: 3.11.24 n.

20   **Sisyphus**: son of Aeolus and craftiest of mortals, punished for outwitting the gods by having to push a rock uphill in Hades, which rolled down again on reaching the top.

24   **cypress**: a funeral tree in antiquity too.

25   **worthier**: presumably implies that Postumus does not know how to enjoy his possessions.

28   **pontiffs' banquets**: cf 1.37.2–4.

15

Horace attacks the building mania of the rich and their purely ornamental estates, contrasting their selfish ostentation with early Roman public spirit.

Metre: Alcaics (for the third time running and like 2.13 without an addressee).

Added: 7 once.

3   **Lucrine**: a shallow lagoon near Baiae on the Gulf of Puteoli.

5   Elms were used to support vines, to which they were said to be married; plane trees were unproductive, but shady.

6   Lit. 'every wealth of the nostrils.'

11   **bearded**: lit. 'unshorn;' probably to be taken with Romulus also. 'The Romans did not shave at all before 300 BC and Scipio Africanus Major is said to have been the first who shaved regularly' J. Gow.

        Cato: Marcus Porcius the famous Censor and an authority on agriculture (234–149 BC).

13   **property list**: J. Gow's translation.

15   **private ten-foot rods**: = private survey. *decempedae* were measuring rods used by Roman surveyors.

16   I.e. the colonnade faced north: 'the cool' comes from the arctic suggestion of *Arcton*.

18   **Fortuitous turf**: turf that happened to be available — for private building and roofing.

16

A meditation on the meaning of *otium*. It is calm as opposed to storm, peace as opposed to war. It is more valuable than conventional 'valuables.' A state of mind not at the mercy of fear, desire, or worry, it lives in the present, recognizing that nothing is perfect and that one can't have everything. In short, it comes closest to the Epicurean ideal of *ataraxia* or 'undisturbance.'

Metre: Sapphics.

Added: 3 no longer, 12 rich.

1–6   The triple anaphora of *otium* looks like a corrective reminder of Catullus 51 (in the same metre):

> *Otium, Catulle, tibi molestum est;*
> *otio exultas nimiumque gestis;*
> *otium et reges prius et beatas*
> *perdidit urbes*
> Leisure, Catullus, does not agree with you.
> At leisure you're restless, too excitable.
> Leisure in the past has ruined rulers and
> Prosperous cities

where *otium* is a bad thing — idleness and enervated ease.

7   **Grosphus**: probably the Pompeius Grosphus of *Epistles* 1.12.22. The family was Sicilian.

13   'The "good life" is not what the *bon viveur* supposes' N–H.

17   *iaculamur:* N–H see a reference to the name Grosphus here, because the Latin *iaculum* 'throwing spear' is *grosphos* in Greek.

18–19   *quid ... patriae?:* lit. 'Why do we exchange lands heated by another \<sun\> for the sun of our country?' The vulgate punctuation is *mutamus? patriae* and *mutamus* is supposed to mean 'take in exchange \<for home\>.' But *patriae* is not needed with *exul.*

21   **galley**: the rich man's yacht, cf. 3.1.39 *aerata triremi.*

29–30   Swift-footed Achilles had glory but a short life (death was too quick for him), Tithonus eternal life but not youth.

38   **Camena**: the Latin word for Muse, so that the paradox 'Greek Camena' represents the Horatian fusion of Latin words and Greek metre.
        tenuem: recalls the 'slender' (*leptaleē*) Muse of Callimachus and his stylistic ideal.

39   *Parca:* lit. 'the Sparing One,' the Roman goddess of Fate identified with the Greek *moira.*
        non mendax: because (a) she does not belie her name, and (b) her decrees are the truth.

40   Closer: 'The spiteful vulgar,' cf. 3.1.1 *Odi profanum uulgus.*

17

Ostensibly a semi-humorous attempt to reassure Maecenas the hypochondriac, this ode advertises the close and enduring friendship between the poet and his patron. The scholia suppose that Horace is sitting by the sickbed while Maecenas thinks he is dying; Porphyrio: *haec dicit Maecenati adsidens aegroto grauiter querenti de periculo salutis suae.*

Metre: Alcaics.

1   **complaints**: according to Pliny (*Natural History* 7.51) Maecenas suffered from a chronic fever (*perpetua febris*) and insomnia.

2   **God's pleasure ... mine**: lit. 'friendly to the gods or to me.'

10   *sacramentum:* especially the oath of loyalty to the *princeps* as sole *imperator* taken by every soldier on his enlistment and renewed annually on the first of January.

11   *supremum:* also 'supreme.'

13   **Chimaera**: 1.27.24 n.
14   **Gyas**: one of the mythical giants who fought against the gods and were pegged down in Tartarus.
16   **Parcae**: 2.16.39 n.
17–24 This astrological excursion is presumably due to Maecenas' interest in 'Babylonian numbers' (1.11.2–3).
25–26 See 1.20.3–5
27–28 See 2.13.11–12. Faunus, the Latin Pan, was Mercury's son.
30   'Properly speaking the Mercuriales were a *collegium* that took Mercury for its patron' N–H. Horace counts himself as a member because Mercury rescued him from Philippi (2.7.13–14) and had been instrumental in giving Horace his Sabine farm (*Satires* 2.6.4–5). He must be suggesting here that Mercury was predominant in his horoscope.
32   **offering**: lit. 'striking.'

18

A diatribe against luxury, building mania, and the greedy and inhuman acquisition of land (cf. 2.15). There is no named addressee, and the *tu* addressed in 17ff. is not any particular person but the customary anonymous opponent in the genre of diatribe, representing here a class of *nouveaux riches* entrepreneurs.

Metre: Hipponactian; trochaic dimeter + iambic trimeter (both catalectic).

1   Cf. 1.31.6 *non aurum aut ebur Indicum.*
3–5   Marble from Hymettus in Attica was grey-blue and from Africa yellow.
6   **Attalus**: 1.1.13 n. His bequest according to some marked the beginning of Roman decadence.
7–8   Roman millionaires no doubt had clients whose wives wore expensive purple dresses.
9   *fides*: OLD *fides*[1] 5 'credit,' 6 'honesty;' *fides*[2] 1 'lyre,' 2 'lyre-strings.' The word-play cannot be kept in English.
14   Maecenas had given Horace a small Sabine estate in about 33 BC.
20   **Baiae**: a seaside holiday resort on the Gulf of Puteoli (3.15.3 n.).
26–28 A memorable picture of the dispossessed.
31   **Orcus**: 1.28.10 n.
34–36 **Orcus' henchman**: Charon (2.3.28 n.). — This story about Prometheus is otherwise unknown (cf. 2.13.37 n.); perhaps Maecenas had told it in his *Prometheus* (a satire or a tragedy?).
37   **Tantalus**: 1.28.7 n.

19

A vision (presumably in imagination) of the god Bacchus teaching Nymphs and Satyrs in wild mountain scenery terrifies the poet but simultaneously inspires him to break into a hymn of praise to the god, in fact a dithyramb in the metre of personal, not choral, lyric.

Metre: Alcaics.

Added: 2 Lord.

1–2   *carmina ... docentem:* lit. 'teaching songs.' Quinn sees the god 'as a *grammaticus* declaiming to his class, who repeat the declaimed text after him ... as part of the process of learning the right way to accent the lines.' Fraenkel 199,

N–H and others see him as a 'chorus-master' training his retinue in the performance of a new choral lyric — a dithyramb, say, to be sung at his *orgia*.

5   **Euoi**: this Greek form of the Bacchic cry is usually represented in Latin by *evoe*.

7   **Liber**: 1.12.22 n. Maybe in this line we are meant to take Bacchus as the power of wine.

9   **Thyades**: the Bacchantes.

10–12   Miracles associated with the god's first arrival in Greece and mentioned in Euripides *Bacchae*.

13–14   Ariadne, when deserted by Theseus, was rescued by Bacchus, who placed her crown in heaven.

14–16   Pentheus, king of Thebes, and Lycurgus, king of Thrace, both denied the divinity of Bacchus and were duly punished.

17–21   The repeated *tu* is characteristic of hymnic style.

18   *separatis*: Porphyrio explains as *secretis ac remotis*.

20   **Bistonids**: female Bistones, a Thracian tribe who were enthusiastic worshippers of Bacchus.

21–24   A reference to the war of the Giants against the Gods, 2.12.6–8 n.

29   **Cerberus**: 2.13.33 n. Bacchus went down to Hades to bring back his mother Semele.

30   **golden horn**: Bacchus was given bull's horns in art as a symbol of strength.

20

This amusing ode on Horace's 'olorification' enlarges upon Ennius' famous epigram: *Nemo me dacrumis decoret nec funera fletu/ faxit. cur? uolito uiuu' per ora uirum* 'Let no one honour me with tears or conduct my funeral in grief. Why? I am alive and flitting over men's lips.' It dedicates the book to Maecenas, carrying on from 2.17 and balancing 1.1.

Metre: Alcaics again.

1   *tenui*: pejorative here, despite 2.16.38 *spiritum Graiae tenuem Camenae*; 'chic' implies criticism of Catullus and the Neoterics. Perhaps 'weak' is safer.

2   *penna*: birds fly on wings (or feathers), the wings of the poet (incarnate in his work) are words that fly through the air when his verse is read aloud and travel out through the sky.
      biformis: because he is both a lyric and a hexameter poet (Porphyrio).

5   **the cities**: or *urbis* can be read as a genitive, 'the City's' understanding 'envy' with it.

6   *uocas*: cf. Catullus 44.21 *qui tunc uocat me cum malum librum legi* 'whose invitation means reading bad books.'

9–12   It would be nice if one could take this as allegorical for becoming a papyrus roll or a parchment codex, but though 'rough skin' might refer to a parchment what can one make of 'feathers sprouting on fingers and shoulders'? There is a similar strange description of the soul of a lover sprouting feathers at Plato *Phaedrus* 251B.

13   **Icarus**: 1.1.15 n.

14ff.   Copies of his works are available throughout the Empire and beyond.

15   The swan is a frequent symbol for the poet in antiquity and Horace refers to Pindar as 'the swan of Dirce' (4.2.25). Swans were believed to sing before their death.— Metamorphosis was a poetical subject at the time, though Ovid's epic of that name was written later.
      Gaetulan: poetical for African.

16   **Syrtes**: 2.6.3 n.
      Hyperborean: an ideally happy race of Apollo-worshippers in the far north.
17   **Colchians**: at the south-east end of the Black Sea. For metrical purposes
      pronounce here as three distinct syllables, Col-chi-ans.
      Dacians: 1.26.3–4 n.
18   **Marsian**: 1.2.39 n.
19   **Geloni**: 2.9.23 n.
20   **Drinkers of**: a figure of speech for 'dwellers by.' *Hiber* is literally an Iberian.
21   *inani funere:* could also mean 'at my empty corpse;' he lives on in his poetry.

BOOK THREE

For the first six odes of this book see Introduction p. xiv.

1

The first ode is really about right ambition. Despite extreme differences in wealth, birth and reputation we all have to die. Power and prosperity bring fear and worry; luxury is no consolation for pain and sorrow. One should therefore aim not to make a fortune but to have enough and to be content.

Metre: Alcaics

Added: 36 tons of, 37 As filling-in.

1–4 Horace gives this poetry a religious flavour and as priest of the Muses turns two religious formulae uttered at the beginning of a sacrifice to new use (cf. *Aeneid* 6.258 *procul este profani* 'Stand off, you uninitiated' and 5.71 *ore fauete omnes* 'Keep silence, all').

5–8 Horace follows religious tradition and begins with Jove, cf. Virgil *Eclogues* 3.60 *ab Ioue principium Musae* 'with Jove the Muse begins.' — One should remember that *rex* 'king' is used in Latin of the rich patron with his herd of clients.

7 *Giganteo triumpho:* see 3.4.53ff.

10–11 Elections to curule magistracies were held in the Campus Martius.

17–20 Dionysius, tyrant of Syracuse, threw a luxurious banquet for his sycophant Damocles but suspended a sword by a horsehair over his head to illustrate the danger always threatening a tyrant. By the adjective 'impious' Horace makes the sword symbolize a guilty conscience.

24 *tempe:* originally the proper name of a beauty spot in Thessaly, a wooded valley where, between Mts Ossa and Olympus, the river Peneus flows down to the sea.

26 **never worried**: because he is not an overseas trader or an owner of large estates.

27–28 I.e. by the beginning of bad weather in autumn (referring to the merchant whose ship is at sea).

47 **Sabine vale**: 2.18.14 n.

2

Not money but manliness (*uir-tus*) is the message here, and the way to it is a military career.

Metre: Alcaics

4 *eques:* 1.8.5–6 mention the training of a cavalry officer.

13 This famous line has shocked certain 20th-century poets, e.g. Wilfred Owen 'The old Lie' (Dulce Et Decorum Est) and Ezra Pound 'Died some, pro patria,/ non "dulce" non "et decor" .../ walked eye-deep in hell/ believing in old men's lies ...' (Hugh Selwyn Mauberley IV).— Tyrtaeus, the 7th-century BC Spartan elegist, has the couplet: 'For to die is noble when a good man falls/ Among the foremost fighting for his country.'

14   Cf. Simonides of Ceos (556–468 BC) 'But death overtakes the coward too' (Fragment 524).

17–20 The honours won in war do not depend like those of politics on election by the fickle populace.

19   **axes**: carried by the lictors in the *fasces*, symbolizing the *imperium* of consul or praetor.

21–24 refer to the deification of heroes such as those mentioned in 3.3.9ff. 'The forbidden path' is the return to life as a god after death; Propertius 2.27.16 (of the lover) *concessum nulla lege redibit iter* 'he will return by the route no law allows.'

25   Cf. Simonides (Fragment 582) 'Silence too has a safe reward,' according to Plutarch a favourite saying of Augustus. Its relevance here is not obvious, but the previous stanza has religious overtones and could lead naturally into the topic of the mysteries. Augustus was initiated into the Eleusinian mysteries of Demeter/ Ceres (Suetonius *Augustus* 93). Later the Mithraic mysteries were specially associated with the Roman army.

29   **Diespiter**: 1.34.5 n.

3

The first line makes the connexion with *Virtus* (Manhood) in the preceding ode, and stanzas 3–4 record the names of those *immeriti mori* (3.2.21), leading up to Romulus and through him to Juno's long speech. She is at pains to show that Rome's empire is based on *pietas*, not money, and on disinterested inquiry, not love of conquest. Her veto on the rebuilding of Troy seems to be a purely poetic point, neither historical (despite the rumour reported by Suetonius *Julius* 79.3 that Caesar intended to move the capital of the empire to Alexandria or Troy), nor symbolic (unless Troy represents the Roman Republic as opposed to the Principate).

Metre: Alcaics

Added: 12 Later, 20 paired, 28 onset, 30 now, 36 now, 53 of ours.

9–16 A list of deified sons of gods by mortal mothers.

9   *hac arte:* lit. 'with this characteristic,' *OLD ars* 4.

11   **Augustus**: dates the ode to after January 27 BC. — 'The justice and pertinacity of Augustus were shown in his 14 years war against his uncle's murderers' J. Gow.

15   **Quirinus**: 1.2.46 n.

18   *Ilion, Ilion*: reminiscent of the Greek lament *ailinon, ailinon*.

19–20 refer to Paris and Helen; cf. 1.15.7 n.

21   **Laomedon**: Priam's father. He refused payment to Apollo and Neptune for building the walls of Troy; as punishment they demanded the annual sacrifice of a virgin to a sea-monster sent against Troy by Neptune. One year the lot fell on Laomedon's daughter Hesione. Hercules rescued her, but Laomedon again refused the promised reward. Hercules came with an army, sacked Troy, and killed Laomedon with all his sons save Priam.

22–23 **accursed/ By me ...**: because of the Judgement of Paris (1.15.7 n.).

30–33 Juno had hated her grandson Romulus because he was the son of Ilia, daughter of the Trojan Aeneas, by Mars, who supported the Trojan side in the war against Troy, whereas Juno supported the Greeks.

38   **exiles**: Aeneas and his Trojan followers and their descendants in Italy.

45   **her name**: not her rule, cf. 54 below, where we find *uisere* not *uincere*.

49	**More resolute**: a condition on which 53–54 depend; in effect 'If more resolute ..., then whatever confines ....'
67	**my Argives**: Argos was Hera/Juno's most ancient place of worship. Cf. 1.7.8 n.
69–72	Cf. 2.1.37–40. But in the very next stanza here (3.4.1–4) the Muse receives a very formal invitation, which lends *Descende caelo* a double meaning and touches the following stanzas with ironic humour.
72	**quatrains**: the metre of personal as opposed to public lyric; the latter would normally display strophe, antistrophe, and epode.

4

This ode, the longest in the four Books, stresses the power of music and poetry as a civilizing and protecting force both in Horace's own and in public life. It is contrasted with the aggressive force of the enemies of civilization. Fraenkel 276ff. enlarges on the ode's likeness to and its difference from Pindar's *First Pythian*.

Metre: Alcaics

Added: 10 cottage, 32 distant, 38 country.

4	*fidibus citharaque:* hendiadys ('one thing by means of two').
5	The plural 'you' addresses his audience, the *uirgines puerique* of 3.1.4. 'Her' or 'it' must be supplied, referring to Calliope's music.
10	In the *Satires* Horace mentions his father but never his mother; perhaps she died in childbirth. There is nothing strange about the name *Pullia*; it occurs in inscriptions.
13–15	The places mentioned are all in Horace's native Apulia.
21–22	*in arduos/ tollor Sabinos:* humorous exaggeration, referring to his Sabine farm (cf. 3.1.45–48).
23–24	Fashionable resorts: Praeneste, the modern Palestrina, is high up in the Apennines east of Rome; for Tibur see 1.18.1 n. and for Baiae 2.18.20 n.
26	*Philippis:* Introduction p. xi.
27	*arbos:* see 2.13 introduction.
	Palinurus: a promontory on the west coast of Lucania, named after Aeneas' steersman who was drowned there. Horace mentions this third escape nowhere else.
32	Presumably the Persian Gulf.
34	**Concani**: a Cantabrian tribe.
35	**Geloni**: 2.9.23 n.
36	**Scythian river**: the Tanais (modern Don).
38	This was after Actium. At the time of Octavian's triple triumph in 29 BC he gave his discharged veterans (120,000) in their colonies 1,000 sesterces each (*Res Gestae* 15).
40	**Pierian cave**: metaphorical for some quiet spot suitable for literary pursuits (because the Muses came from Pieria, cf. 4.3.18). On his return from the east in 29 BC Octavian rested at Atella in Campania and there on four consecutive days Virgil and Maecenas read the recently completed *Georgics* to him.
43	**Titanes**: represent the older gods who ruled before the Olympians, six sons and six daughters of Heaven and Earth.
	Giant gang: sons of Earth and Tartarus, some of whom (the Hecatoncheires) were hundred-handed (see lines 50 and 69 below); their names appear in 53–56.
51	**brothers**: Otus and Ephialtes, sons of Aloeus, the Aloidae.

opaco: for 'tree-grown' cf. Virgil *Georgics* 1.282 *frondosum ... Olympum* 'leafy Olympus.'

57   **Palladis aegida:** 1.12.19 n. and 1.15.11 n.
59   **Vulcanus:** 1.4.8 n.
      Juno: 1.7.8 n.
60   Because he is either shooting with his bow or carrying it.
61   **Castalia:** a spring on Mt Parnassus.
64   **Apollo:** 1.2.32 n. He was specially associated with Delos, his birthplace, and Patara in Lycia. Augustus regarded him as his protector and ascribed to him his victory over Antony and Cleopatra at Actium in 31 BC.
65   **counsel:** picks up 41 'advice.'
      mole ruit sua: or closer 'falls by its own brute weight.'
69   **Gyas:** 2.17.14 n.
71   **Orion:** 2.13.39 n.
      Diana: Artemis, Apollo's sister.
73   They had mountains piled on top of them.
75   **Orcus:** 1.28.10 n.
76   Typhoeus was the Giant under Etna.
78   **Tityos:** 2.14.8 n.
80   **Pirithous:** 4.7.28 n.

5

The subject is really *uera uirtus* 'true manliness' (29) as exemplified in the figure of Regulus. The structure, with the main body of the ode occupied by an epic speech, resembles that of 3.3, with which there is the further connexion of Regulus as *iustum et tenacem propositi uirum* (3.3.1).

Metre: Alcaics

Added: 22 in shackles, 26 simply, 46 (*auctor* omitted).

2   **Augustus:** dates the poem to after 16 January 27 BC when on the motion of Munatius Plancus the Senate gave Octavian this name; cf. 3.3.11–12.
4   **Persians:** 1.2.22 n.
5   **Crassus:** Marcus Licinius Crassus, the *triumuir*, had been disastrously defeated by the Parthians at Carrhae in northern Mesopotamia in 53 BC.
9   *Marsus et Apulus:* 1.2.29 n. and 1.22.14 n.
10   *ancilia:* twelve small figure-of-eight sacred shields kept by the Salii in the temple of Mars. One had fallen from heaven in the reign of Numa and on it the safety of Rome was said to depend. Numa caused eleven copies of it to be made to make theft of it more difficult.
11   **Vesta:** the Roman goddess of the hearth in whose small round temple in the Forum a sacred fire was kept continually alight by the Vestal Virgins. Its going out threatened disaster to the state.
13   **Regulus:** in 255 BC in the First Punic War Marcus Atilius Regulus was defeated and captured by the Carthaginians. Legend further recorded that he was sent to Rome to arrange for an exchange of prisoners, having sworn to return to Carthage, that he advised the Senate to vote against the proposal and returned to die by torture in Carthage.
15   **conditions:** Horace does not make it clear what these were. Were they for peace including a ransoming (25) or for an exchange of prisoners? Or is the plural poetic?

25   This suggests that Regulus was sent to obtain a ransom and not an exchange of prisoners.
35   *lora:* leather thongs for tying up prisoners.
37   In war he should fight for his life and not negotiate for it.
42   *capitis minor:* for prose *capite deminutus.* Regulus lost his civic rights when he was taken prisoner.
46   'The *auctor* of a senatus consultum was the senator who first proposed it: those who spoke in favour of it were *suasores*' J. Gow.
53–54 Lit. 'than if, a law-suit settled, he were leaving behind the lengthy business of his clients ....'
55   **Venafran acres**: 2.6.15–16 n.
56   **Tarentum**: 2.6.10–12 n. It was originally a Spartan colony. — Regulus returns to his death like some rich but conscientious *patronus* going to his country villa or to a holiday resort after dealing with all the tedious business of his clients.

6

The importance of religion is the theme of the last and most pessimistic poem in the cycle. Writing perhaps in 29 BC (see note on the first stanza), Horace ascribes to neglect of the gods Rome's recent military defeats and the present corruption of family life. Roman history for him is not progress but degeneration.

Metre: Alcaics

Added: 3 Great, 12 Rich Roman, 21 depraved, 33 Roman, 34 Sicilian, 36 King.

1–4   'Two and eighty temples of the gods in the city as consul for the sixth time (i.e. in 28 BC) on the authority of the Senate I restored' *Res Gestae* 20.4.
8   **Hesperia**: 1.28.26 n.
9   **Monaeses**: the Parthian general who defeated Oppius Statianus, one of Antony's commanders, in 36 BC during the disastrous Parthian expedition of that year.
      Pacorus: a Parthian prince who defeated Decidius Saxa, Antony's legate in Syria, in 40 BC.
12   **chokers**: the Parthians wore collars and armlets of twisted metal.
13–16 Horace is thinking of the situation just before Actium in 31 BC when Antony was supported by the Dacians under their king Cotiso (see 3.8.18) and by Cleopatra's Egyptian fleet (for rhetorical effect here referred to as Ethiopian).
17–20 'Plus ça change, plus c'est la même chose.'
22   **Ionic**: Ionians had a reputation for *mollitia*, soft living and immorality, so 'depraved' is added here.
24   *de tenero ungui: a prima infantia* 'from earliest childhood' (Porphyrio).
25   **younger**: than their husbands.
33–36 refer to the naval battles of the First Punic War (Mylae 260 BC and Ecnomus 256 in Sicily), to the defeat of Antiochus, the Seleucid monarch, at Magnesia in 190, to the defeat of Hannibal at Zama in 202 and of Pyrrhus at Beneventum in 275.
38   At *Epistles* 1.16.49 after describing his Sabine farm Horace refers to himself as a Sabellian, presumably because of his ownership of that farm. The Sabelli, Oscan speakers, originated from the Sabini (Strabo 5.4.12).
45–48 An amazingly pessimistic ending to the series.

7

After the solemnity of the Roman Odes and the pessimism of their concluding stanza this poem comes as a welcome contrast, but at the same time 'affirms their moral standards' (Santirocco 125). The romantic plot reveals the two young men concerned as responsible people; Gyges is a successful businessman as well as a faithful husband, and Enipeus, unlike Sybaris in 1.8, is no shirker of manly sports.

Metre: Third Asclepiad.

1   **Asterie:** Greek, lit. 'Starry.' (Pronounced with four syllables, As-ter-i-ē.)
3   **Thynian:** he has been trading in the Roman province of Bithynia where Catullus served under Memmius (Catullus 10.6–13).
4   *fide:* genitive.
5   **Oricum:** a port in Illyricum opposite Otranto in the heel of Italy.
6   **rose:** towards the end of September.
10   **Chloe:** Gyges' hostess, wife of the friend he is staying with. We are not supposed to ask how the poet has got all this information.
10–11   *tuis/ ... ignibus uri:* could also mean 'is in love with your love,' *OLD ignis* 9b.
13–16   Sthenoboea, the Greek equivalent of Potiphar's wife (Genesis 39). She fell for Bellerophon who refused her, whereupon she accused him of attempted rape.
14   **Proetus:** king of Argos, sent Bellerophon to the king of Lycia with a sealed letter requesting him to kill the bearer. But Bellerophon caught the winged horse Pegasus and with his help managed to perform all the fatal tasks that he was set.
17–20   **Magnessan Hippolyte:** Magnesia was in Thessaly; the adjective distinguishes her from the Amazon Hippolyte. This one was married to Acastus king of Iolcos and fell in love with Peleus, who rejected her advances. She then accused him to Acastus of trying to seduce her and he tried, unsuccessfully, to have Peleus killed.
18   **Tartarus:** for Hades, cf. 1.28.10.
21   **Icarian rocks:** 1.1.15 n.
26   *gramine Martio:* on the Campus Martius, cf. 1.8.4.
28   **Tuscan stream:** the Tiber rises in Etruria.

8

A humorous variant of the invitation poem. Maecenas and his party arrive to find Horace preparing a sacrifice on the day of the Matronalia, a women's festival in honour of Juno.

Metre: Sapphics.

1   *Martiis ... Kalendis:* the date of the annual festival of the foundation of the temple of Juno Lucina, goddess of childbirth, celebrated by married women.
5   *sermones:* strictly 'discussions' but 'researches' makes the humorous point clearer. Maecenas had himself written Dialogues and Menippean Satires.
  either language: Greek and Latin.
6   *Liber:* 1.12.22 n. Like Apollo a god of poetry and poets, cf. 2.19.
7–8   See 2.13.
11   Smoke was thought to mellow wine, which was stored in the *apotheca* so as to catch the heat and smoke of the bath-furnace.
12   A Lucius Volcacius Tullus was consul in 66 BC, the year before Horace was born, and another was consul in 33.
17–24   'So the convivial poem grows imperceptibly into a *carmen civile* and, while setting Maecenas' mind at ease, it extols the *pax Augusta*' Fraenkel 223.
18–19   1.26.3–4 n.

21   **Cantabri**: 2.6.2 n.
23   **Scyths**: 2.9.23 and *Res Gestae* 31 *nostram amicitiam appetiuerunt per legatos Bastarnae Scythaeque* ... ; see 4.14.42 n.
25-28 The picture of Maecenas that Seneca paints in *Epistle* 114.4ff. suggests that Horace is humorously advising him to behave as he always does.

9

This delightful love-duet is Horace's answer to Catullus 45 'Acme and Septimius.'

Metre: Fourth Asclepiad.

Added: 16 darling.

8   **Ilia**: 1.2.17 n. and 3.3.30–33 n. 'Lydia caps the man's 'Persarum vigui rege beatior' with a more patriotic variant on the same model' Quinn.
10   *dulcis docta modos:* lit. 'trained in sweet measures,' referring to musical 'modes,' poetic 'metres' and 'ways of love-making.'
13   **Thurian**: Thurii was a highly civilized Greek colony on the Gulf of Tarentum, founded by Pericles. Lydia's young man is much superior socially to Horace's Thracian. — In the Latin the epithet goes with Ornytus, who is being complimented here.
18   **brazen yoke**: 1.33.11.
22   **angrier**: at *Epistles* 1.20.25 Horace describes himself as *irasci celerem, tamen ut placabilis essem* 'quick to anger but easily placated.'

10

Horace's ironical version of the serenade of an excluded lover, a type of poem technically known by the Greek name that Plutarch gave it as a paraclausithyron (sc. *melos*) or song at the closed door.

Added: 4 All, 7 this, 14 poor ... with cold.

1   Lit. 'If you drank of remotest Tanais' i.e. were you a Scythian, cf. 2.20.20 *Rhodanique potor*.
      Lyce: lit. 'she-wolf,' cf. 1.32.11 *Lycus*.
5-6   *nemus ... tecta:* lit. 'the grove planted between the fine buildings,' referring either to the garden surrounded by the peristyle or cloister of an expensive Roman house, or to the trees between such houses.
10   'A proverbial expression meaning "lest in attempting too much you lose the whole" ' J. Gow. — There will come a point when Lyce's disdainful treatment of her lover will drive him away altogether.
11   **Tyrrhenian**: the Etruscans were reputed to be luxury-loving and loose-living.
      Penelope: 1.17.20.
14   *tinctus uiola:* lit. 'tinged with purple.'
15   **Pierian**: for 'Macedonian' (4.3.18 n.). 'Macedonia had been a Roman province since 146 BC; both government and trade would have provided reasons for Romans to be absent there for long periods.' G. Williams.
20   *latus:* implying sexual powers, cf. Ovid *Ars Amatoria* 2.413.

11

A serio-comic poem ostensibly attempting to persuade a virginal Greek girl to take a lover (the speaker himself). A grandiose invocation of Mercury and the lyre he had invented leads into examples of the miraculous power of its music. In this connexion the Danaids are introduced and used as a warning to Lyde of what can happen to persistent virgins; she should revere Hypermnestra, the right sort of virgin.

Metre: Sapphics.

Added: 37–38 Quick and now.

1   **Amphion**: his lyre music was fabled to have moved into position the stones that built the walls of Thebes.
3   **Turtleshell**: 1.10.6 n.
5   **once**: before Mercury's invention of the lyre.
6   Good evidence for its use at symposia and religious ceremonies.
7   **Lyde**: the name reappears from 2.11 and cf. 3.28.3.
9   **three-year-old**: this was the usual age for training horses (Virgil *Georgics* 3.190–191).
11 **wedlock**: here probably used loosely for sexual intercourse (with a concubine) and 'husband' similarly for a male lover, cf. 2.5.16.
13–24 refer to the power of Orpheus' music and to his descent into the Underworld to win back Eurydice.
13 *tu*: i.e. *testudo*.
15 *immanis*: goes with *aulae*; cf. Matthew Arnold *Requiescat* 'The vasty hall of death.'
17 **Cerberus**: 2.13.33 n. — This stanza is regarded by some as spurious because *eius* is very rare in poetry (despite 4.8.18) and not needed here. For a full discussion see Williams (1969).
21 **Tityos**: 2.14.8 n.
    Ixion: a king of the Lapiths, who tried to seduce Juno. Jupiter punished him by fastening him to an ever-revolving fiery wheel in the Underworld.
24 Danaus king of Argos had fifty daughters, his brother Aegyptus king of Egypt fifty sons. It was arranged that they should marry, but Danaus suspected his nephews of wishing to kill him and persuaded his daughters to kill their husbands on the wedding night. This they all did, except Hypermnestra who saved her husband Lynceus; the other daughters were punished eternally in the Underworld by having to try to fill up a leaking cask. — Between the columns of the portico of Apollo's temple on the Palatine, dedicated by Augustus in 28 BC, were statues of the fifty Danaids.
29 **in Orcus**: strictly 'under Orcus,' here regarded as a person rather than a place, see 1.28.10 n.
33 **One alone**: Hypermnestra.
37 **her youthful husband**: Lynceus.
40 *sorores*: *OLD soror* 1c.
48 **Numidia**: Danaus was also king of Libya.
51 **a tombstone**: lit. 'on tomb' with no pronominal adjective. Some prefer to supply 'my,' taking *nostri* with *sepulcro* as well as with *memor*; others understand 'your' with 'tomb.'

12

This ode appears to have been inspired by a poem of Alcaeus in the same metre, of which what survives (Fragment 10B) proves that the poem was a soliloquy by the girl, and probably the Horatian imitation is also a self-address. It is interesting that the ancient commentator Porphyrio takes it as the poet addressing the girl, which would throw a different light on the description of Hebrus.

Metre: Ionics *a minore* ($\sim$ — —), in four stanzas of ten Ionic feet each, which can be arranged in lines of various lengths, limited by avoidance of word division and convenience of printing.

Added: 2 due, 3 all.

1	**It's a girl's fate***: lit. 'It is for wretched women ....'*
3	**or**: i.e. if they do have a love affair.
4	**an uncle***: lit. 'father's brother,' who was proverbially a strict moralist.
7	**Minerva**: goddess of spinning and weaving.
8	*Liparaei nitor Hebri*: most edd. regard this as the subject of *aufert*, but it is odd to say that Cupid takes away her basket and Hebrus her hand-loom etc. It is more sensible to take the phrase as subject of *lauit*, though placed before *simul*. — *nitor Hebri* = *nitidus Hebrus* and can be qualified by *eques*, cf. Propertius 1.20.15–16 where *error Herculis* 'Hercules' wandering' = *errans Hercules* and can suffer hardship and shed tears.
	Lipara (modern Lipari) is the largest of the Aeolian islands, north of Sicily.
9–16	Hebrus is undergoing all the strenuous exercise (and more) that Sybaris shirks in 1.8.
11	**Bellerophon**: 3.7.13–16 n.
15	**the quickest**: lit. 'quick.'
	extracting: or 'receiving (the attack of).'

13

One of his best known and most beautiful poems, part hymn, part dedicatory epigram.

Metre: Third Asclepiad.

Added: 2 Most, 5 head to head, 6 this, 7 Caprine, 8 his dark, 16 in their ... rush.

3	**Yours**: lit. 'you shall be given.'
	tomorrow: probably 13 October, the festival of Fountains or Fontinalia, when wine and flowers were offered to springs and fountains (Varro *De lingua latina* 6.22).
9	**Dog Star**: 1.17.17 n.
11	**ox**: lit. 'bulls.'
13	**the famous springs**: the poetically inspirational Greek springs, Aganippe, Arethusa, Castalia, Hippocrene etc.
14–15	Lit. 'the ilex planted on the hollow rocks whence ....'

14

In the summer of 24 BC after an absence of three years Augustus returned to Rome from NW Spain where he had been engaged in waging a gruelling war against the Cantabri. His victory was not lasting and they were not finally defeated until 19 BC by Agrippa. Horace composes this ode to greet the Princeps in gratitude for the peace he has brought to the Mediterranean world.

Metre: Sapphics.

1	Hercules' tenth labour was the killing of the three-headed monster Geryon of Gades, whose flocks and herds he drove back to Argos. On the way he called at

the site of Rome and established his worship at the Ara Maxima. The story is told in Virgil *Aeneid* 8 and Propertius 4.9.

5   **his wife**: Livia Drusilla, who had married Augustus in 38 BC after divorce from her first husband Tiberius Claudius Nero, father of the future emperor Tiberius.

7   **sister**: Octavia, mother of Gaius Claudius Marcellus (1.12.46 n.).

11   A famous crux. *expectate* is J. Gow's emendation of MSS *expertae*, avoiding hiatus between *male* and *ominatis*.
     uirum: here emphatic (*OLD uir* 3) = Augustus.

13–16 This stanza is the connecting link between the public and private sections of the ode.

18–20 A reminder of earlier horrors, the Marsian or Social War (91–87 BC) which forced Rome to enfranchise the Italians, and the slave revolt led by the Thracian gladiator Spartacus from 73–71 when he was defeated and killed by M. Licinius Crassus, who crucified the prisoners he took.

19   *si qua:* or 'if somehow,' *OLD qua* C9.

21–24 Cf. 2.11.21–24.

22   *murreum:* may also refer to colour — 'reddish brown' (*OLD*).

24   **give up**: *OLD abeo* 14.

28   *consule Planco:* 42 BC the year of Philippi when Horace fought on the losing side.

15

It makes sense to connect this poem with 2.5.17–20; we now learn that Chloris is Pholoe's mother and that Pholoe was *fugax* 'flighty' because she was young and inexperienced. Time has passed and now Pholoe is mature and keen, while Chloris has had her day and is advised to behave like a respectable *matrona*.

Metre: Fourth Asclepiad.

1   **indigent**: a bit too strong for *pauper* 'not well off.'

11   **Nothus**: the name appears in inscriptions; it is Greek for 'bastard' (cf. the Latin name Spurius) and used of the offspring of a citizen and a slave.

13   Cf. the sepulchral epitaph in praise of a Roman matron: *domum seruauit, lanam fecit* 'She kept house, made wool' (*Corpus Inscriptionum Latinarum* 1.1007).

14   **Luceria**: in Apulia; produced particularly fine wool.

16

'Placed at the beginning of the second half of Book III, it serves as the dedication of this book to Maecenas' Fraenkel 229. It expresses Horace's gratitude to his patron, while at the same time emphasizing his contented independence. One senses humour in his implied imitation of Maecenas (18–20) and in his claim to be free from desire and a deserter from the ranks of the rich (21–23). 1.31, 2.2, 2.16 and 18 are comparable.

Metre: Second Asclepiad.

Added: 7 quite

1–8 Acrisius, king of Argos, was warned by an oracle that he would be killed by his grandson. He therefore immured his only daughter in a brazen tower, but Jupiter, entering as a shower of gold, made her pregnant with Perseus. The Stoics interpreted the story as an allegory of the power of money.

12   **The Argive soothsayer**: Amphiarus knew that if he joined the Seven against Thebes he would be killed, so he went into hiding. His wife Eriphyle was bribed

by a necklace of gold and diamonds to betray his whereabouts and cause his death. Her son Alcmaeon killed her to avenge his father and like Orestes was pursued by the Furies.

13 **Macedonia's king**: Philip, father of Alexander the Great. He used to say that any fort could be taken if it could be reached by a donkey loaded with gold (Cicero *Ad Atticum* 1.16.12).

16 **Admirals**: such as Sextus Pompey's admiral Menas, who was twice won over to Octavian's side by a bribe.

20 Cf. 1.20.5.

21 **can do without**: lit. 'had denied himself.'

22 **Gods**: 1.17.13 n.

23 **Who have mastered desire**: lit. 'who desire nothing.'

28 Lit. 'resourceless amid great resources.'

29–30 His Sabine farm.

31–32 Lit. 'escape the notice of one resplendent with *imperium* as more blest than the lot of fertile Africa;' lots were drawn for governorship of the provinces and the richest province was Africa.

35 **Formian**: Formiae was believed to be the Homeric Laestrygonia.

36 **Gallican**: Cisalpine Gaul produced fine white wool.

41 **Alyattes**: king of Lydia, father of Croesus.

42 **Mygdonia**: 2.12.22 n.

17

A humorous genethliacon or birthday poem. Horace constructs for his friend Lamia (cf. 1.26.8 and 36.7) a spoof genealogy of the kind fashionable in Roman aristocratic circles; e.g. Cluentii, Memmii, and Sergii traced their descent to the Trojans Cloanthus, Mnestheus, and Sergestus respectively. So Horace derives Lamia from Lamus, king of the Laestrygonians, cannibal giants in Homer's *Odyssey*, who were associated with Formiae (3.16.35 n.) in whose neighbourhood Lamia's estate must have lain. Spoof genealogy is followed by spoof weather forecast for Lamia's birthday when he would by tradition make offerings to his Genius.

Metre: Alcaics.

1 *nobilis:* in a genealogical context refers to someone whose family has produced a consul. The consul in Aelius' case is a cannibal king.

7 *princeps:* here both 'first' and 'as chief.'
Liris: now Garigliano.

8 **Marica**: the Nymph of the river Liris, worshipped at Minturnae where it flows into the sea through marshland.

9 **Wide-ruling king**: refers back to 5 *that founder who* (= Lamus).

16 **Genius**: each man's guardian spirit. 'The Companion who tempers the star of our birth, the God of human nature, subject to death in each individual life' Horace *Epistles* 2.2.187–9. He was also identified with the Lar by many.

18

A prayer to Faunus (cf. 1.17.1–12) to prosper the poet's farm in return for the due celebration of his festival, the Faunalia, on 5 December each year.

Metre: Sapphics.

Added: 7 and.

5   *si:* either for *si modo* 'provided that' or *siquidem* 'inasmuch as.'
       falls: as a sacrifice.

10   **Nones**: by inclusive counting the ninth day before the Ides which were the 13th of every month except March, July, October, May when they fell on the 15th. So the Nones were on the 5th of every month except these four when they fell on the 7th.

13   **prowling**: lit. 'wandering,' without hurting them.

19

A difficult ode to interpret. The scene appears to be a *cena* at which arrangements are to be made for a future symposium, but the host has been boring the company with remote questions of genealogy and early history (1–8). The poet can stand it no longer and takes over as master of ceremonies, introducing the carousal (*comissatio*) that often follows a dinner (9–28). Alternatively one imagines a time-gap between lines 8 and 9 and can take 9–28 as the actual party for which the arrangements called for in 5–8 have been made. In any case the ode celebrates the co-option to the augural college of Murena, presumably the Licinius of 2.10.1.

Metre: Fourth Asclepiad.

Added: 8 all this, 12 for us, 17 in this.

1   **Inachus**: 2.3.21 n.

2   **Codrus**: the last king of Athens; he brought about his own death because of an oracle that the Dorians would defeat the Athenians if Codrus survived the battle.

3   **issue of Aeacus**: Telamon and Peleus with their descendants Teucer, Achilles, Neoptolemus etc.

5   **Chian**: a choice Greek wine from Chios.

6   **heating the water**: for mixing with the wine in cold weather. But some take it as referring to bath-water.

8   **Pelignian cold**: Ovid, a Pelignian, calls Sulmo *gelidus* 'icy.' The phrase here is probably proverbial.

9   **pour**: so that the company can drink the three toasts mentioned. With the genitive of the toast understand *cyathos*, cf. 3.8.13–14.

10   It is midnight on 31 December and Murena's augurate begins on 1 January.

11–17 There are two mixing-bowls; in one the wine is mixed in the proportion of three measures of wine to nine of water, in the other in the proportion of nine measures of wine to three of water. Alternatively the choice does not refer to proportion but to simple quantity. The wine is already mixed in the *cratera* and the guest can choose to have either three or nine *cyathi* of the mixture poured into his wine-cup for each toast.

12   *miscentor:* 3rd person plural of imperative passive of *miscere.*

19   **Berecynthian**: 1.18.14 n.

26   **serene**: lit. 'cloudless.'
       Vesper: 2.9.10 n.
       Telephus: also at 1.13.1–2 and 4.11.21. Some interpreters suppose that he is the host here.

27   **Rhode**: only here; a Greek name = 'rose' (the plant rather than the flower, *rhodon*).

28   **Glycera**: re-appears from 1.19, 1.30 and 33.

20

The subject is taken from Hellenistic epigram. Horace advises the young man Pyrrhus, who has fallen for the beautiful boy Nearchus, not to try to steal him from the anonymous woman who loves him.

Metre: Sapphics.

Added: 13 of victory, 15 the boy.

11–16 Nearchus, supremely confident in his beauty, tramples on the palm-leaf because he knows that in fact he is the winner.

15–16 **Nireus**: after Achilles the best-looking of all the Greeks at Troy (*Iliad* 2.673).
 the boy ... Ida: Ganymede, see 4.4.4 n.

21

'It soon becomes clear that the poem is in prayer-form' writes Gordon Williams. In fact it was not until 1913 when Eduard Norden published his famous discussion of the ode in his book *Agnostos Theos* that this important point was recognized and the ode was seen to be a light-hearted parody. For a similar parody of hymnic style see Catullus 44 *O funde noster seu Sabine seu Tiburs ...* 'Our Farm, which art or Sabine or Tiburtan ....'

Metre: Alcaics.

Added: 16 too, 18 of defiant pride.

1 **Manlius**: Lucius Manlius Torquatus was consul in 65 BC.
2–4 *seu ... siue ... seu ... seu:* the noun-verb pairs here represent Greek compound adjectives as titles of a divinity.
5 *quocumque ... nomine:* for a prayer to be answered it was important to address the god by the right name and this formula is intended to cover any omissions. The other meaning of *nomen* here is probably 'reason' (*OLD nomen* 26).
6 *Massicum:* 1.1.19 n.
7 **Come down**: as god from Heaven, as wine-jar from the wine-loft (see 3.8.11 n.).
 Corvinus: Marcus Valerius Messalla Corvinus (64 BC – AD 9), consul 31 BC, triumphed over the Aquitani 27, orator, historian, literary critic and patron of Tibullus and others.
9 Philosophy was another of Messalla's interests and he had been a student at Athens with Horace when Caesar was murdered.
11 **old Cato**: the Censor (234–149 BC), a champion of old Roman *uirtus*.
13 *tu:* its repetition in 14 and 17 (with *te* 10, 19, 21) is characteristic of hymnic style (2.19.17ff.). — Torture makes people talk, so does wine; it is therefore a 'gentle torture.'
15 **Lyaeus**: 1.7.23 n.
18 *cornua:* symbolizing power (2.19.30 n.).
21 **Liber**: 1.12.22 n.

22

This ode is related to the dedicatory epigrams found in Book 6 of the *Greek Anthology*. It has special point if we suppose that Horace is dedicating a pine-tree to Diana in gratitude for the safe birth of a child perhaps fathered by him on one of the slave-girls at his Sabine farm (hence the emphasis on Diana as helping girls in labour). The child is male, hence the sacrifice of a boar rather than a sow. Presumably the sacrifice will take place on the boy's birthday each year. Horace would hardly be so interested in him unless the boy were his own.

Metre: Sapphics.

Added: 7 one.

1–4   Cf. Catullus' hymn to Diana, 34.9 and 13–16.
6   **And … I shall … give it**: lit. 'which I am to give.'

23

Horace addresses a countrywoman whose Greek name suggests 'thrifty,' assuring her that the Lares do not require expensive sacrifices. A garland of rosemary and myrtle is enough (13–16) or even an offering of meal and salt.

Metre: Alcaics.

Added: 12 severed.

1   *supinas:* Greeks and Romans prayed with hands uplifted, palm upwards.
2   *rustica:* some say that Phidyle is the wife of Horace's *uilicus* or farm-manager, but had he wished to make that clear he could have written *uilica* for *rustica*.
8   Lit. 'the sickly season when autumn yields its fruits' (Loeb Classical Library).
10–11 **Algidus … Alban**: 1.21.6 n.
13   *tinget:* lit. 'will stain;' for this type of future tense cf. 1.7.1 *laudabunt alii*.
17   *immunis:* a crux. The ancient commentators Acro and Porphyrio understand *scelerum* and say it means 'innocent,' which would give the best sense but is unparalleled. There is however good warrant for the meaning 'giftless' (cf. 4.12.23 *immunem*), i.e. here 'without a sacrifice' but simply with an offering of *far et sal* 'emmer wheat and salt,' which is here thrown on the altar fire so that the salt-grains jump about.

24

A passionate poetic diatribe against the worship of money in contemporary Rome and an urgent callfor moral reform. It has much in common with the Roman Odes, especially with 3.1 and 6, but was probably written before them, perhaps not long after Octavian's triple triumph in 29 BC.

Metre: Fourth Asclepiad.

Added: 15 twelve months, 36 Public, 42 all, 58 maybe.

4   Text uncertain.
5   **Necessity**: cf. 1.35.17–20.
9–24 An idealized picture of the 'noble savages' of the North whose simple lifestyle contrasts with the greed, luxury and immorality of the Romans.
12   *immetata:* because it was common land.
23   **a second man**: or 'another's man.'
25–32 A reference to Augustus, in support of his proposed moral legislation; see *Res Gestae* 8.5.
27   PATER VRBIVM: a variant of *Pater Patriae*, a title which Augustus was not officially given until 2 BC.
36   I.e. 'unless there is a moral majority.'
       If: continuing the 'If' of 34.
44   **steep**: with 'integrity' in the Latin.

45   Augustus gave the temple of Capitoline Jupiter 16,000 pounds of gold, and jewellery worth 50 million sesterces (Suetonius *Augustus* 30).

56   The wild boar is a formidable antagonist. For the popularity of hunting cf. *Epistles* 1.18.49–52.

60   *hospites*: 'guest-friends' and 'strangers,' to deceive whom was a specially heinous crime.

25

Inspired by Bacchus (presumably literal wine, cf. Propertius 3.17 and 4.6.69ff.) Horace conceives the idea of a new type of poetry, political in praise of Caesar, in the metre of personal lyric. The idea excites him, the more so because of its difficulty and the danger of failure. The ode is connected with the previous one in the same metre, especially with lines 25–32 there; also with the Roman Odes, to which it may look forward (cf. 3.1.1–4).

Metre: Fourth Asclepiad.

Added: 6 in the sky, 16 bare.

4–6   I.e. this new poetry will represent Caesar Augustus as a god.

7   *dicam*: could be future like 4 *audiar*, but subjunctive seems more appropriate here.

9   *Euhias*: title of a female follower of Bacchus, from *euhoe* (*evoe*) the cry of the Bacchantes.

10–11   **Hebrus ... Rhodope**: river and mountain in Thrace.

16   **trees**: lit. 'ash-trees.'

19   **Lenaeus**: title of Bacchus derived from the Greek word for wine-press, *lēnos*.

20   **wearing**: describes the god primarily (cf. 4.8.33), though it could also describe the worshipper.

26

This ode is inspired, in part, by those epigrams in Book 6 of the *Greek Anthology* (cf. 3.22 above) in which a person, usually on the point of retiring, dedicates the tools of his or her trade or profession to its patron deity. Horace claims that his successful career as a lover is over and dedicates to Venus his serenading kit. But the prayer he then makes to her proves that he is still susceptible. The tone is humorous and ironical.

Metre: Alcaics.

Added: 11 Venus.

1   *Vixi*: Gordon Williams quotes Dido at Virgil *Aeneid* 4.653 *vixi et quem dederat cursum Fortuna peregi* 'My life is over and I have completed the course Fortune gave' to suggest the full colour of this perfect tense.

2   *militaui*: cf. Ovid *Amores* 1.9.1 *militat omnis amans* 'every lover is a soldier.'

5   *marinae*: because Venus was sea-born (1.4.5 n.) and maybe also because this imaginary temple is near the sea.

7   **torches**: required on the lover's nocturnal visits.

       crowbars: to force open the locked door of his mistress.

       axes: *securesque* is Bentley's emendation for *et arcus* 'bows' of the MSS, a word which is incomprehensible here.

9   **Cyprus**: 1.3.1 n.

10   **Memphis**: Herodotus 2.12 places a temple of Venus there.

Sithonian: 1.18.9 n. Chloe is Thracian (3.9.9) and Gordon Williams sees here a reference to Thrace's chilly climate and to her chilly treatment of the poet.

11   **whip**: cf. Tibullus 1.8.5–6 *ipsa Venus ... perdocuit multis non sine uerberibus* 'Venus herself ... has flogged me to full knowledge.'

27

An extraordinary propempticon (cf. 1.3) for the girl Galatea whom the speaker loves and for whom he writes a dramatic version of the story of Europa — as a deterrent? If so, the last stanza implies that to be one of Jove's 'wives' and to have a continent named after one is cold consolation for the loss of human love such as the poet's. The poem is similar to 3.11 in its use of myth.

Metre: Sapphics.

Added: 10 well, 17 now, 31 Then, 43 wearisome, 53 Long.

1   *parrae:* identification of this bird of ill omen is uncertain.

3   **Alban hills**: lit. 'fields of Lanuvium,' in the Alban hills south of Rome.

7   *cui:* understand *ei* 'for him' as antecedent to go with *suscitabo*.

9–12   Augural hocus-pocus to help the person he is worried about.

10–11 **that prophetic/ Bird**: the raven.
        oscinem: oscen is 'a bird that gives omens by its cry' (*OLD*). The ancient etymology of the word is from *os oris* 'mouth' and *canere* 'to sing.'

13–14 'Galatea is leaving with her lover. When we realize this we can detect the playful malice in Horace's innocent-sounding valediction.' Quinn (1963) 259.

18   *pronus Orion:* 1.28.22 n.

19   **white**: 1.7.15 n.

20   **Iapyx**: 1.3.4 n. Two syllables in the English here.

22   **Auster**: the south wind.

25   **thus**: the likeness is not immediately apparent. Probably 'Just as you are trusting yourself to your new lover and the storms of the Adriatic, so did Europa trust herself to the bull who took her overseas.' Europa was daughter of Agenor king of Tyre. Jupiter fell for her, appeared to her in the form of a gentle bull and carried her over the sea to Crete. There she bore him Minos and Rhadamanthus. — The Hellenistic poet Moschus (2nd century BC) tells the story in his epyllion *Europa.* Horace treats it quite differently and is more influenced by Catullus' Ariadne (64.132–201).

27   *medias ... fraudes:* strictly 'middle, or intervening, deceits.'

33   The Homeric epithet for Crete is *hekatompolis* 'hundred-citied.'

35   *filiae:* taken as dative of the agent with *relictum.*

37   **virgins' crime**: loss of chastity.

41   Homer (*Odyssey* 19.562–67) says that dreams come from Hades, the true through a gate of horn, the false through a gate of ivory.

50   *Orcum moror:* lit. 'I keep Orcus waiting.' On Orcus, 1.28.10 n.

53–54 Lit. 'Before ugly emaciation attacks my comely cheeks ....'

57–66 Europa imagines her father's reaction.

59   **the belt**: symbol of the virginity she has lost.

65   **concubine**: the husband's concubine would be his wife's slave.

67–68 *perfidum ... arcu:* so Venus has cooked up the whole thing and Cupid as desire in this affair has shot his bolt.

71   *cum:* causal, *OLD cum* 6a.

72   Taken as a Latin imitation of the Greek nominative and infinitive construction;
       but it can also be taken as 'You do not know how to be wife to ....'
75   *sectus orbis:* lit. 'a slice of the globe.' Why Europe was named after Europa is
       obscure.

28

To celebrate the Neptunalia, Neptune's annual festival held on July 23, Horace spends
the day and night with Lyde, whom we have already met in 2.11 and 3.11. One feels the
poem may have some further point which is lost on us.

Metre: Fourth Asclepiad.

Added: 11 Then.

3   *strenua:* military terminology like line 4 and 8 *cessantem.*
       Caecuban: 1.20.9 n.
7   *parcis:* perhaps better as a question 'Are you slow ... ?.'
8   Marcus Calpurnius Bibulus was consul with Julius Caesar in 59 BC, but
       presumably his name is chosen here as a joke (*bibulus* = 'hard-drinking').
12   **Latona**: 1.21 introduction.
       swift: the translation transfers the epithet from Cynthia to her arrows.
       Cynthia: 1.21.2 n. Here as the moon goddess.
13–14 **the Queen of**: lit. 'of her who holds ...' i.e. Venus, cf. 1.30.1.
       fulgentis ... Cycladas: cf. 1.14.19–20 *nitentis ... Cycladas.*
16   I.e. 'we shall make love.'

29

A grander and much enlarged version of 3.8, finally endorsing the dedication to
Maecenas of all three books of Odes. In 1685 Dryden published a fine paraphrase 'in
Pindaric Verse' Here is his expansion of 41–43 (text as in J. Sargeaunt ed. *The Poems of
John Dryden*, Oxford, repr. 1945):

> Happy the Man, and happy he alone,
>   He, who can call to day his own:
>   He who, secure within, can say,
> To morrow do thy worst, for I have liv'd to-day.

Metre: Alcaics.

Added: 5 So, 17 till lately, 58 weak.

1   **Tyrrhenian**: Etruscan, see 1.1.1 n.
4   *balanus:* a nut producing fragrant oil, whose identification is uncertain.
6   **simply**: lit. 'always.'
       well-watered: because of its famous falls.
7   **Aefulae**: in the hills between Tibur (Tivoli) and Praeneste (Palestrina).
8   **Telegonus**: Ulysses' son by Circe. When sent by her to find his father he
       unwittingly killed him. Legend made him the founder of Tusculum, another
       fashionable place for the country-houses of the rich.
10   Maecenas' town-house on the Esquiline had a famous tower, the *turris
       Maecenatiana*, from which Nero was later to watch Rome burning. The places in
       stanza 2 were all visible from it.

17–20 give the time of year as July during the unhealthy Dog Days. Andromeda's father is Cepheus; Procyon the Lesser Dog heralds the rising of Canis Major (Sirius). The traditional dates for Leo are 23 July to 23 August.

23   **Silvanus**: Latin god of the woods and the wild country, sometimes identified with Pan.

        while: lit. 'and.'

27   **Cyrus**: 2.2.19 n.

        Bactrian: Bactria was the NE province of the Parthian empire, roughly the modern Balkh in Afghanistan.

28   **Tanais**: the river Don, cf. 3.10.1.

33   *aequus:* i.e. *aequo animo.*

        the rest: i.e. the future, as opposed to *quod adest.* The *carpe diem* theme again.

35–41 He is thinking of the Tiber, which was prone to floods.

43   *uixi:* some editors limit the direct speech to this word, others carry it on to 48 *uexit*, or even to the end of the ode.

54–55 Horace humorously claims that virtue (also 'manliness,' cf. 3.2.17 and 21) is his *abolla*, or philosopher's cloak.

62–64 His imaginary treasure-ship may founder but he will escape in its dinghy, rowing himself — an amusing picture.

64   **Pollux**: he and his twin Castor were protectors of sailors.

30

It was customary for ancient poets to give a brief personal account of themselves at the end of a work or in the last poem of a collection; see, for example, Virgil *Georgics* 4.559–566 and Propertius 1.22. Such an epilogue was known as a *sphragis* (Greek for 'seal,' or 'signature' as we might say). Horace combines this with the proud claim that his Odes are an intellectual monument that will outlast all merely physical monuments. Shakespeare makes a similar claim for his Sonnets (55.1–2, text as in Thorpe's 1609 Quarto):

> Not marble, nor the guilded monument,
> Of Princes shall out-live this powrefull rime.

Metre: First Asclepiad, answering 1.1.

Added: 9 Vesta's.

1   **bronze**: often used for public inscriptions and statues.

2   **rubble**: *situs* can also mean 'placement' and 'structure.'

        altius: OLD *altus* 13.

3   *impotens:* the opposite of 3.29.41 *potens sui.*

7   **Libitina**: the Italian goddess of death. At her temple in Rome (HQ of the undertakers' guild) a register of deaths was kept.

8–9   The Pontifex Maximus and the chief Vestal Virgin ascending to the temple of Jupiter Optimus Maximus on the Capitol represent Roman religious observance. Horace was not to know that all such pagan observance would be abolished by Theodosius in AD 392.

10   **Aufidus**: a river (now Ofanto) in Apulia, Horace's native country.

11   **Daunus**: 1.22.14 n.

        pauper aquae: cf. *Epodes* 3.16 *siticulosae Apuliae* 'of thirsty Apulia.'

12–13 *ex humili potens/ princeps:* words from the political vocabulary. Horace is proud of having overcome the handicap of his birth as son of a former slave. Cf.

Epistles 1.20.23 *me primis Vrbis belli placuisse domique* 'I found favour with Rome's leading men in war and at home.'

Aeolium carmen: see Introduction p. xiii.

14   *deduxisse:* the translation follows *OLD deduco* 12d, but the word is also used of spinning (*OLD* 4), of founding a colony (*OLD* 9) and of bringing to Rome (*OLD* 10), so there is an implied comparison between Daunus colonizing Apulia and Horace naturalizing Greek lyric metres in Latin.

    rhythms: or 'tunes' *OLD modus* 8.

15   **Melpomene:** 1.24.3 n.

16   Apollo's Delphic bay as poetic crown reminds one of the bay-wreath worn by triumphing Roman generals.

BOOK FOUR

Suetonius in his *Vita Horati* explains the origin of Book 4 of the Odes thus: 'He (Augustus) was so impressed by his (Horace's) writings and so convinced of their immortality that he employed him not only to compose the *Carmen Saeculare* but to celebrate the Vindelician victory of Tiberius and Drusus his stepsons and on this account compelled him to add a fourth book after a long interval to the three books of the *Odes*.'

1

A variation on the theme of 1.19 and 3.26, with the important addition of a description of a young Roman noble. 'The portrait of Paullus Fabius Maximus is to be the first in a series of similar ones, and this gallery of portraits is the most distinctive element of the fourth book' Fraenkel 413. He was consul in 11 BC, an intimate of Augustus, an accomplished orator and patron of literature, some twenty years younger than Horace. Syme is convinced that this ode is an epithalamium for his marriage in 16 or 15 BC to Marcia, a cousin of Augustus (*Roman Papers* 6.241).

Metre: Fourth Asclepiad

Added: 21 rich, 22 sweet, 25 every, 32 garlands, 36 embarrassment, 40 as you swim past.

4   **Cinara**: she is mentioned in 4.13.21–23, *Epistles* 1.7.28 and 14.33, and must be a real person.
5   Cf. 1.19.1 *Mater saeua Cupidinum.*
6   *circa lustra decem:* Horace was born in 65 BC, which dates this ode to about 15 BC.
9   *in domum:* with *comissabere* in imitation of the Greek construction with *kōmazein* 'to go revelling.'
10   *purpureis ales oloribus:* lit. 'winged by lustrous swans.'
12   *torrere iecur:* lit. 'to roast a liver.'
15   *puer:* lit. 'boy,' 'strictly till the seventeenth year, but frequently applied to those who are much older' L&S.
18   **extravagant**: transferred from the rival to his gifts.
19   'On that ridge of the Alban hills which overlooks the Lago di Albano on the one side and the Lago di Nemi on the other' Fraenkel 412. Paullus must have had a villa in the neighbourhood.
20   He will dedicate a shrine and a marble statue to you.
22–24 Lit. 'and you will be delighted by mingled tunes of lyre and Berecynthian flute, not without pan-pipes.'
24   **Berecynthian**: 1.18.14 n.
28   **In the Salian style**: 1.36.12 n.
33   **Ligurinus**: lit. 'the Ligurian,' reappears in 4.10.
35–36 *decoro/ inter:* T.E. Page writes of this hypermetric line with elision of *-o* before *inter* 'Horace clearly designs it to express the effect of a lover breaking off in the middle of a word.' It is certainly *parum decorum*, 'improper' metrically!
38–40 Ligurinus is engaging in the sports that Sybaris in 1.8 is shirking; see the introduction to that ode.

2

Another recusatio; cf. the introduction to 1.6 and 2.12. It reads as though Iullus Antonius (for whom see note on line 26) had suggested to Horace that he should write a Pindaric ode in honour of Augustus' triumph over the Sygambri, a powerful German tribe who had defeated Marcus Lollius, the governor of Gaul, in 16 BC. In the summer of 16 BC Augustus left Rome to deal with the situation in Gaul, but after that was occupied in Spain and did not return to Rome until 13 BC. Horace spends five stanzas describing Pindaric verse in one long Pindaric-style sentence (5–24), contrasting with it his own type of lyric (25–32). In the name of Iullus he goes on to celebrate Augustus and his supposed future triumph, describing himself as one of the spectators.

Metre: Sapphics.

Added: 5 heavy (representing the plural *imbres*), 34 crown of, 38 ever ... this, 43 honouring, 57 horned ... young, 58 now.

1   **Pindar**: the Greek choral lyric poet, born about 520 BC.
2–3   He will fall like Icarus who gave his name to the Icarian sea. See 1.1.15 n.
7   *immensus:* lit. 'unmeasured' cf. 11–12 *numeris ... lege solutis.* It appears that Pindar's metrical systems were not properly understood in Horace's time.
10–24   describe various kinds of Pindaric poetry: 10–12 dithyrambs in honour of Dionysus, 13–16 hymns and paeans to gods and heroes, 17–20 epinicians celebrating victors in various events at the various Greek Games, 21–24 *threnoi,* or dirges.
14–16   Pirithous killed the Centaurs (1.18.8 n.), Bellerophon the Chimaera (1.27.24 n.).
17   **Elean palm**: 1.1.3–6.
18   *caelestis:* accusative plural.
22–23   *moresque ... nigroque:* two consecutive hypermetric lines, perhaps suggesting Pindar's metrical boldness.
24   **Orcus**: 1.28.10 n.
25   **Swan of Dirce**: Pindar was a Theban, Dirce a spring near Thebes, and swan a frequent metaphor for poet, cf. 2.20.
26   Iullus Antonius, son of Mark Antony, married to a niece of Augustus, praetor in 13 BC, consul in 10 BC. As one of Julia's lovers he was condemned to death in 2 BC. He is also said to have been a poet who wrote a *Diomedea* in twelve books of epic hexameters.
27   **Matine**: must here be a trope for Apulian, Apulia being Horace's *patria*; cf. 1.28.3 n.
31   **Tibur**: 1.18.1 n.
33   **You**: Iullus Antonius.
35   **up the Via Sacra**: i.e. 'up the sacred slope' on the way to the Temple of Capitoline Jupiter.
36   **Sygambri**: see introductory note. In fact they withdrew from Gaul before the arrival of Augustus, gave hostages and made peace.
37   *nihil maius meliusue:* a clear allusion to Jupiter's title Optimus Maximus.
39–40   **to ... gold**: to the mythical Golden Age.
42   **Public Games**: gladiatorial Games held specially for this occasion.
46–47   *O Sol/ pulcher! O laudande!:* the first half of a trochaic tetrameter catalectic, skilfully appearing in a Sapphic stanza. This popular metre was used by soldiers at triumphs, e.g. Suetonius *Julius* 51 *Vrbani, seruate uxores! moechum caluum adducimus.* 'City-dwellers, guard your wives! We bring the bald adulterer.' The second half of Horace's tetrameter could be *iam recepto Caesare.*
49   A famous crux here. The text printed is Bentley's.

54–60   A fine example of Horace's *operosum carmen* 'elaborate poetry.'
54   **release**: from my vow.

3

The poet is born, not made, and his poetry is a gift from some power other than his conscious self. The ode links up with 3.30 in naming Melpomene as his lyric Muse, but Horace in his fifties, with Odes 1–3 (23 BC) and *Carmen Saeculare* (17 BC) behind him, has become, as virtual poet laureate, more modest about his achievement.

Metre: Fourth Asclepiad.

Added: 20 poetic.

1–2   Horace is thinking of Callimachus *Aetia* 1.37–38, roughly 'If the Muses have looked on a child with no disapproving eye, they remain his friends in old age.'
3   **Isthmian toil**: the Isthmian games held at Corinth every second year in honour of Poseidon.
4–5   Cf. 1.1.3–6 and 4.2.17–19.
7   **Delian**: Apolline, Delos being the god's birthplace.
8–9   I.e. in a Roman Triumph.
10   Horace had a house at Tibur in addition to his Sabine farm (Suetonius *Vita Horati ad fin.*).
11   Cf. *Epistles* 2.2.77 *scriptorum chorus omnis amat nemus et fugit urbem* 'the whole choir of authors loves the woods and flees the city' and Tacitus *Dialogus* 9 *Adice quod poetis ... in nemora et lucos, id est in solitudinem recedendum est* 'Add that poets ... have to withdraw into woods and groves, i.e. into solitude.'
12   *Aeolio carmine*: 2.13.24–28 n.
        nobilem: also 'noble' cf. 4.1.13 of Paulus Maximus. Horace, the freedman's son, had none the less become a *nobilis* in Rome's hierarchical society.
17–18   The Muses were *Pierides* as coming from Pieris in Macedonia.
        turtleshell: 1.10.6 n.
24   *quod spiro*: cf. 4.6.29–30 *spiritum Phoebus mihi ... dedit*. The English scansion is tricky here: 'My' elides with 'in-,' 'ation and' becomes 'aysh nand.'

4

Despite his claim in 4.2.1–4 that Pindar is inimitable, Horace here produces a virtual epinicion, not in a Pindaric choral metre but in Alcaics, a metre of personal lyric. Otherwise the ode has all the features of a Pindaric victory ode: praise of the victor Drusus and his family, lengthy similes (1–16), a learned parenthesis (18–22), moral maxims (29–36) and Hannibal's speech (taking the place of the usual myth). — The campaign of Augustus' stepsons Drusus and his elder brother Tiberius (the future emperor) against the Alpine tribes took place in 15 BC, opening up the route to Germany; Tiberius' part is celebrated in 4.14.

Metre: Alcaics.

Added: 25 soon, 26 well, 46 all, 48 overturned, 50 natural, 60 renewed, 64 magical, 69 town.

1   The eagle sometimes appears in Graeco-Roman art as carrying Jove's thunderbolt in his talons.
4   Jove employed the eagle to kidnap Ganymede, the beautiful son of Tros, king of Troy, to be his cup-bearer.

13 This picks up from line 1.
17 The Vindelici were a Bavarian tribe, north of the Rhaeti; the latter lived in an area extending from eastern Switzerland through the Tyrol to the Brenner Pass.
18 **Drusus**: a cognomen of the *gens Liuia*. Nero Claudius Drusus was the son of Livia Drusilla by her first husband Tiberius Claudius Nero, who divorced her so she could marry Augustus in 38 BC.
28 Nero was a cognomen of the *gens Claudia*; it was first used as a praenomen by Drusus (see n. 18). On Roman nomenclature, *OCD*[3] names, personal, Roman.
29 *fortes:* the connexion is that Nero in the Sabine language = *fortis ac strenuus* (Suetonius *Tiberius* 1.2).
38 **Metaurus**: the Umbrian river where Hannibal's brother Hasdrubal was defeated and killed by the consul Gaius Claudius Nero in 207 BC.
42 *dirus ... Afer:* Hannibal.
53–56 The *Aeneid* had been published soon after Virgil's death in 19 BC.
54 **Tuscan waters**: the *mare Tyrrhenum* between the west coast of Italy, Siciliy and Sardinia.
 to emigrate/ ... Deities: lit. 'safely carried its sacred things.'
56 **Ausonian**: poetical for Italian.
58 **Algidus**: 1.21.6 n.
61 **hydra**: a monstrous many-headed watersnake in the marshes of Lerna near Argos. As fast as one head was cut off another grew in its place. Hercules killed it with the help of Iolaus who cauterized each decapitated neck.
63 **Colchis**: refers to the armed men that sprang from the dragon's teeth sown by Jason in his labour for the Golden Fleece.
 Echion: one of the survivors of the armed men that sprang from the dragon's teeth sown by Cadmus. He married Cadmus' daughter Agave and succeeded him as king of Thebes.
73–76 The Oxford Text makes this stanza a comment by Horace, but it is often read as part of Hannibal's speech.

5

'One of his most perfect poems' says Fraenkel (440), and compares it with 3.14 which 'seems to be moving on two different planes. In *Diuis orte bonis*, on the other hand, every thought, every picture is an organic part of a living whole' (448).

Metre: Second Asclepiad

Added: 7 Roman, 14 every day, 27 our, 29 vineyard, 37 peace and.

1 *Diuis orte bonis:* so Augustus is called *Veneris ... sanguis* at *Carmen Saeculare* 50. He was grandson of Caesar's sister Julia, the dictator's great-nephew and adopted son. Some, however, prefer to render 'born when gods were gracious,' comparing *Satires* 2.3.8 *iratis natus ... dis* 'born when gods were angry.' 'Born when gods were benign' is Leishman's happy solution.
2 Augustus had gone to the Rhine frontier after Lollius' defeat there in 16 BC and thereafter to Spain; he did not return to Rome till the summer of 13 BC.
3–4 Lit. 'the august assembly of the fathers' i.e. the Senate.
17 The ox is probably ploughing; there are no cattle thieves.
18 *Faustitas:* the only occurrence of this word.
19 The sea is free of pirates, cf. *Res Gestae* 25.1 *mare pacaui a praedonibus* 'I made the sea peaceful, ridding it of pirates.'

20–24 cover Augustus' moral legislation. *Res Gestae* 6.1 records his appointment as *curator legum et morum summa potestate solus* 'supervisor of laws and morals without a colleague and with supreme power'and 8.5 describes this legislation in general terms.

23 A paraphrase. Literally 'Wives in childbirth are praised because of like offspring.' Cf. Hesiod *Works and Days* 'Wives bring forth children like their fathers.'

25 Cf. *Res Gestae* 29.2 *Parthos trium exercitum Romanorum spolia et signa reddere mihi supplicesque amicitiam populi Romani petere coegi* 'I compelled the Parthians to restore to me the spoils and standards of three Roman armies and to ask as suppliants for the friendship of the Roman people.' The three armies were those of Crassus (53 BC), Decidius Saxa (40 BC) and Antony (36 BC). Also 26.2 *Gallias et Hispanias prouincias, item Germaniam ... pacaui* 'I brought peace to the Gallic and Spanish provinces as well as to Germany.'

30 Cf. 2.15.5 n.

31 **for his wine**: at the evening meal at home.

32 **second course**: the *secundae mensae* were really our dessert. After the *cena* the tables were removed and another lot brought in for the wine. Before the drinking began a libation was poured to the Lares, gods protecting hearth and home. Libations had been offered to Augustus at private as well as public banquets since 24 BC (Dio Cassius 51.19).

34 *pateris*: patera was a shallow bowl used for libations.

35 *Castoris*: represents his twin brother Pollux too, cf. 3.3.9.

38 **Hesperia**: 1.28.26 n.

6

First, a hymn to the god of poetry, stressing his punishment of hubris and praying him to grant success to the *Carmen Saeculare*. Then Horace turns to the chorus of boys and girls that he represents himself as rehearsing, ascribes his lyric inspiration and technique to Phoebus and asks the chorus to follow his beat.

Metre: Sapphics.

Added: 19 the babe, 26 long.

1–2 Lit. 'God whom Niobe's offspring experienced as punisher of big talk ....' According to *Iliad* 24.602–609 Niobe, mother of six sons and six daughters, boasted she was superior to Leto who had only two children, Apollo and Diana; in revenge Apollo killed the sons and Diana the daughters. Horace, commissioned to write the *Carmen Saeculare*, is anxious to avoid divine jealousy. — The sentence that begins here is interrupted by a lengthy Pindaric-style parenthesis (9–24) and completed in 25–28.
Tityos: 2.14.8 n.

3 **near captor**: Achilles slew Hector on whom the safety of Troy depended, but himself was slain by Apollo.

4 **Phthian**: Achilles' father Peleus was king of Phthia in Thessaly.

7 **Dardanian**: 1.15.10 n.

10 **Eurus**: cf. 1.25.20.

11 **Teucrian**: Trojan. A Teucer was ancestor of the Trojan kings through his daughter who married Dardanus (see line 7).

13–16 A reference to the famous Wooden Horse, whose part in the capture of Troy by the Greeks is told in *Aeneid* 2. — Achilles, though cruel (17–20), was not a trickster like Ulysses.

17 Or taking *palam* with *captis*: 'But to captives openly taken harsh.'

21–24 Judging by the *Aeneid* this is poetic licence. Jupiter was not won over by Venus at *Aeneid* 1.229–296; he simply assures her that Aeneas is fated (in effect) to found the Roman empire; Apollo is not mentioned.

25 **Thalia**: the Muse of festivity.

26 **Xanthus**: a Lycian river, cf. 3.4.64 n.

27 **Daunian**: of Apulia, Horace's birthplace, cf. 1.22.14 and 3.30.10–12.

28 Apollo was eternally youthful. Greek *agyia* 'street' produces the cult title Agyieus 'Lord of the Ways,' but its presence here is obscure.

33 **Delian goddess**: Diana, born with Phoebus Apollo on the island of Delos.

protected: refers to 'maidens and boys.'

35 **the Lesbian foot**: here Sapphics, named after Sappho the 6th-century BC poetess of Lesbos.

36 **thumb-stroke**: Horace is probably not conducting with his thumb but accompanying on the lyre or snapping his finger.

38 **Noctiluca**: Diana as moon-goddess.

39 *pronos*: OLD *pronus* 5b.

41 Horace ends by addressing one of the girls.

43–44 **by that skilled metrician ...**: takes *docilis* as genitive. With *docilis* as nominative we get 'Having learnt the measures/ Of the bard Horace.'

7

A spring song in epodic metre like 1.4, but much graver. Housman regarded it as 'the most perfect poem in the Latin language' and produced a fine rhyming imitation of it (see Wilkinson pp.40–42). Lines 13–16 can be seen as a Horatian expansion of Catullus 5.4–6:

> soles occidere et redire possunt;
> nobis cum semel occidit breuis lux,
> nox est perpetua una dormienda.

> Suns can set and rise again;
> For us, once our brief light has set,
> There's one unending night for sleeping.

Metre: Second Archilochian; a dactylic hexameter + dactylic trimeter catalectic.

Added: 3 swollen, 4 confined, 16 Then.

5 The plural *Gratiae* being a cretic (— ⌣ —) is unavailable in dactylic verse (contrast 1.4.6); Horace had a good solution to the difficulty.

7 **life everlasting**: lit. 'things eternal.'

13 I.e. every month after waning and disappearing the moon returns.

15 There is a choice of reading here between *pater* and *pius*, Aeneas' standing epithet in the *Aeneid*, though he is often *pater* there too. *pius* is picked up by *pietas* (24). — For Tullus Hostilius' wealth see Livy 1.31.1; he was the third king of Rome and Ancus Marcius the fourth.

19 *amico:* is said to be a Latin imitation of Greek *philos* 'dear,' which is used in Homer in the sense of 'one's own.' Some take as ablative 'with friendly

intention;' the dative is also possible in the sense of 'to a friendly mind,' 'to the mind of a friend,' perhaps 'to give pleasure to a friend.'

21–22 **splendida ... arbitria**: grandiose to suit the standing of Torquatus, who we gather from the next line is *nobilis, eloquens* and *pius*.
Minos: legendary judge of the dead, see also 1.28.9 n.

23 **Torquatus**: may be the same as the addressee of *Epistles* 1.5, perhaps a Manlius Torquatus and descendant of Catullus' aristocratic friend (61.209).

26 **Hippolytus**: dedicated to the virgin goddess Diana and a single life, was falsely accused by his stepmother Phaedra of trying to seduce her. His father Theseus banished and cursed him, causing his death.

27–28 Theseus and his friend Pirithous were chained to a rock in Hades for their attempt to kidnap Proserpine, with whom Pirithous had fallen in love. Hercules rescued Theseus.

8

The ode has been placed at the centre of Book 4 and uses the same metre as 1.1 and 3.30, which are also concerned with poetry, but especially with Horace's own lyric achievement. Here he keeps himself more in the background and argues that poetry can immortalize and even deify. — This is the only Horatian ode to break Meineke's law, which finds that all the rest of the odes consist of multiples of four lines. But editors are unable to agree about which lines here, if any, are spurious.

Metre: First, or Lesser, Asclepiad.

Added: 19 North, 20 but a splendid, 24 just, 25 fine, 31 among the clouds.

2 **Censorinus**: perhaps C. Marcius Censorinus, consul in 8 BC.
sodalibus: possibly here fellow members of the *sodalicium poetarum* or association of poets; in which case read not 'closest friends' but 'poet friends.'

3 **tripods**: prizes for Greek athletic contests as early as Homer (*Iliad* 23.259).

6 **Parrhasius**: famous 5th-century BC Greek painter. ˙
Scopas: famous 4th-century BC Greek sculptor.

8 The first *perhaps* must be pronounced *p'r'aps*.

9–10 **nec tibi ... egens**:I.e. either 'you could buy such luxuries if you wished' or 'you already possess such luxuries and have no desire for more.'

15 **swift flight**: at Zama in 202 BC where Hannibal was defeated by Scipio Africanus Major. The plural *fugae* is probably poetic, cf. 3.5.52 *reditus*.

17 refers to the destruction of the city by Scipio Africanus Minor in 146 BC. — The line is metrically unique in lacking the break between words after the sixth syllable in this metre.

18 **Calabrian Muse**: the epic *Annales* of Quintus Ennius who was born at Rudiae in Calabria in 239 BC and died in 169 BC, long before the destruction of Carthage.

19 I.e. the elder Scipio Africanus (see 15 above).

20 I.e. his only personal profit from the victory was his cognomen Africanus.

22–23 1.2.17 n.

26 **Aeacus**: 2.13.22 n.

27 **Fortunate Isles**: or Isles of the Blest in the Ocean beyond the Pillars of Hercules, to which favoured heroes were translated without dying and where Rhadamanthus was usually said to rule.

29 **Hercules**: after his famous labours and death on the pyre on Mt Oeta, was translated to Olympus, married Hebe, the goddess of youth, and sat at the gods' table.

31   **Tyndarids' star**: the constellation of the Twins, Castor and Pollux, sons of Tyndareus, and protectors of sailors to whom they appear in the form of St Elmo's fire.
     Tyndaridae: nominative plural, has *sidus* in apposition.
34   **Liber**: 1.12.22 n. The third example here of the deified sons of mortal mothers.

9

Continues the theme of 4.8, the poet's power to immortalize, leading up to the magnificent seventh stanza, which is followed by a eulogy of Marcus Lollius, for whom see the note on line 33.

Metre: Alcaics.

Added: 5 Reflect that, 10 and 21 and 28 all, 39 only, 43 and, 49 all.

2   **Aufidus**: 3.30.10 n.
5   **Maeonian**: 1.6.2 n.
6   **Pindaric**: 4.2.1 n.
7   **Cean**: 2.1.38 n.
8   **Stesichorus**: of Himera in Sicily, composer of narrative choral lyric (6th century BC), the lyric Homer.
     Alcaeus: 1.32.5–12.
     the rebel: lit. 'menacing,' a reference to his public poetry attacking tyrants, cf. 2.13.26–28.
9   **Anacreon**: 1.17.18 n.
11   **passion en-**: for scansion see 4.3.24 n.
12   *fidibus:* lit. 'lyre-strings;' for *barbitos* see 1.1.34 n.
     that Aeolian girl: Sappho, cf. 2.13.24–25.
14   **adulterer**: Paris.
17   **Teucer**: 1.7.21 n.; the best archer among the Greeks at Troy (*Iliad* 13.313–314).
     Cydonian: Cretan, Cydonia (modern Khania) being in NW Crete and Crete being famous for its archers.
18   **Ilios**: can be taken as 'an Ilios,' i.e. cities like Troy.
20   **Idomeneus ... Sthenelus**: minor Homeric heroes. The scansion of the first is *metri gratia*.
21   **Hector**: 2.4.10 n.
22   **Deiphobus**: a son of Priam, who married Helen after Paris' death.
25   **Agamemnon**: commander of the Greek army at Troy, 2.4.7 n.
28   **sacred poet**: cf. 3.1.3 *Musarum sacerdos*.
29   **cowardice**: or 'laziness, indolence.'
30   **courage**: or 'virtue.'
33   **Lollius**: a rich and trusted supporter of Augustus, legate of Galatia in 25 BC, consul in 21 BC, proconsul of Macedonia 19–18 BC, governor of Belgic Gaul 17–16 BC, when he was defeated by the Sygambri (4.2 introduction).
37   **it**: i.e. Lollius' 'mind' (34 *animus*) which remains the subject throughout 34–44.
44   **Factions**: lit. 'groups.'
46   **happy**: *beatus* also means 'rich' (*OLD* 3), e.g. 1.29.1–2 *beatis ... Arabum ... gazis*.

10

Ligurinus re-appears from 4.1.33ff. The theme of time punishing the cruelty of a pretty boy comes in the *Greek Anthology*. For Fraenkel 'the real theme ... is something more simple and touching, regret for the bygone days of youth' (414) — on the part of Horace too.

Metre: Greater Asclepiad.

Added: 1 all, 4 even, 6 Then ... there.

2 **winter:** *bruma* is Bentley's conjecture; the MSS all read *pluma* 'plumage,' which is said to refer to the down of the first beard, coming when he is proud of his pre-pubescent looks.

3 **cut off:** a sign of manhood on the assumption of the *toga uirilis* between the ages of 15 and 18.

6 **ask:** to avoid fortuitous rhyme; lit. 'say.'

8 **matching:** lit. 'for.'

11

Horace's one, but warm, tribute in Book 4 to his friend and patron Maecenas, cleverly combined with an invitation (cf. 1.17 and 3.28) to his last love to console her for losing Telephus.

Metre: Sapphics.

Added: 1 vintage, 11 Even, 18 same, 22 another, 23 Both, 30 all.

1 **Alban:** a good wine from the Alban Hills SE of Rome.

3 **Phyllis:** also at 2.4.14.

8 *spargier:* archaic form of *spargi* in a religious context.

15 **Ides:** 3.18.10 n.

19 *Maecenas meus: meus* 'my' emphasizes their closeness and puts them on the same level; cf. Catullus 10.1 *Varus meus* and 53.3 *meus Calvus.*
    adfluentis: lit. 'on-flowing,' also suggesting affluence.

21 **Telephus:** also at 1.13.1–2 and 3.19.26.

25 **Phaëthon:** son of Helios, the Sun-god, drove his father's chariot off course, burnt up the world, and was killed by Jupiter with a thunderbolt.

26 **Pegasus:** 1.27.24 n.

28 **Bellerophon:** 3.7.13–16 n. Pegasus threw him off when he tried to ride up to heaven (Pindar *Isthmian* 7.44–47).

12

For the first three stanzas the ode describes the return of spring in the manner of epigrams in Book 10 of the *Greek Anthology*. A surprise ensues in the middle stanza: spring also brings thirst. This turns the ode into a light-hearted invitation — again with a difference: the guest must earn his wine with an expensive unguent. The last three stanzas develop the theme.

Metre: Second Asclepiad.

Added: 2 Gentle, 9 young, 10 and repeat their songs, 12 pine-, 16 from me, 17 one.

5–8 Procne, daughter of Pandion king of Athens, married Tereus king of Thrace and had by him a son Itys, or Itylus. Tereus raped Procne's sister Philomela and cut out her tongue to escape detection, but Philomela depicted the rape on a tapestry.

Procne in revenge murdered Itys. Tereus on the point of killing Procne was turned into a hoopoe, Procne into a swallow and Philomela into a nightingale. (In another version Philomela became the swallow and Procne the nightingale.)

7   **Cecrops**: the first king of Athens. Horace regards Pandion as his descendant.

10   **and repeat their songs**: added to bring in 'songs' as well as 'tunes' for *carmina*.

11   **the God ...**: cf. Virgil *Eclogue* 10.26 *Pan deus Arcadiae* 'Pan Arcadia's god.' This is the only appearance of Arcadia in Horace. The stanza reflects Virgil's *Eclogues*.

13   **Vergilius**: the name occurs 11 times in Horace, in 10 places undeniably referring to the poet. It is surely improbable that Horace should here use it in the company of Maecenas (4.11) and Augustus (4.14 and 15) of some complete nonentity. Just as Book 1 begins with odes addressed to Maecenas, Augustus and Virgil, so Book 4 ends with odes addressed to Maecenas, Virgil and Augustus. The ode could have been written long before Virgil's death in 19 BC. Porphyrio takes *iuuenum nobilium* (15) to refer to Octavian and Maecenas or possibly to Augustus' Neronian stepsons. Horace is making fun of Virgil, as he is in accusing him of *studium lucri* (25), a ludicrous suggestion (though Virgil died a rich man, *Vita Donati* 13). 'H. intended [the ode] to be recognised as an early poem, published after Virgil's death to recall the easy intimacy that had existed between old friends' Quinn.

14   **in Campania**: lit. 'at Cales,' see 1.20.9 n.

16   *merebere*: the future is jussive, 'must.' — This reverses the exchange in Catullus 13 where Fabullus the guest is to bring the dinner and Catullus as host will provide the unguent. For *nard* see 2.11.16 n.

18   **Sulpicius**: Porphyrio says that this is Sulpicius Galba and that the *horrea Galbae* were still in use in his day (2nd/3rd century AD).

19   **that**: strictly the antecedent is 'donor,' not 'hopes.'

24   Lit. 'Not like a rich man in a well-stocked house,' qualifying 'I.'

28   The ode itself is an example of such *desipientia*.

13

Just as the Lydia of 1.13 receives her come-uppance from a jealous Horace in 1.25, so the Lyce of 3.10 who shuts him out in a winter gale is duly punished here, both for that and for acting like Chloris in 3.15. Horace has small mercy for ageing courtesans unwilling to retire.

Metre: Third Asclepiad.

Added: 2 middle-aged, 24 for many moons, 27 old.

6   *uirentis*: cf. 1.9.17.

8   *excubat*: lit. 'lies out,' of an outpost or watchman who spends the night outside and so keeps vigil, is on the alert. Lyce tries to arouse male desire, but Chia is desirable all the time and looks for answering desire.

9   **desiccated oaks**: cf. 1.25.19 *aridas frondes*.

12   **snowy thatch**: lit. 'head's snows.'

13   **Cos**: the island, off Halicarnassus, was famous for its silks.

21   **Cinara**: 4.1.4 n.

14

This ode forms a pair with 4.4 in the same metre, which celebrates the victory of Drusus over the Vindelici and the contribution of the Claudian family to Roman history. Here, after a brief mention of Drusus, his elder brother Tiberius' victory over the Rhaetians is celebrated. But the ode as a whole is dedicated to Augustus and his military achievements.

Metre: Alcaics

Added: 8 before, 10 warrior, 32 all, 34 very.

7–9   *quem ... Vindelici didicere ... quid Marte posses:* the construction is like that at Mark 1.24 'I know thee who thou art.' For the Vindelici see 4.4.17 n.
10   **Genauni**: a tribe in and around the valley of the river Inn.
11   **Breuni**: a neighbouring tribe, after whom the Brenner pass between Italy and Austria is named.
13   *plus uice simplici:* understand *quam* with *plus* (*OLD* 2a) and see *OLD uicis* 5; literally 'with requital more than onefold' (Page).
14   **elder Nero brother**: Tiberius.
16   **Rhaetians**: another tribe in the central Alps, defeated by Tiberius coming from Lake Constance. — It looks as though Horace regards Vindelici as a generic name for these individual tribes.
17–19 *spectandus ... quantis fatigaret ruinis:* lit. 'worth watching ... with what destruction he wore down ...;' the construction is related to that in 7–8.
20   **Auster**: the south wind.
21   **Pleiades**: the seven daughters of Atlas forming a constellation whose setting in November brought stormy weather and an end to the sailing season. They were used for navigation.
     dance: or maybe 'troupe.'
25   **tauromorphic**: river-gods were thought of as bulls when in spate.
     Aufidus: the river of Horace's birthplace, see 3.30.10.
26   **Daunus**: 1.22.14 n.
29   **Claudius**: Tiberius.
35–36 Alexandria fell to Octavian (Augustus) on 1 July 30 BC
38   **prosperous**: perhaps also 'second,' Actium in Sep. 31 being the first.
40   *arrogauit:* here = *assignauit* (*OLD arrogo* 4).
41   **Cantabrians**: 2.6.2 n.
42   See *Res Gestae* 31: *Ad me ex India regum legationes saepe missae sunt ... Nostram amicitiam appetiuerunt per legatos Bastarnae Scythaeque ... Albanorumque rex et Hiberorum et Medorum.* 'Embassies from kings in India were frequently sent to me ... The Bastarnae, Scythians ... and the kings of the Albanians and the Iberians and the Medes sent embassies to seek our friendship.'
46   **Hister**: the Danube.
51   **Sygambri**: 4.2.36 n.

15

Horace ends his book with another poem in praise of Augustus, not this time as a victorious general but as bringer of peace to the Roman world, the architect of the *Pax Augusta*.

Metre: Alcaics.

Added: 2 jangling, 7 Our captured, 15 now, 18 armed, established. 19 pride, 29 We then, 32 famous.

2   *increpuit lyra:* reminding Horace that he was a lyric and not an epic poet.
3   **over Tyrrhene seas**: Horace gives the impression that he had considered writing about Augustus' campaigns in Spain.
7   Cf. 1.2.23 n. and 4.5.25 n.
9   *Ianum Quirini:* his usual title was 'Ianus Quirinus' identifying Janus with the ancient Sabine god Quirinus. The doors of Janus' temple were closed only when the Roman world was at peace. This happened three times under Augustus but only twice before, since the foundation of Rome.
10–12 refer to Augustus' moral legislation, see 4.5.20–24 n.
17   **us**: lit. 'things, the state.'
21–22 The assonance of *-undum ... uuium ... -um-* is remarkable.
23–24 Danube and Rhine formed the northern border of the Roman empire. These peoples were outside it.
24   **Tanais**: the river Don.
26   **Liber**: 1.12.22 n.
29   *more patrum:* 'In his *Origines* Cato said it was customary among our ancestors at banquets for those dining to sing to flute accompaniment the praises and virtues of distinguished men' Cicero *Tusculans* 4.3.
32   **offspring**: Aeneas and the *gens Iulia* culminating in Augustus.

CARMEN SAECULARE

At Rome in September 1890 an inscription was discovered recording in detail the celebration of the Saecular Games in 17 BC and confirming that Horace wrote this hymn for performance on the occasion by twenty-seven boys whose mothers and fathers were alive and the same number of girls. It falls into two halves (1–36 and 37–76), each of which is subdivided into three triads (1–12, 13–24, 25–36, and 37–48, 49–60, 61–72), the final quatrain forming a coda. See also the introductory note to Book 4 above and Fraenkel 364ff.

Metre: Sapphics

Added: 14 our, O, 17 us, 19 that's designed, 25 ever, 55 so, 56 us, 59 now, 62 friend, 68 in the future.

2   *caeli decus:* in apposition to both Phoebus and Diana as sun and moon.
5   The Sibylline books containing prophecies of the various Sibyls in Greek dactylic hexameter verse were kept in the temple of Palatine Apollo in the care of the *Quindecimuiri* (see line 70), who consulted them when instructed to do so by the Senate.
6   *lectas ... castos:* both adjectives go with both nouns in this line.
7   *septem ... colles:* the seven hills of Rome.
14–16 **Ilithyia ... Lucina ... Genitalis:**of Diana as goddess of childbirth. It was important to address a deity by the right name, cf. 3.21.5 n. Augustus prayed to Ilithyia on the second night of the festival.
14   *lenis:* governs *aperire*, cf. 1.24.17 *non lenis ... recludere.*
17–20 refer to Augustus' moral legislation, the *Leges Iuliae de maritandis ordinibus* and *de adulteriis* ('Julian laws on the Marriage of the Orders' and 'on Adultery'); see *Res Gestae* 6 and 8.5.
19   *feraci:* with genitive *prolis*, cf. 29 *fertilis frugum.*
21–24 A *saeculum* represents the longest human life and the *Quindecimuiri*, probably at the suggestion of Augustus, made it 110 years.
25   *Parcae:* 2.16.39 n. Augustus sacrificed to them on the first night of the festival.
29   *Tellus:* Terra Mater received her sacrifice on the third and last night.
31–32 *salubres ... Iouis:* both go with both *aquae* and *aurae.*
37   *si:* 'For this use of *si* in appeals, not implying any doubt as to the fact, and founding the appeal on it, cf. 1.32.1 ... 3.18.5 ... and below, line 65' Page.
     uestrum: looks forward to *di* (45).
38   *turmae:* a military word usually applied to a troop of cavalry consisting of 30 men. At *Aeneid* 5.754 Virgil tells us that the Trojans who actually left Sicily for Italy were very few: *exigui numero, sed bello uiuida uirtus.* Perhaps there is some connexion with the *lusus Troiae* in which two *turmae* took part, see Suetonius *Julius* 39 *Troiam lusit turma duplex, maiorum minorumque puerorum* 'the troop for the Trojan Game was double, older boys and younger boys.' The *Aeneid* had been published in 18 BC.
41   *cui:* the antecedent is *pars* (39). For *sine fraude* cf. 2.19.20.
45   *probos mores:* 'a sense of duty' is Professor Crook's fine paraphrase; roughly, 'approved behaviour.'

49–50   *Venerisque sanguis:* by poetic licence is Augustus, adopted as his son by Julius
        Caesar who claimed descent from Iulus, Aeneas' son and grandson of Venus and
        Anchises. — The word play *ueneratur ... Veneris* perhaps implies that the prayer
        is in conformity with Julian origins and therefore deserves to be granted.
51–52   Cf. Virgil *Aeneid* 6.853 *parcere subiectis et debellare superbos* 'spare the
        submissive and war down the proud.'
54   *Albanas ... securis:* see 3.2.19 n. *axes.* Alba Longa was the city founded by Iulus
        on the site where the white sow was discovered (Virgil *Aeneid* 3.390–393).
55–56   Cf. *Res Gestae* 31 quoted at 4.14.42 n.
58   *redire:* cf. Virgil *Eclogue* 4.6 *iam redit et Virgo, redeunt Saturnia regna* 'Now
        too returns the Virgin; Saturn's rule returns.' Aratus *Phaenomena* 128–136 had
        described how the virgin goddess of Justice left the earth in the Bronze Age
        because of human wickedness. Her return announced the return of the Golden
        Age when Saturn ruled.
61–64   represent the four concerns of Apollo: augury, archery, music and poetry,
        medicine.
69   Diana had an ancient temple on the Aventine in Rome and another at Nemi,
        where Frazer begins *The Golden Bough*, see 1.21.6 n.
70   *quindecim ... uirorum:* see 5 n.

ABBREVIATIONS AND BIBLIOGRAPHY

Abbreviations

c.	circa
CS	*Carmen Saeculare*
lit.	literally
L&S	C.T. Lewis and C. Short *A Latin Dictionary*
N–H	R.G.M. Nisbet and M. Hubbard *A Commentary on Horace's Odes. Book 1* 1970, *Book 2* 1978. Oxford
OCD³	*Oxford Classical Dictionary* 3rd edn 1996
OCT	Oxford Classical Text
OLD	*Oxford Latin Dictionary* 1968–1982
Res Gestae	*Res Gestae Diui Augusti. The Achievements of the Divine Augustus* edited by P.A. Brunt and J.M. Moore. Oxford 1967

Select Bibliography

When the works listed in this bibliography are referred to in the Introduction and Notes, it is by the author's name only, or by author's name and year of publication.

Texts, Commentaries and Translations of Horace

Bennett C.E. (1927). *Horace: Odes and Epodes*. Loeb: London, revised reprint

Bentley R. ed. (1869³). *Q. Horatius Flaccus*. 2 vols., Berlin

Garrison D.H. ed. (1991). *Horace Epodes and Odes*. Norman and London

Gow J. ed. (1896). *Q. Horati Flacci Carmina*. Cambridge

Hauthal F. ed. (1864). *Acronis et Porphyrionis Commentarii in Q. Horatium Flaccum*. Vol. 1, Berlin

Kiessling A. and Heinze R. (1955⁸). Horaz: *Oden und Epoden*. Berlin

Klingner F. ed. (1959³). *Horatius: Opera*. Teubner: Leipzig

Leishman J.B. (1956). *Translating Horace*. Oxford

Michie J. (1964). *The Odes of Horace*, verse translation with Latin text. London

Moore C.H. ed. (1902). *Horace: Odes, Epodes and Carmen Saeculare*, with introduction and commentary. New York

Müller L. ed. (1900). *Horaz: Oden und Epoden*. St Petersburg and Leipzig

Nisbet and Hubbard: see Abbreviations N–H

O'Brien R.W. (1857). *The Odes of Horace: translated into English verse with the original measures preserved throughout*, Book 1. Dublin and London

Orelli J.C. revised by J.G. Baiter and W. Hirschfelder (1886⁴). *Q. Horatii Carmina*. Vol.1

Page T.E. ed. (1896). *Q. Horatii Flacci Carminum Libri IV*, with introduction and notes. London

Porphyrio: see Hauthal (1864) above.

Putnam, M.C.J. (1986). *Artifices of Eternity. Horace's Fourth Book of Odes*. London

Quinn K.F. ed. (1980). *Horace: the Odes, with introduction, revised text and commentary*. London

Shackleton Bailey D.R. ed. (1985). *Horatius: Opera*. Teubner: Stuttgart

Schmidt E.A. and Killy W. eds. (1981). *Horaz: Oden und Epoden*. Artemis: Zürich and Munich. Latin Text with German translation and notes

Shepherd W.G. (1983). *Horace: the complete Odes and Epodes with the Centennial Hymn*. Penguin Classics: London

West D. ed. (1995). *Horace: Odes I.*. Latin text translated line for line with commentary. Oxford

Wickham E.C. (1903). *Horace for English Readers*. Oxford

Wickham E.C. and Garrod H.W. eds. (1912). *Horati Opera*. Oxford Text

Williams G.W. (1969). *The Third Book of Horace's Odes*. Latin text, prose translation and running commentary. Oxford

Other Works

Barr W. (1962) 'Horace, *Odes* i. 4' *The Classical Review* n.s. 12 (1962) 5–11

Bonavia-Hunt N.A. (1969). *Horace the Minstrel*. Kineton

Brink C.O. (1969 and1971). 'Horatian Notes I and II' *Proceedings of the Cambridge Philological Society* n.s.15.1–6 and 17.17–29

Brunt P.A. and Moore J.M. eds. (1967). See Abbreviations *Res Gestae*

Cairns F. (1971). 'Five "Religious" Odes of Horace (1.10; 1.21 and 4.6; 1.30; 1.15)' *American Journal of Philology* 92.433–452

— (1972). *Generic Composition in Greek and Roman Poetry*. Edinburgh

— (1977). 'Horace on Other People's Love Affairs (*Odes* I 27; II 4; I 8; III 12)' *Quaderni Urbinati di Cultura Classica* 24.121–147

Campbell A.Y. (1924). *Horace*. London

Campbell D.A. ed. (1982–1993). *Greek Lyric*. 5 vols. Loeb: London

Collinge N.E. (1961). *The Structure of Horace's Odes*. London

Connor P.J. (1987). *Horace's Lyric Poetry: the Force of Humour*. Berwick, Victoria

Costa C.D.N. ed. (1973). *Horace*. London

Crook J.A. (1996). 'Political History 30 BC to AD 14' and 'Augustus: Power, Authority, Achievement' Chaps. 2 and 3 in *Cambridge Ancient History* Vol.10^2

Currie H. MacL. (1996). 'Horace's epigraphic poetry: some comments on Odes IV' *Latomus* 55.78–86

Doblhofer E. (1992). *Horaz in der Forschung nach 1957*. Darmstadt

Du Quesnay I.M.LeM. (1995). 'Horace, *Odes* 4. 5' in Harrison (1995) 128–187

Fraenkel E. (1957). *Horace*. Oxford

Glover T.R. (1932). *Horace: a return to allegiance*. Cambridge

Griffin J. (1985). *Latin Poets and Roman Life*. London

Harrison S.J. ed. (1995). *Homage to Horace. A Bimillenary Celebration*. Oxford

Levi P. (1997). *Horace: a Life*. London

Lyne R.O.A.M. (1980). *The Latin Love Poets from Catullus to Horace*. Oxford

— (1995). *Horace: Behind the Public Poetry*. London

Maltby R. (1991). *A Lexicon of ancient Latin Etymologies*. Leeds

Martindale C.M. and Hopkins D. eds. (1993). *Horace Made New*. Cambridge

Murgatroyd P. (1989). *Melpomene: translations of selected Greek Lyrics with notes*. Amsterdam

Moritz L.A. (1968). 'Some Central Thoughts on Horace's Odes' *Classical Quarterly* 18.116–131

Noyes A. (1947). *Portrait of Horace*. London

Nussbaum G. (1981). 'Sympathy and Empathy in Horace' in *Aufstieg und Niedergang der römischen Welt* ed.H. Temporini and W. Haase, II.31.3.2093–2158. (Berlin 1972–)

Res Gestae: see Abbreviations

Roberts M. (1991). 'Reading Horace's Ode to Postumus (2.14)' *Latomus* 50.371–375

Rudd N. (1982). 'Horace' in *Cambridge History of Classical Literature* 301–319

— ed. (1993). *Horace 2000: essays for the Bimillennium*. London

Santirocco M.S. (1986). *Unity and Design in Horace's Odes*. Chapel Hill and London

SELECT BIBLIOGRAPHY

Shackleton Bailey D.R. (1982). *Profile of Horace*. London

Syme R. (1939). *The Roman Revolution*. Oxford

— (1979–). *Roman Papers*. Oxford

Syndikus H.P. (1972–73). *Die Lyrik des Horaz*. 2 vols. Darmstadt

Wilkinson L.P. (1951^2). *Horace and his Lyric Poetry*. Cambridge

— (1963). *Golden Latin Artistry*. Cambridge

Wille G. (1967). *Musica Romana*. Amsterdam

Williams G. (1970). *The Nature of Roman Poetry*. Oxford

— (1972). *Horace* (Greece and Rome New Surveys in the Classics No.6). Oxford

Woodcock E.C. (1959). *A New Latin Syntax*. London

Woodman A.J. (1974). 'Horace Odes 3.30' in *Quality and Pleasure in Latin Poetry* ed. T. Woodman and D. West, 115–128. Cambridge